A Practical Guide to Ethics in Public Relations

Regina Luttrell
Syracuse University

Jamie Ward
Eastern Michigan University

ROWMAN & LITTLEFIELD
Lanham • Boulder • New York • London

Executive Editor: Elizabeth Swayze
Assistant Editor: Carli Hansen
Senior Marketing Manager: Kim Lyons

The decision guide at the end of chapters 2–8 is based on Kathy Fitzpatrick, "Ethical decision-making guide helps resolve ethical dilemmas," accessed November 2, 2016, http://www.prsa.org/AboutPRSA/Ethics/documents/decisionguide.pdf.

Published by Rowman & Littlefield
A wholly owned subsidiary of The Rowman & Littlefield Publishing Group, Inc.
4501 Forbes Boulevard, Suite 200, Lanham, Maryland 20706
www.rowman.com

Unit A, Whitacre Mews, 26-34 Stannary Street, London SE11 4AB, United Kingdom

British Library Cataloguing in Publication Information Available

Library of Congress Cataloging-in-Publication Data

Names: Luttrell, Regina, 1975– author. | Ward, Jamie, 1977– author.
Title: A practical guide to ethics in public relations / Regina Luttrell,
   Syracuse University, Jamie Ward, Eastern Michigan University.
Description: Lanham : Rowman & Littlefield, [2018] | Includes bibliographical references and index.
Identifiers: LCCN 2017046341 (print) | LCCN 2017051276 (ebook) | ISBN 9781442272750 (electronic) | ISBN 9781442272736 (cloth : alk. paper) | ISBN 9781442272743 (pbk. : alk. paper)
Subjects: LCSH: Public relations—Moral and ethical aspects.
Classification: LCC HM1221 (ebook) | LCC HM1221 .L87 2018 (print) | DDC 659.2—dc23
LC record available at https://lccn.loc.gov/2017046341

Printed in the United States of America

Contents

Foreword

A Practical Guide to Ethics in Public Relations

Teresa N. Dougherty

Early in my corporate communications career as a new hire at a large firm, I was asked to accompany a senior leader to an industry conference where he would be the keynote speaker. It was my first such trip for the firm, and I was looking forward to building a rapport with the executive and establishing my credibility with him as a communications advisor. The speech was written, attending reporters were contacted, and the senior leader was prepared to deliver the opening address.

What could go wrong?

The evening before the conference, a well-known celebrity was invited to speak to a small group of conference attendees at a dinner event where, I would later learn, he made several derogatory remarks. The senior leader called me the next morning concerned that the comments might have offended some of the attendees, and if the comments were made public, reporters could get sidetracked.

"Should we modify the speech to proactively address the offending remarks, apologize, and stress that our industry does not endorse such comments?" he asked me. "Or should we ignore the remarks, hope no one is offended, and chance that reporters will not hear about the prior evening's comments?"

As I look back on that day, I realize how easily and without warning ethical dilemmas can infiltrate our everyday work as PR practitioners. Bad situations that require tough decisions are not just for the C-suite. When moral dilemmas collide with communications, it's our job as public relations professionals to advise clients, staff, and senior leaders on sound ethical practices.

I counseled the senior leader that he should be transparent and honest with the audience because honesty engenders trust, which, after all, is at the heart of good communications. Besides, it was the right thing to do for the audience he was trying to reach. We modified the speech accordingly, attendees were gratified, and the press covered the speech without mention of the dinner or of the celebrity's comments.

Honesty is one of six core values outlined in the Public Relations Society of America (PRSA) Member Code of Ethics, the official guide that members pledge to uphold. As a member of PRSA, I understand that especially today—as communications become more fractionalized and truth is often under pressure—moral decision making underscores the way we must skillfully practice our profession with our internal constituents and external stakeholders.

A Practical Guide to Ethics in Public Relations is an engaging, hands-on text that provides readers with the tools and practices to help identify and resolve ethical dilemmas that practitioners may face during their PR careers.

Dr. Regina Luttrell and Dr. Jamie Ward present a reliable and contemporary resource that will inform practice whether one works in a start-up company, Fortune 500 corporation, nonprofit agency, marketing firm, or independent consultancy by detailing the principles, theories, and applications of PRSA's Member Code of Ethics.

Each chapter opens with an "Expert on Ethics," and then delves into real-world ethical dilemmas, how they were handled, and what implications can be inferred. In addition, each chapter concludes with a decision-making guide, allowing readers to directly apply what they've learned. Drawing from the Member Code of Ethics, *A Practical Guide to Ethics in Public Relations* aims to show readers how core values, such as advocacy, honesty, expertise, independence, loyalty, and fairness, help define our profession and sustain our reputation.

Because the book is written for twenty-first-century practitioners, readers will gain insight into how ethical principles can be applied to everyday challenges, such as:

- Serving the best interest of clients without compromising integrity and the public trust
- Protecting against conflicts of interest
- Revealing violations that may impact reputation
- Providing objective counsel
- Promoting transparency
- Safeguarding employee confidences and protecting privacy rights
- Ensuring honesty, accuracy, and the integrity of communications, including when posting, tweeting, snapping, and pinning

As stewards of the profession, we are often called upon to act as both voice and conscience of those we represent. With technology at our fingertips and society just one click away, a more connected public requires PR practitioners to be diligent about the moral underpinnings of our messaging and of our behavior.

Ethical practice is the most important obligation of all public relations and communications professionals, and this book provides the know-how and techniques to understand, exercise, and pursue ethical communications in a world that moves at lightning speed.

Teresa N. Dougherty, APR
Ethics Chair
Colorado Chapter of the Public Relations Society of America

Preface

APPROACH

Throughout our years of teaching public relations ethics at the university level, we have come to understand the difficulties in identifying a text that is all-encompassing. We struggled to find a book that was a "must-have" in our classrooms. Our desire for a collection of appropriately diverse ethics-related content led to a master list of resources for students to reference, many of which reside in different publications. This text eliminates that process.

A Practical Guide to Ethics in Public Relations discusses public relations ethics from both traditional and social media contexts, while also providing specific examples that relate back to the PRSA Member Code of Ethics. This text includes the necessary content to understand ethical values, to put ethical principles into practice, and to reflect on those decisions.

ORGANIZATION AND PEDAGOGICAL FEATURES

Each chapter opens with an interview from a respected professional in the field and closes with a section on Solving the Ethical Dilemma. The entirety of the book guides readers through the process of making sound ethical decisions as they relate back to the PRSA Member Code of Ethics.

- Systematic treatment of the PRSA Member Code of Ethics. The code is a set of core professional values that should guide practitioners through all ethical concerns.

- Case studies illustrating the varied ethical dilemmas that public relations practitioners are faced with in the profession. The cases serve as models for students to enhance their understanding of theory and guide their decision making by offering ethical challenges.
- "Experts on Ethics" who share their views about ethics in the field offering additional perspectives and insights into how the PRSA Member Code of Ethics is applied in the field.
- Implications within social media and on the social sphere.
- PURE ethical decision model—First-time introduction to an innovative ethical model that provides practitioners with a method of applying traditional ethical theory to present-day ethical practice.
- Ethical decision guides to help readers' decision-making abilities when analyzing through ethical difficulties. An emphasis is placed on encouraging student thinking, reasoning, and decision making rather than on providing specific answers or driving students to a foregone conclusion.

CHAPTER 1: WHY ETHICS MATTER

Chapter 1 sets the stage for the text. The chapter covers definitions, origins, and ethical theories while also delving into ethical situations that were handled both positively and negatively, and the implications of each situation.

Expert on Ethics: Peter Verrengia, President and Senior Partner, Communications Consulting Worldwide, FleishmanHillard

Solving the Ethical Dilemma: Hill & Knowlton Controversy

CHAPTER 2: ETHICS IN PUBLIC RELATIONS

Chapter 2 discusses how ethics is applied in public relations while also giving an overview of the history and application of the public relations code of ethics. This chapter explores the negative connotations associated with practitioners who solely rely on the code of ethics for their decision making without understanding the larger ethical frameworks.

Expert on Ethics: Rosemary Benzo-Bonacci, Vice President, Foundation and Communications, Sitrin Health Care Center

Solving the Ethical Dilemma: *Call of Duty: Black Ops 3* Stunt

CHAPTER 3: ADVOCACY

Chapter 3 examines the role that advocacy plays in the public relations decision-making process. Using case studies and ethical dilemmas, this chapter looks at the ways in which public relations practitioners advocate on behalf of their company, client, organization, or brand. In order to offer open public discourse, PR practitioners provide various perspectives, thoughts, and statements on organizational stances.

Expert on Ethics: Alison Kangas, Social Media and Marketing Specialist, Pioneer State Mutual Insurance Company

Solving the Ethical Dilemma: Prevention Project Dunkelfeld

CHAPTER 4: HONESTY

Chapter 4 hones in on the premise that good character is at the center of public relations. Practitioners who exhibit a commitment to open and honest communication can establish authentic relationships with a variety of publics. Honesty, truth, and the accurate dissemination of information can be seen as the highest ethical standard by which relations practitioners hold themselves and their respective organizations when communicating with their publics, stakeholders, and community members.

Expert on Ethics: Jason Mollica, Owner, JRM Comm

Solving the Ethical Dilemma: Flint Water Crisis

CHAPTER 5: EXPERTISE

Chapter 5 examines the role that expertise plays in public relations decision making. Continuous professional development through educational opportunities advances a public relations practitioner's knowledge in an effort to maintain trust with C-suite colleagues as well as constructing mutually beneficial relationships with organizations, clients, stakeholders, and the general public. Each of these areas requires a thoughtful ethical application.

Expert on Ethics: Jack Pflanz, Development Associate, ACR Health

Solving the Ethical Dilemma: The White House

CHAPTER 6: INDEPENDENCE

Chapter 6 considers how the value of independence provides public relations practitioners with the ability to not only provide sound guidance but to also take responsibility for our professional activities.

Expert on Ethics: Hope Brown, Principal and Owner, PublicCity PR

Solving the Ethical Dilemma: TV Anchor Leslie Roberts Scandal

CHAPTER 7: LOYALTY

Chapter 7 delves into the complexities of loyalty as it relates to upholding organizational responsibilities while balancing public complexities of duty to self, client, employer, profession, and society.

Expert on Ethics: Daniel Cherrin, Esq., Northcoast Strategies
Solving the Ethical Dilemma: Paula Pedene, Veteran Whistle-Blower

CHAPTER 8: FAIRNESS

Chapter 8 explores the role of fairness in public relations decision making—specifically, looking at how public relations practitioners strive for objective and equitable treatment of various publics including individuals they work alongside and represent, internal and external constituents as well as the larger populous while supporting an open marketplace.

Expert on Ethics: Brianna Neace, Public Relations Specialist, Blue Cross Blue Shield of Michigan
Solving the Ethical Dilemma: SeaWorld

CHAPTER 9: ETHICS MATTER; CHOOSE ACTION

This final chapter illuminates the need to take action when unethical situations arise. The text provides a working grasp of important philosophical principles and their application in ethical situations in public relations. Resources including websites, journals, and blogs are provided so that students can remain well informed of current communication situations. The chapter culminates with five in-depth case studies from the Arthur W. Page Society that examine ethical boundaries practitioners can face. Readers delve into applicable material that will challenge them to think critically while working to understand and resolve the issues on principled preparation.

Truth, honesty, empathy, and character are foundational to ethical communications and the profession of public relations. We hope that you find *A Practical Guide to Ethics in Public Relations* not only an engaging textbook, but also a book that helps you recognize and understand ethical dilemmas while providing the knowledge and tools to help you solve ethical dilemmas in a way that results in a principled outcome.

I

ETHICS IN PUBLIC RELATIONS

1

Why Ethics Matter

experience that facts will be questioned, and those that cannot be proven may need to be corrected. Any person or organization that routinely presents or defends false information will harm its reputation. It may take time for consequences to arrive, but if you violate the expectation of your audience that you will be truthful, you create the expectation that you will lie in the future. Ultimately, those who stretch or abuse the truth will lose access to the audiences they want to persuade. As the famous twentieth-century journalist Edward R. Murrow said, "To be persuasive we must be believable. To be believable we must be credible. To be credible we must be truthful." As communications consultants or employees of organizations that present information, we are not in a position to play Sherlock Holmes with every fact our clients present. We can, however, make sure that due consideration has been given to the question, can this information be established as false? In other words: Is it accurate? That has always mattered and still matters to credibility, persuasion, and reputation.

What skills are necessary to demonstrate expertise in public relations?

It's important to distinguish between skills and personality traits or characteristics. It's true that some of the best public relations people are curious and creative. Many of the best also have perseverance and resilience. These are valuable traits, because it is difficult to break through competing noise to reach audiences, and it takes time, and sometimes rejection, before trust is earned in public relationships. But in contrast to those characteristics, the learned skills in highest demand are excellent writing (which reflects clear thinking); attention to detail; ability to acquire and analyze information (secondary research, quickly assembled and summarized with your own insights or conclusions, as well as primary research for evaluating awareness and opinion); an understanding of planning and project management; knowledge of the way traditional and social media operate; an appreciation of the basics of business management (since no one pays for public relations people who don't support business or organizational objectives—communications is not an end in itself); and a sense of urgency and responsiveness in teamwork (few public relations people work entirely alone). It is also useful to understand the industry or public policy sector that your organization or client works in.

Can you provide an example of a time when you had to disagree with what the client felt was necessary and guide them in another direction?

This happens frequently. Quite often, people in management or operating roles, or those involved in paid marketing activities, want results that take longer in an "earned" communications environment than they expect. In most programs that public relations teams carry out, we do not pay for time or space, and we cannot control the timing and words used by third parties. Clients often get frustrated when top media won't immediately report on a product that the client feels is innovative. And they may demand a confrontation with an editor or an event organizer, or blogger, when remarks about the company or its products are unflattering. In those situations, we often have to disagree with the request and propose a more effective alternative. It isn't clear to people outside of our discipline that when we ask an audience, or an intermediary like traditional media or a social influencer, to carry our client's message, money is not changing hands. Many people in other functions still do not understand the difference between an advertisement, a news story, an op-ed, or a blog post. We have to help them understand that the currency we use to earn visibility and valuable persuasion is timely, fresh information and a clear point of view. Convincing people in management roles to share information, or take a clear point of view to earn credibility, either with employees or with outside audiences, can be difficult. We also have some clients who do not want to tell their own stories. They think the PR people are there to do that. Ultimately we have to say to a senior executive or leader of an institution, "We can create the messages, the story line, and the occasion for communications, but you have to stand and deliver before the audience you wish to persuade." Those who will not, cannot have the benefits of effective communications. Very rarely, a client will want us to distract audiences from the truth, or will want to provide misleading information. There are so many examples of this backfiring on products or companies, that it is not difficult to change their minds. However, it is fairly common for brands and organizations to refuse to engage with external critics, or respond to questions. This sometimes happens when the benefits of public transparency conflict with the potential legal consequences of sharing information publicly. Generally, the most successful companies take a balanced approach to those situations, but often, the financial consequences of losing a lawsuit outweigh the benefits of corporate or brand reputation.

How do you balance loyalty to the client and loyalty to society?

The lines are generally clear in a paid relationship. We work for a client, or those who are employed in internal roles work for an organization. The interests of that organization come first. Our role is not altruistic. We do not work for "society." Even those public relations people who work in government, not-for-profit, or religious institutions have a role that is carried out on behalf of the objectives of those institutions. However, we have a duty not to lie or communicate information in circumstances where public harm might result from our communications activities. In those cases, we have an ethical responsibility to society to disengage. That could mean asking the client or company to reconsider, based on the possible negative consequences of that kind of communications. Or it could mean resigning, because the ethical standards of PRSA, and for public relations firms, the PR Council, and our own standards as individuals, are violated.

Can you discuss how you deal with differing opinions or maintain free expression of ideas?

Communications in general, and public relations as a discipline, requires a high degree of collaboration in most organizations. This is important both for the internal dialogue and the external dialogue. Internally, communications is a function that has to collect and refine many points of view that represent the institution. In a product launch, the engineers, sales staff, marketing team, and investor relations staff may all have different views on what is most important to communicate. If their views are not sought out and represented, the resulting communications activities—like a media story, third-party product review, or analyst report—may not look successful to the function that ultimately owns the relationship with that audience. At the same time, the opinions of outside audiences need to be understood and addressed, in any effective communications initiative. This is where techniques like opinion polling, content analysis of media coverage, or social media analytics create real value. With an accurate view of outside awareness and perception, a brand or organization has a good starting point to create a dialogue with the marketplace. Despite the need for input and benchmarking, a successful effort cannot work without a clear understanding of the purpose of the organization, its values, the differentiation of its product or service, and the specific objective of the communications initiative. With these criteria, the communications professional can assemble all the input from important internal and external contributors, and screen out instructions or desires that are not specifically relevant to the focused outcome that communications is meant to create. To the extent that the process is transparent, and those criteria and objectives are clear to all, the communicator can facilitate an effective public dialogue. This applies even to political or organizational communications at times of conflict. If the values and the objectives of all parties are clear, it is possible for communicators to structure and maintain a dialogue. The most difficult dynamic to manage is lack of respect between the organization and its audiences, or among audiences. Communicators can try to pull back the conversation to common ground, as a way to restart mutual respect, but that can be difficult. This is equally true for companies that mislead or ignore their customers and stimulate displays of anger in the marketplace, as it is for political advocates who disrespect opponents publicly. The solution is to stop the conversation, reset expectations—often through a gesture of reconciliation (like refunding money for those who have purchased a defective product, or creating an advisory board that includes opponents of a public project), restate objectives, and commit to mutual respect. In those situations, it is not purely a communications problem that needs to be solved, and communications professionals cannot resolve the situation alone.

What types of ethical issues are entry-level public relations practitioners likely to encounter?

Entry-level practitioners often encounter confusion between personal and professional ethics and between ethical problems and business problems. In most organizations—especially PR firms, where assignments are not always easy to anticipate—individuals might find themselves assigned to work for products, or for organizations, that they are morally opposed to. In most PR firms, anyone who has a personal objection to a product or company can rotate off onto another assignment. For example, a new hire who is vegan might not want to work on a hot dog account. However, it is not practical for that staff member to say that the entire PR firm is unethical if it agrees to represent the hot dog company, after he or she is moved to other business. Hot dogs are legal to sell and consume, and as long as they meet ingredient disclosure and food safety standards when they are sold, they are not an unethical product. The decision to represent the food company that makes hot dogs is a business decision for the agency, and making the product is a business decision for the company. Until a majority of people, or the government on the people's behalf, decide that the product can't be sold, doing so is not unethical. An individual with strong views against the product can always decide to look for a job elsewhere, as an expression of his or her personal position. Another common problem is that an entry-level person may be asked to attend a competitor's press conference, or a briefing from an opposition group, posing as students, in order to gather information. This is clearly unethical and should never be done, but people unfamiliar with PR ethics will often make this request. Often, entry-level PR people are asked to do research or monitor for news stories or social media posts. When they do so, they may assemble a collection of content that is the intellectual property of someone else—for example, a media outlet. This is also true for images that might be found online, and incorporated into a presentation or used as illustrations in content for a client. In these cases, the entry-level person may not be familiar with rules, and his or her supervisor might be either unaware, or intentionally looking the other way. It is unethical to use someone else's content, and ignorance is no defense. The solution is for the entry-level person to ask if the use of the content is permissible, and it is the job of a supervisor or in-house legal staff to address the intellectual property question from that point until resolution.

WHAT ARE ETHICS?

When discussing the topic of public relations ethics within today's classroom, students are commonly asked to contemplate and explain their perception of what ethics are and why they are important. Inevitably, responses follow a similar theme. "Ethics means the difference between right and wrong." "Ethics are never clear. They are never black-and-white." One such reply to these questions affirms, "Ethics are what people follow to stay out of trouble." An obvious, discussion-initiating retort to this statement follows as "do you believe most businesses are ethical?" to which the reaction is typically a resounding "no." At this point, it is important for students and professionals alike to understand that, as a public relations practitioner, it is your job to help organizations act ethically. The primary aim of this text is to assist the reader in recognizing and understanding ethical dilemmas while also providing the knowledge and tools to help resolve those dilemmas in a way that results in an ethical outcome.

By definition, "ethics provide a set of standards for behavior that helps us decide the appropriate way to act in a range of differing situations."[1] In essence, ethics is all about making choices and being able to provide justifications as to why particular choices are made. Ethics is sometimes conflated or confused with religion, law, or morality; however, there are important distinctions.[2] You are likely to face decisions that may be considered unethical but are completely legal. For example, it is unethical to embellish claims that a film is the number one family movie in the country, but it is not illegal. It also may be contrary to certain religious principles to support organizations that uphold a woman's right to choose; however, it is not illegal. Ethical decisions can stand in contrast with popular religious beliefs and even moral codes.

Many industry experts claim that "public relations professionals should have 'unimpeachable ethical standards' that develops trust from clients and the public."[3] The reason experts argue that PR practitioners require strong ethics is because PR practitioners play an integral role in issues management and in the development of society as a whole through the shaping of perception. "Every profession has a moral purpose. Medicine has health. Law has justice. Public relations has harmony—social harmony."[4] It is imperative that entry-level public relations practitioners learn how to make ethically sound decisions before being placed in problematic situations. Ethics research and professional practice highlight that pre-establishing ethical boundaries prior to being involved in tough situations helps to guide young practitioners as opposed to forcing new practitioners to create their own personal ethical values in the heat of the moment. Heath and Coombs suggest that proper ethical choices will "foster community by creating, and maintaining mutually beneficial relationships."[5] Researcher Richard Nelson states, "The lack of a single common framework for deciding what is ethical and what is not thus ultimately influences the outcome of public policymaking and the reputation of public relations."[6]

PROFESSIONAL VALUES DRIVE THE PROFESSION

Instances requiring a specific decision, whether ultimately right or wrong, inundate our everyday lives. Ethics should apply to all levels of behavior and judgment: acting properly as individuals, creating responsible organizations and governments, and bettering our society as a whole. This text has been developed as an introduction to the principles of making ethical decisions. Individuals who have received training in ethical decision making and who understand various ethical theories and their applications have an easier time not only selecting the appropriate courses of action in morally challenging situations but in applying their knowledge and ability to guide others on the professional standards of ethical behavior.

ORIGINS OF PR ETHICS

In reviewing the history of modern public relations, it is easy to see why today's practitioners are still struggling to shake the profession's ties to propaganda and the manipulation of public opinion.

It may surprise you to learn that an industry that largely prides itself on building, maintaining, and restoring images suffers from a fairly significant image problem itself. The field of public relations has historically been associated with unethical practices. While current practitioners follow the Public Relations Society of America Code of Ethics[7] and typically regard truth as paramount to success, it is important to note that PR is a practice built on propaganda, manipulation, and outright lies. This historical perspective currently influences how many practitioners are received by other industries, as well as the general public.

The late 1800s and early 1900s piloted the rise of the press agent. During this period, press agents commonly relied on sensationalism, exaggeration, and blatant mistruths in order to capture the attention of the American public. Phineas Taylor (P.T.) Barnum is one of the most well-known press agents of this era. Barnum was a master at packaging and promoting entertainment and understood that people wanted to be entertained. He consistently found innovative ways to garner the attention of both the general public and the media with shrewd pseudo-events.

Barnum initially gained notoriety by introducing Joice Heth, an African American slave who he claimed to be the 161-year-old former nurse to George Washington. "The Greatest Natural and National Curiosity in the World" read one of Barnum's handbills.[8] Joice Heth was in fact an elderly woman in her seventies. Barnum began exhibiting Heth in 1835 and earned nearly $1,500 per week, leveraging clever publicity schemes and media manipulation.[9]

Barnum also expanded his reputation when he presented the FeeJee Mermaid. Using clever publicity materials featuring the buxom, goddess-like mermaids of today and the assistance of his partner, Levi Lyman, masquerading as a naturalist, Barnum "concocted quite an elaborate scheme to expand the curiosity into 'mermaid fever.'"[10] Barnum convinced the public that he had the body of a real mermaid in his possession, when he actually had the bodies of a monkey and a fish that had been carefully sewn together. Barnum had a keen understanding of media manipulation and used it to his advantage.[11] Once the novelty of the mermaid diminished, Barnum continued to expand his empire with his largest claim to fame, the "Barnum & Bailey Circus."

In addition to the sensationalism and manipulation ushered into the field of public relations by P.T. Barnum and other press agents, several additional historical figures have also added to the industry's perception.

Ivy Lee is likely most well known for his "Declaration of Principles." Lee's principles assisted in moving the field of public relations from one of exaggeration and hype to one of accuracy and openness. "In brief, our plan is frankly, and openly, on behalf of business concerns and public institutions, to supply the press and public of the United States prompt and accurate information concerning subjects which it is of value and interest to the public to know about."[12]

As a former journalist, Lee had a high regard for truth. He is well regarded for his representation of Standard Oil and its founder, John D. Rockefeller. Lee is also credited with pioneering what many public relations practitioners deem as the modern-day press release.

Furthermore, Edward Bernays, who is often referred to as the father of modern public relations, believed that public relations were to be used for influencing public opinion. "The conscious and intelligent manipulation of the organized habits and opinions of the masses is an important element in democratic society. Those who manipulate this unseen mechanism of society constitute an invisible government which is the true ruling power of our country."[13] Bernays referred to his opinion molding technique as "the engineering of consent."[14]

With this historical perspective in mind, and knowing that perceptions of the field have evolved since its inception, there continue to be numerous ethical lapses afflicting various high-profile public relations agencies. For example, in a well-publicized case against Edelman Public Relations, the PR firm created the "Walmarting Across America" campaign. The idea was to follow a couple who were traveling across the country in their RV and spending each night in a Walmart parking lot. The participants planned to blog about their exploits along the way. The challenge here was that the entire campaign was actually a PR stunt created by Edelman to garner attention for Walmart. Consumers were never made aware that the participants were being compensated for their blog entries. This tactic tends to create doubts from the general public. A second example, included as a case study at the end of the chapter, highlights the instance wherein Hill & Knowlton masterminded a campaign to send the United States to war with Iraq.

As you can see, current practitioners have to overcome the sins and indiscretions of the industry's past in order to be viewed as a viable, entity service for the public good. It is for this reason that ethics is paramount to public relations.

VARIETIES OF ETHICAL THEORY

In order to best understand how ethics can be aptly applied to both the field of public relations and to other areas of life, professionally and personally, we must establish a solid foundation of classic ethical theories to ground our ethical understanding and decision making. We will focus on three distinct theoretical areas; consequentialist theories, nonconsequentialist theories, and virtue ethics.

ETHICS OF CONSEQUENCES

Consequentialist moral theories are primarily concerned with the aftereffects of a specific action. The consequences determine whether the action was morally acceptable or not. It is important to note that the action itself is not necessarily the determining factor in assigning morality; however, the result of the action does determine whether an action can be considered right or wrong.

One classical example of consequentialism is often referred to as the trolley car dilemma.[15] Consider that a trolley car is barreling down the track. If the trolley car stays the current course, it will likely run into five individuals that are working near the end of the track. If the trolley car is redirected onto an adjacent track, it will only run into a single individual at work. The brakes have stopped working. What do you do? For those of you struggling with the idea of a runaway trolley car, this example can also be updated to include a self-driving, autonomous vehicle that has been programmed to drive a particular route. Using the same challenge and consequences, what would you do? Either five people will most likely lose their lives if the vehicle stays the course or one will perish with your intervention.

When looking at this dilemma from a utilitarian perspective, the conductor of the trolley or the programmer of the autonomous vehicle might decide to deliberately steer the vehicles onto the course with the single individual in order to spare the five. The basic tenet of utilitarianism is the greatest good for the greatest number. Therefore, the harm of one individual is justified if you saved five others.

Let's look a bit more closely at one of the most well-known and influential consequentialist moral theories: utilitarianism.

Utilitarianism

British philosopher Jeremy Bentham introduced the Western world to the concept of utilitarianism in his book *An Introduction to the Principles of Morals and Legislation*.[16] "Utilitarians believe that the purpose of morality is to make life better by increasing the amount of good things (such as pleasure and happiness) in the world and decreasing the amount of bad things (such as pain and unhappiness)."[17] Utilitarianism follows the principle of utility, which holds that the action that provides the highest levels of satisfaction in addition to the most benefit over harm to everyone involved, is the morally correct one. In other words, utilitarianism supports what is considered the "greatest happiness principle" or that the morally correct action affords the greatest good for the greatest number of people.

There are two types of utilitarians: act utilitarians and rule utilitarians. Act utilitarians seek to follow the principle of utility and to maximize happiness. Rule utilitarians are interested in understanding the rules behind an action and whether following the rules maximizes happiness. To apply this to a real-world situation, let's explore cheating on a test. For an act utilitarian, a justification for cheating on a test could be that cheating produces the greatest amount of happiness. Cheating would grant the student the ability to not only pass the test but to also graduate on time and fulfill the requirements of a scholarship. A rule utilitarian would look at this situation differently. A rule utilitarian would evaluate the rule that was being called into question. In this instance it could be the rule of not cheating or perhaps it involves the rule of an honor code. Rule utilitarians would evaluate happiness based on what would happen if everyone cheated on tests and essentially received grades they did not deserve. It could throw the current system into chaos; thus, it would not be maximizing happiness despite what it appears to present on the surface.

Bentham believed that "happiness is the primary moral good." The preferred governing structure for utilitarianism or "right course of action" is to first identify the possible courses of action, then determine the benefits and harms that would come out of the course of action for everyone affected by it, and lastly, choose the course of action that results in the greatest good for the greatest number of people.[18]

British philosopher John Stuart Mill further elevated Bentham's notions of utilitarianism. Bentham argued that the pleasure providing the ultimate amount of happiness is the pleasure that one should heed toward. However, Mill argued that not all pleasures were on the same level, that there were higher pleasures and lower pleasures, and that if a morally responsible person had experienced both pleasures, they would always choose the one resulting in higher pleasure over the lower pleasure.[19] The low pleasures would be connected to the body, while the high pleasures would be associated with the mind. Individuals should resist their animalistic urges, which he considered lower pains and pleasures, such as physical pain, sexual desire, euphoria, and adrenaline rushes, and instead, embrace higher pleasures that involve more qualitative experiences of the mind.

A recent example of utilitarianism relates to the US government's decision to financially bail out General Motors, a casualty of the 2007 economic downturn. Initially, the administration had to carefully identify all available options. They could (a) allow General Motors to go bankrupt or (b) infuse a large amount of taxpayer money in order to firm up their ongoing operations. Next, the individuals involved had to identify the harms and utilities in this decision, as well as the parties that would be directly affected by the decision. To simplify a complicated situation, the harms of the bailout ultimately related to the use of billions of taxpayer dollars to buy stock in the company. On the flip side, the harms of not offering General Motors a bailout could potentially lead to millions of autoworkers being left without jobs, their families left without support, and households losing billions of dollars. At this point, the administration had to make a decision leading to the best possible outcome, and also positively affecting the largest number of people. Because US workers must pay taxes anyway, their happiness in this situation doesn't necessarily rest with winning or losing money, but primarily with where the money is going. The individuals that are directly affected by this decision are those working for the auto industry and their families. The utilitarian decision, considered the best decision, was to bail out General Motors. In the long run it brought the most benefits to the most people.

One of the greatest strengths of utilitarian theory is also its greatest weakness. Individual needs are often ignored in favor of providing the greatest amount of collective happiness for all involved. A great example of this is a cost-benefit analysis. A cost-benefit analysis determines a project's total cost by adding up the perceived benefits and subtracting the costs. This comparison assists an organization in determining if the proposed project is worth implementing. On a business level, a cost-benefit analysis is commonly used when initiating new projects, or in many cases, applied when determining if a company should recall a product and make updates/alterations. For example, if you are a dog food manufacturer and are notified that a small batch of your dog food may have been contaminated, it would be prudent to weigh the cost of a recall of all dog food versus the potential lawsuits or loss of sales from dog owners who had animals that were made ill by the product or who were concerned by media reports of contamination. Oftentimes, it is more cost-effective for a company to work with individuals who may have sick animals than to go through a costly recall. Therefore, in this example, the greatest amount of utility comes from protecting the company and ignoring the needs of individual consumers.

ETHICS OF DUTY

Now that we have been introduced to the concept of consequentialism and ethics based on the potential penalties of one's actions, let's take a look at an opposing view on ethics. Deontological (duty-based) ethics are concerned with the actions themselves, not with the consequences. There are two primary styles of duty-based ethics: Kantian ethics and libertarianism.

Kantian Ethics

While some individuals believe that consequences should be the determining factor in guiding one's ethical decision making, and that as long as the majority of people affected by your decision received more pleasure than pain, others might focus on a different set of rules to govern their behavior. These individuals focus on Kantian ethics.

Philosopher Immanuel Kant deems it important to recognize that humans are rational beings. He also notes that making a person happy is much different than making him or her good.[20] As humans, we have an ability to determine our own will and determine what our motive is behind our actions. Kant's biggest detour from utilitarianism lies in that he focuses on elements to consider as a rational being beyond simply looking at whether the act will provide pleasure or pain.

The primary tenet of Kantian ethics is the categorical imperative. The categorical imperative states that moral principles should be followed without exception.[21] To demonstrate Kant's stance on principles, from a public relations standpoint, let's look at the idea of "truth." From a Kantian standpoint, it is never permissible to tell a lie; regardless of the circumstances, there are universal principles that need to be followed. According to Kant's Formula of Universal Law, an individual should "Act only on that maxim which you can at the same time will to become a universal law of nature."[22] To better understand this concept, let's look at a case involving Disney.

In 2016, a Disney worker was fired after tweeting a photo of a poster directing employees to mislead customers when responding to questions regarding alligators on the property.[23] Specifically, the poster stated that if employees were asked if there were alligators in the water they were to respond with, "Not that we know of, but if we see one, we will call Pest Management to have it removed."[24] The poster was in direct response to the death of a two-year-old child who was killed by an alligator at a Disney resort. Kant would deem that misleading visitors is highly unethical. The moral thing to do in this instance, according to Kant, would have been to explain to visitors that alligators had been seen on the property but that there was protocol in place to protect guests and to immediately remove animals from the premises if one was seen.

Natural-Rights Libertarianism

Often referred to as the "Father of Liberalism,"[25] John Locke helped to usher in libertarian ideas about natural rights and minimal government. Libertarians see the individual as a fundamental unit of society to be valued above all else. Since the individual is held in such high esteem, to a libertarian, individual rights and responsibilities are also valued.

According to Locke, all individuals are moral agents who have a right to be secure in their life, liberty, and property. You may notice this statement is similar to the the phrase *life, liberty, and the pursuit of happiness* as included in the Declaration of Independence. Several scholars trace the phrase back to Locke's theory of rights.[26]

Furthermore, these rights are not granted by the government, so the government or in Locke's day, the monarchy, cannot take them away from the individual. If, however, someone was to violate those rights, then they would be deemed immoral and worthy of contempt. If the only guiding principle in life was to be happy then that would not be productive. Thus for libertarians, individuals should have the freedom to pursue their own interests as long as they do not infringe on the rights of others.[27] A staple of libertarianism is freedom.

Let's look at a case that illustrates the importance of rights ethics. Sweet Cakes by Melissa, a bakery in Gresham, Oregon, refused to sell a wedding cake to a same-sex couple. According to the co-owner, Aaron Klein, the bakery refused to sell the cake to the couple because it was against their religious beliefs to do so. According to Oregon law, businesses cannot discriminate or refuse to provide services based on a customer's sexual orientation. The couple filed a complaint with the Oregon Bureau of Labor and Industries, who then brought charges against the business owners, Melissa and Aaron Klein. "The business owners in the case believed they had the right to deny services because of their religious beliefs," said Nancy Haque, a co-director at Basic Rights Oregon. "Religious freedom is a fundamental part of America, and is written into our state's constitution already. But those beliefs don't entitle any of us to discriminate against others. Religious liberty should not be used to discriminate against people."[28] As a result, the bakery had to shut its doors, and it is reported that the owners could be fined up to $135,000 in damages.[29]

If you analyze this case from an individual rights standpoint, do you find in favor of the same-sex couple that was denied service or do you find in favor of the bakery? Justify your stance and then play devil's advocate for the opposite viewpoint.

ETHICS OF CHARACTER

Kohlberg's Stages of Moral Development

It is important to discuss Lawrence Kohlberg's stages of moral development in this section because one of the primary beliefs of Kohlberg's work is that people make different ethical judgments based on the ethical stage that they are in. In other words, students just entering the field of public relations are likely to make and justify ethical decisions differently than seasoned professionals. Experience and understanding make all the difference.

Expanding on the theories originally developed by Jean Piaget, Kohlberg developed six stages of moral development. The six stages can be grouped into three levels, each consisting of two stages: preconventional, conventional, and postconventional.[30] Kohlberg's first developmental stage is Obedience and Punishment. In other words, the very lowest stage of moral development is one where an individual is solely concerned with punishment and matters of obedience. This stage of morality is primarily engulfed by the fear of consequences and is most commonly seen in children.[31] Kohlberg's second developmental stage is Instrumental Purpose and Exchange. This stage of moral development is one where an individual is concerned with how a set of rules provides advantages or disadvantages to them, according to Kohlberg. Behaviors are typically based on self-interests.

The third and fourth stages move to the next bracket in Kohlberg's psychological groupings, the conventional level. Kohlberg's third stage deals with Interpersonal Accord. This stage of moral development is one where human beings base moral judgments on personal relationships and favorable treatment by others. In this stage, individuals work to conform to traditional social standards. The fourth stage is labeled the Social Accord and Conscience stage of morality, wherein the individual holds true to the duties accepted by him or her as part of a larger social system.[32] The fifth stage for Kohlberg is Social Contract and Individual Rights. In this stage, individuals accept that they are a part of a social contract and do their best to avoid infringing on the individual rights of others. Lastly, the sixth stage for Kohlberg is Universal Ethical Principles. In this stage, a person adheres to universal principles including the freedom of speech or the right of persons to have a vote in who rules their lives.

Stages of Moral Development

Lawrence Kohlberg

Level 1

Pre-Conventional Morality

Right and wrong determined by reward or punishment.

Stage One:
Punishment over obedience.
Whatever leads to punishment is wrong.

Stage Two:
Rewards.
The right way to behave is is rewarded.

Level 2

Conventional Morality

Views of other matter.
Avoidance of blame; seeking approval

Stage Three:
Good intentions. Behaving in ways that conform to "good behavior."

Stage Four:
Obedience to authority. An importance of fulfilling a duty to others.

Level 3

Post- Conventional Morality

Abstract notions of justice. The rights of others can override obedience to laws and rules.

Stage Five:
Differentiating between moral and legal right.

Stage Six:
Individual principles of conscience. Considers the views of others and everyone potentially affected by a moral decision.

Virtue Ethics

According to virtue ethics, what's most important to ethical life is the commitment to being a good and virtuous person. Not surprising, virtue ethics is concerned more with character and less with actions or rules. To commit yourself to becoming a virtuous person, you have to dedicate yourself to being an excellent human being. For most virtue ethicists, being an excellent human being entails realizing your nature, which leads to living a life in accord with the good.

Taking all of these traditional ethical theories into consideration, it is important to remember that the primary focus of this text is to help distinguish rationalization from reasoning. Throughout each chapter, you will learn to recognize and apply the various ethical theories in the categories of consequences, duty, and character; however, there is also an emphasis on demonstrating how you can make publicly defensible decisions that you can personally live with.

For the vast majority of practicing public relations professionals, there is most likely not a single "silver bullet" moral theory that should be followed to the letter in every instance. Something that is moral in one situation might not be morally applicable in another. Moral theory should be constantly reviewed, amended, and adhered to on a case-by-case basis, and in most cases, there is not an ultimate moral truth for all.

SITUATIONAL ETHICS

Ethical dilemmas that public relations practitioners commonly face are, by nature, inherently different. Each individual situation, circumstance, or condition poses a multitude of questions, actions, and reactions. The theory of situation ethics, pioneered by Joseph Fletcher, addresses this variability by providing a framework for decision making based upon the circumstances of a particular situation, and also the associated laws. Fletcher intended to offer a straightforward approach to ethical problems and the subsequent decisions required to resolve complex situations.[33]

Throughout this text, the reader will be introduced to various ethical dilemmas ranging from catastrophic to nearly insignificant, depending on your moral code. Kim Harrison, author and public relations consultant, warns that practitioners may not realize just how many ethical dilemmas they are faced with on a daily basis. In fact, Harrison compiled a list of seven ethical situations a practitioner could face on any given day. She urges practitioners to think about how they would handle some of these real-life scenarios:[34]

1. Do you wait to return the telephone call from a journalist requesting sensitive information until just after their deadline so they are not able use the information?
2. What angle do you take in writing an article on a staff member you do not necessarily respect?
3. Do you avoid saying no to a senior manager or client whose expectations of communication are unrealistic, because you do not want to jeopardize the relationship?

4. Your boss hypes up your draft of a media release. You know the reporter receiving it will not use it now. Do you say anything to your boss?

5. Your marketing department has made dubious claims about a new product. How do you handle this?

6. Your organization is in the middle of a difficult issue and your CEO decides to make public statements only after the lawyers have watered down your draft statement. What can you do?

7. You have been recruited by a competitor of your previous employer. To what extent can you use your knowledge of your previous employer's work in your new job?

These questions highlight just a few of the ethical situations that drive the practice of public relations. According to the Arthur W. Page Center, "Situational ethics is the most common ethical orientation used by public relations professionals."[35] Professionals tend to make consequence-based choices that vary based on the situation, but they do so using subjectivism, meaning that public relations professionals respond differently to the same ethical situation. Situational ethics suggests that every dilemma must be evaluated in its particular context or situation. Rather than applying a rigid set of rules in each decision, situational ethics suggests that decisions are made on a case-by-case basis. "This approach can be helpful when there are several ethical obligations to resolve in the one issue and when blindly following rules would cause significant harm."[36]

As a matter of practice, public relations professionals need to be able to assess a situation, identify the personal values at play, and consider the most appropriate ethical orientation.[37] When rationalizing a decision, we must consider the premise that just because a decision or action is made, it does not necessarily mean that it is right. Every situation is different; thus, every decision is distinctive.

CORPORATE SOCIAL RESPONSIBILITY

Corporate social responsibility (CSR) refers to voluntary business initiatives that benefit local communities. Businesses can benefit their communities by being good corporate citizens. Examples of socially responsible programs include projects designed to help the environment or contribute to education. Consumers are demanding that organizations become increasingly socially responsible. According to the 2015 Cone Communications/Ebiquity Global CSR Study, "the leading ways that consumers want to get engaged with companies' CSR efforts are actions tied directly to their wallets; with nine-in-10 just as likely to purchase (89 percent) as to boycott (90 percent) based on companies' responsible practices."[38]

Consumers have grown leery of most corporations and will no longer simply trust that these organizations desire to provide a benefit to society. Consumers expect to see the results of initiatives designed to support and promote their values. "Global consumers have high demands for companies to address social and environmental issues, but they now also understand they have an obligation to make change, as well. It's critical for companies to understand the nuanced drivers, barriers and opportunities that resonate among discerning global audiences."[39]

APPLYING CASE STUDIES

Readers are presented with a section titled "Solving the Ethical Dilemma" at the close of each chapter. These chapters offer details related to ethics, providing background on varieties of ethical theory, ethical consequences, or the PRSA Code of Ethics. The readers will also be introduced to the many "gray" areas inherent in PR ethics, and see how one decision leads to a series of other decisions before finally reaching a conclusion. Since ethical decisions are rarely black-and-white in nature, it is important for readers to understand how one decision can affect various results.

These dilemmas are deliberately constructed to deliver several outcomes. Discuss how each outcome was brought about and the positive or negative implications inherent in each ethical decision.

SOLVING THE ETHICAL DILEMMA: HILL & KNOWLTON CONTROVERSY

During the 1990s, the United States was attempting to gain public support for a rapidly escalating conflict, ultimately known as the Iraq War. It is often said that no matter how many troops you can put on the ground or planes in the air, before the United States goes to war, it has to first win the war (or the rationale for the war) in the hearts and minds of the American people, for without their support, taking up arms will not happen.

How Bush Sr. Sold the Gulf War, by Mitchell Cohen

"The U.S. has a new credibility. What we say goes."

President George Bush, *NBC Nightly News*, February 2, 1991

In October, 1990, a 15-year-old Kuwaiti girl, identified only as Nayirah, appeared in Washington before the House of Representatives' Human Rights Caucus. She testified that Iraqi soldiers who had invaded Kuwait on August 2nd tore hundreds of babies from hospital incubators and killed them.

Television flashed her testimony around the world. It electrified opposition to Iraq's president, Saddam Hussein, who was now portrayed by U.S. president George Bush not only as "the Butcher of Baghdad" but—so much for old friends—"a tyrant worse than Hitler."

Bush quoted Nayirah at every opportunity. Six times in one month he referred to "312 premature babies at Kuwait City's maternity hospital who died after Iraqi soldiers stole their incubators and left the infants on the floor," and of "babies pulled from incubators and scattered like firewood across the floor."[40] Bush used Nayirah's testimony to lambaste Senate Democrats still supporting "only" sanctions against Iraq—the blockade of trade which alone would cause hundreds of thousands of Iraqis to die of hunger and disease—but who waffled on endorsing the policy Bush wanted to implement: outright bombardment. Republicans and pro-war Democrats used Nayirah's tale to hammer their fellow politicians into line behind Bush's war in the Persian Gulf.[41]

Nayirah, though, was no impartial eyewitness, a fact carefully concealed by her handlers. She was the daughter of one Saud Nasir Al-Sabah, Kuwait's ambassador to the United States. A few key Congressional leaders and reporters knew who Nayirah was, but none of them thought of sharing that minor detail with Congress, let alone the American people.

Everything Nayirah said, as it turned out, was a lie. There were, in actuality, only a handful of incubators in all of Kuwait, certainly not the "hundreds" she claimed. According to Dr. Mohammed Matar, director of Kuwait's primary care system, and his wife, Dr. Fayeza Youssef, who ran the obstetrics unit at the maternity hospital, there were few if any babies in the incubators at the time of the Iraqi invasion. Nayirah's charges, they said, were totally false. "I think it was just something for propaganda," Dr. Matar said. In an ABC-TV News account after the war, John Martin reported that although "patients, including premature babies, did die," this occurred "when many of Kuwait's nurses and doctors stopped working or fled the country"—a far cry from Bush's original assertion that hundreds of babies were murdered by Iraqi troops.[42] Subsequent investigations, including one by Amnesty International, found no evidence for the incubator claims.

It is likely that Nayirah was not even in Kuwait, let alone at the hospital, at that time; the Kuwaiti aristocracy and their families had fled the country weeks before the anticipated invasion.

How did Nayirah first come to the attention of the Congressional Human Rights Caucus, which put her before the world's cameras? It was arranged by Hill & Knowlton, a public relations firm hired to rally the U.S. populace behind Bush's policy of going to war. And it worked!

Hill & Knowlton's yellow ribbon campaign to whip up support for "our" troops, which followed their orchestration of Nayirah's phony "incubator" testimony, was a public relations masterpiece. The claim that satellite photos revealed that Iraq had troops poised to strike Saudi Arabia was also fabricated by the PR firm. Hill & Knowlton was paid between $12 million (as reported two years later on *60 Minutes*) and $20 million (as reported on *20/20*) for "services rendered." The group fronting the money? Citizens for a Free Kuwait, a phony "human rights agency" set up and funded entirely by Kuwait's emirocracy to promote its interests in the U.S.

"When Hill & Knowlton masterminded the Kuwaiti campaign to sell the Gulf War to the American public, the owners of this highly effective propaganda machine were residing in another country"—the United Kingdom—write Sharon Beder and Richard Gosden in *PR Watch*. "Should this give pause for thought? Does it demonstrate a certain potential for the future exercise of global political power—the power to manipulate democratic political processes through managing public opinion, which Hill and Knowlton demonstrated 10 years ago?"[43]

CREATING YOUR PERSONAL CODE OF ETHICS

In order to truly understand your personal ethical code, it is important to think about the components that have shaped your ethical principles up to this point. The majority of individuals subscribe to at least some basic ethical theories. Whether those theories stem from teachings that we received as children from our parents, from our faith or religious beliefs, or simply from life experiences, we all make judgments about the "rightness" or "wrongness" of certain actions based on our own moral values.

Take some time to think about your personal ethical code and the experiences that have shaped your beliefs. The questions below should kick-start your analysis. Learning to identify your current moral code will allow you to better see where your beliefs fit with other ethical theorists and will also assist you in identifying your core values.

- What external influencers (parents, teachers, friends, etc.) have shaped your values?
- What values have you maintained that you were taught as a child?
- Are there any values that you were taught as a child that have been altered as you matured?
- Discuss personal experiences that have shaped your personal values/beliefs.
- What qualities do you value in yourself and/or others?
- What ethical theory or theories do you most closely identify with?
- What ethical systems do you follow on a day-to-day basis?
- What are some of your strongest beliefs about humanity? For example, do you believe that everyone deserves respect? Do you believe that all people are inherently "good"?
- Are there any ethical practices you think are absolutes? For example, it is wrong to lie under any circumstances or it is never permissible to take the life of another living being.

2

Ethics in Public Relations

The same can be said for transparency, a proactive public relations com-munication strategy. Today's publics expect to know more about organizations in which they are involved, including how it operates, its activities, and its finances. Providing observable information builds public trust and support. Transparency is especially significant with fundraising. Donors want to know that their donations are being used as intended and not for other purposes. Public relations practitioners who engage in fundraising should provide annual reports that reflect this information.

What skills are necessary to demonstrate expertise in public relations?
The following skills are necessary to demonstrate expertise in public rela-tions: strategic planning for public relations with knowledge of the RACE and/ or ROPE process—the ability to establish goals and objectives, implement public relations strategies to meet goals and objectives, select and put into action communication tactics to achieve goals and objectives, and evalu-ate the effectiveness of their efforts. The public relations practitioner should also be experienced in building strategic relationships with diverse publics, understand the importance of issue anticipation (environmental scanning and research), manage appropriate responses during crisis situations, counsel senior management, and keep current with all aspects of social media.

Can you provide an example of a time when you had to disagree with what the client felt was necessary and guide them in another direction?
Public relations is a powerful storytelling tool. It's an opportunity for an organization to tell an audience what it's done, what it's doing, and what it intends to do. When trying to make a case for support, a well-crafted public relations campaign can be successful in securing funds from a source unfa-miliar with an organization's services.
During a meeting with legislative representatives in Washington, D.C., to try to obtain federal funding for a multimillion-dollar expansion project, I felt that my client was not providing enough background information about our orga-nization. I could tell from the quizzical look on the person's face with whom we were meeting that he was not following my client's succinct description. I stepped in and guided the presentation in a different direction, which enabled me to tell the whole story. After the meeting, my client expressed his dissat-isfaction with the way I changed course; however, after I explained that my actions were meant to be informational and not disrespectful, he understood. Afterward, I had a lengthy discussion with him about public relations storytell-ing and the impact it can have on fundraising.

How do you balance loyalty to the client and loyalty to society?
I have a copy of the PRSA Code of Ethics on my desk, as should every public relations practitioner. It serves to remind me of my obligation to uphold the integrity of the public relations profession. Also on my desk are my organization's policies and procedures that I must also follow. How do

I balance loyalty to my organization and to society? By building mutual understanding between my organization and its publics through honest and transparent communication.

The PRSA Value of Fairness can also be applied to this question. As a public relations practitioner, I have an obligation to ensure that my organization does not take advantage of its publics, which include patients, family members, board members, donors, and vendors. We must also respect their opinions and their right to express them.

Can you discuss how you deal with differing opinions or maintain free expression of ideas?

Without differing opinions, the world would be a boring place! While I may not always agree with differing opinions, they are a valuable way to learn new ways of doing things. In addition, I'm always interested in learning what other people are thinking.

When dealing with differing opinions, I avoid conflict at all costs. I've learned that open and respectful dialogue between people will result in positive outcomes. I also practice active listening, waiting for the person(s) to finish before talking, and then restating that person's opinion to be sure it is understood.

I always try to keep an open mind to allow for free expression of ideas because I'm a proponent of "out of the box" thinking. If an opinion or suggestion will not work, I always thank the person(s) for expressing it and then provide the reasons why it cannot be implemented. On several occasions, I've taken a few days to research a differing opinion to review all of its aspects.

Embracing the right of free expression is a good thing: it builds stronger employee relations and enhances team spirit. It's also the right thing to do.

What types of ethical issues are entry-level public relations practitioners likely to encounter?

Ethical issues that entry-level public relations practitioners may encounter include:

- A supervisor instructing an entry-level practitioner to embellish a story, or worse, to lie about it.
- Instructing an entry-level practitioner to ignore a reporter's call or email, especially during a crisis.
- Telling an entry-level practitioner that it's all right to say "no comment" to a reporter when litigation is not involved.
- A supervisor telling an entry-level practitioner to remove a contradictory comment from the organization's Facebook page.
- Telling the entry-level practitioner to exclude certain media from covering events.
- Texting, tweeting, surfing the Internet, or posting on Facebook during work hours for personal pleasure.

- Gossiping about a supervisor or fellow employee.
- Divulging bid amounts to competing vendors.
- Complaining about a reporter who wrote an unflattering story about the entry-level PR person's organization.
- A supervisor who asks you to post false reviews online about your company's product.
- Complaining about your job online.

This chapter will discuss the manner in which ethics are applied in public relations and review the history and application of the PRSA code of ethics. Additional attention will highlight many of the negatives associated with practitioners who rely solely on the code of ethics for their decision making without understanding the larger ethical frameworks.

PRACTITIONERS' GUIDING CODE

Possessing a familiarity with a few of the more prominent ethical theories provides an opportunity to discuss ethical decision making and also begin developing a personal code of ethics. Let's take a moment to break down how those theories truly apply to varying areas of public relations.

As a start, we will begin by looking at five professional codes of ethics, the Public Relations Society of America (PRSA) Professional Code of Ethics, American Marketing Code of Ethics, Chartered Institute of Public Relations Code of Conduct (UK), the Society for Professional Journalists Code of Ethics, and the code of ethics for the Public Relations Institute of South Africa.

As you read through the codes, take the time to highlight some of the common themes prevalent within each. Try to recognize how some of the traditional ethical theories, consequentialist ethics, deontological ethics, and ethics of character have assisted in the formation of these codes.

- Do you notice mention of the aftereffects of specific actions?
- Can you identify specific principles that focus on collective happiness?
- How do the ethical codes deal with the categorical imperative or with trust/ honesty?
- Are there principles that focus on rights or freedoms? Can you link that back to the ideas presented in chapter 1 on libertarianism?
- Lastly, can you identify virtues in the various ethical codes? How do the codes reference personal character?

PUBLIC RELATIONS SOCIETY OF AMERICA'S CODE OF ETHICS

The PRSA Member Code of Ethics[1] is a set of ethical guidelines that apply to members of the Public Relations Society of America (PRSA), the world's largest and foremost organization for public relations professionals. According to the PRSA newsroom, there are more than twenty-two thousand professional members and more than ten thousand student members.[2] Recognizing that the level of public trust sought by its members requires a special obligation to operate ethically, PRSA wrote its first code of ethics in 1950.[3] Today, ethical practice is the most important obligation of PRSA members. The PRSA Code of Ethics is a guide for PRSA members as they carry out their professional responsibilities. This document is designed to anticipate and accommodate, by precedent, ethical challenges that may arise.[4]

PRSA Member Statement of Professional Values[5]

This statement presents the core values of PRSA members and, more broadly, of the public relations profession. These values provide the foundation for the Member Code of Ethics and set the industry standard for the professional practice of public relations. These values are the fundamental beliefs that guide our behaviors and decision-making process. We believe our professional values are vital to the integrity of the profession as a whole.

Advocacy

We serve the public interest by acting as responsible advocates for those we represent. We provide a voice in the marketplace of ideas, facts, and viewpoints to aid informed public debate.

Honesty

We adhere to the highest standards of accuracy and truth in advancing the interests of those we represent and in communicating with the public.

Expertise

We acquire and responsibly use specialized knowledge and experience. We advance the profession through continued professional development, research, and education. We build mutual understanding, credibility, and relationships among a wide array of institutions and audiences.

Independence

We provide objective counsel to those we represent. We are accountable for our actions.

Loyalty

We are faithful to those we represent, while honoring our obligation to serve the public interest.

Fairness

We deal fairly with clients, employers, competitors, peers, vendors, the media, and the general public. We respect all opinions and support the right of free expression.

PRSA Code Provisions

Free Flow of Information

Core Principle: Protecting and advancing the free flow of accurate and truthful information is essential to serving the public interest and contributing to informed decision making in a democratic society.

Intent:

- To maintain the integrity of relationships with the media, government officials, and the public.
- To aid informed decision-making.

Guidelines:

- A member shall: Preserve the integrity of the process of communication.
- Be honest and accurate in all communications.
- Act promptly to correct erroneous communications for which the practitioner is responsible.
- Preserve the free flow of unprejudiced information when giving or receiving gifts by ensuring that gifts are nominal, legal, and infrequent.

Examples of Improper Conduct Under This Provision:

- A member representing a ski manufacturer gives a pair of expensive racing skis to a sports magazine columnist, to influence the columnist to write favorable articles about the product.
- A member entertains a government official beyond legal limits and/or in violation of government reporting requirements.

Competition

Core Principle: Promoting healthy and fair competition among professionals preserves an ethical climate while fostering a robust business environment.

Intent:

- To promote respect and fair competition among public relations professionals.
- To serve the public interest by providing the widest choice of practitioner options.

Guidelines:

- A member shall: Follow ethical hiring practices designed to respect free and open competition without deliberately undermining a competitor.
- Preserve intellectual property rights in the marketplace.

Examples of Improper Conduct Under This Provision:

- A member employed by a "client organization" shares helpful information with a counseling firm that is competing with others for the organization's business.
- A member spreads malicious and unfounded rumors about a competitor in order to alienate the competitor's clients and employees in a ploy to recruit people and business.

Disclosure of Information

Core Principle: Open communication fosters informed decision making in a democratic society.

Intent:

To build trust with the public by revealing all information needed for responsible decision making.

Guidelines:

- A member shall: Be honest and accurate in all communications.
- Act promptly to correct erroneous communications for which the member is responsible.
- Investigate the truthfulness and accuracy of information released on behalf of those represented.
- Reveal the sponsors for causes and interests represented.
- Disclose financial interest (such as stock ownership) in a client's organization.
- Avoid deceptive practices.

Examples of Improper Conduct Under This Provision:

- Front groups: A member implements "grass roots" campaigns or letter-writing campaigns to legislators on behalf of undisclosed interest groups.

- Lying by omission: A practitioner for a corporation knowingly fails to release financial information, giving a misleading impression of the corporation's performance.
- A member discovers inaccurate information disseminated via a website or media kit and does not correct the information. A member deceives the public by employing people to pose as volunteers to speak at public hearings and participate in "grass roots" campaigns.

Safeguarding Confidences
Core Principle: Client trust requires appropriate protection of confidential and private information.

Intent:
To protect the privacy rights of clients, organizations, and individuals by safeguarding confidential information.

Guidelines:

- A member shall: Safeguard the confidences and privacy rights of present, former, and prospective clients and employees.
- Protect privileged, confidential, or insider information gained from a client or organization.
- Immediately advise an appropriate authority if a member discovers that confidential information is being divulged by an employee of a client company or organization.

Examples of Improper Conduct Under This Provision:

- A member changes jobs, takes confidential information, and uses that information in the new position to the detriment of the former employer.
- A member intentionally leaks proprietary information to the detriment of some other party.

Conflicts of Interest
Core Principle: Avoiding real, potential or perceived conflicts of interest builds the trust of clients, employers, and the publics.

Intent:

- To earn trust and mutual respect with clients or employers.
- To build trust with the public by avoiding or ending situations that put one's personal or professional interests in conflict with society's interests.

Guidelines:

- A member shall: Act in the best interests of the client or employer, even subordinating the member's personal interests.
- Avoid actions and circumstances that may appear to compromise good business judgment or create a conflict between personal and professional interests.
- Disclose promptly any existing or potential conflict of interest to affected clients or organizations.
- Encourage clients and customers to determine if a conflict exists after notifying all affected parties.

Examples of Improper Conduct Under This Provision:

- The member fails to disclose that he or she has a strong financial interest in a client's chief competitor.
- The member represents a "competitor company" or a "conflicting interest" without informing a prospective client.

Enhancing the Profession
Core Principle: Public relations professionals work constantly to strengthen the public's trust in the profession.

Intent:

- To build respect and credibility with the public for the profession of public relations.
- To improve, adapt and expand professional practices.

Guidelines:

- A member shall: Acknowledge that there is an obligation to protect and enhance the profession.
- Keep informed and educated about practices in the profession to ensure ethical conduct.
- Actively pursue personal professional development.
- Decline representation of clients or organizations that urge or require actions contrary to this Code.
- Accurately define what public relations activities can accomplish.
- Counsel subordinates in proper ethical decision making.
- Require that subordinates adhere to the ethical requirements of the Code.
- Report practices not in compliance with the Code, whether committed by PRSA members or not, to the appropriate authority.

Examples of Improper Conduct Under This Provision:

- A PRSA member declares publicly that a product the client sells is safe, without disclosing evidence to the contrary.
- A member initially assigns some questionable client work to a non-member practitioner to avoid the ethical obligation of PRSA membership.

AMERICAN MARKETING ASSOCIATION STATEMENT OF ETHICS[6]

Preamble

The American Marketing Association commits itself to promoting the highest standard of professional ethical norms and values for its members (practitioners, academics and students). Norms are established standards of conduct that are expected and maintained by society and/or professional organizations. Values represent the collective conception of what communities find desirable, important and morally proper. Values also serve as the criteria for evaluating our own personal actions and the actions of others. As marketers, we recognize that we not only serve our organizations but also act as stewards of society in creating, facilitating and executing the transactions that are part of the greater economy. In this role, marketers are expected to embrace the highest professional ethical norms and the ethical values implied by our responsibility toward multiple stakeholders (e.g., customers, employees, investors, peers, channel members, regulators and the host community).

Ethical Norms

As Marketers, we must:

1. Do no harm. This means consciously avoiding harmful actions or omissions by embodying high ethical standards and adhering to all applicable laws and regulations in the choices we make.
2. Foster trust in the marketing system. This means striving for good faith and fair dealing so as to contribute toward the efficacy of the exchange process as well as avoiding deception in product design, pricing, communication, and delivery of distribution.
3. Embrace ethical values. This means building relationships and enhancing consumer confidence in the integrity of marketing by affirming these core values: honesty, responsibility, fairness, respect, transparency and citizenship.

Ethical Values

Honesty—to be forthright in dealings with customers and stakeholders. To this end, we will:

- Strive to be truthful in all situations and at all times.
- Offer products of value that do what we claim in our communications.
- Stand behind our products if they fail to deliver their claimed benefits.
- Honor our explicit and implicit commitments and promises.

Responsibility—to accept the consequences of our marketing decisions and strategies. To this end, we will:

- Strive to serve the needs of customers.
- Avoid using coercion with all stakeholders.
- Acknowledge the social obligations to stakeholders that come with increased marketing and economic power.
- Recognize our special commitments to vulnerable market segments such as children, seniors, the economically impoverished, market illiterates and others who may be substantially disadvantaged.
- Consider environmental stewardship in our decision-making.

Fairness—to balance justly the needs of the buyer with the interests of the seller. To this end, we will:

- Represent products in a clear way in selling, advertising and other forms of communication; this includes the avoidance of false, misleading and deceptive promotion.
- Reject manipulations and sales tactics that harm customer trust.
- Refuse to engage in price fixing, predatory pricing, price gouging or "bait-and-switch" tactics.
- Avoid knowing participation in conflicts of interest.
- Seek to protect the private information of customers, employees and partners.

Respect—to acknowledge the basic human dignity of all stakeholders. To this end, we will:

- Value individual differences and avoid stereotyping customers or depicting demographic groups (e.g., gender, race, sexual orientation) in a negative or dehumanizing way.
- Listen to the needs of customers and make all reasonable efforts to monitor and improve their satisfaction on an ongoing basis.
- Make every effort to understand and respectfully treat buyers, suppliers, intermediaries and distributors from all cultures.
- Acknowledge the contributions of others, such as consultants, employees and coworkers, to marketing endeavors.
- Treat everyone, including our competitors, as we would wish to be treated.

Transparency—to create a spirit of openness in marketing operations. To this end, we will:

- Strive to communicate clearly with all constituencies.
- Accept constructive criticism from customers and other stakeholders.
- Explain and take appropriate action regarding significant product or service risks, component substitutions or other foreseeable eventualities that could affect customers or their perception of the purchase decision.
- Disclose list prices and terms of financing as well as available price deals and adjustments.

Citizenship—to fulfill the economic, legal, philanthropic and societal responsibilities that serve stakeholders. To this end, we will:

- Strive to protect the ecological environment in the execution of marketing campaigns.
- Give back to the community through volunteerism and charitable donations.
- Contribute to the overall betterment of marketing and its reputation.
- Urge supply chain members to ensure that trade is fair for all participants, including producers in developing countries.

Implementation

We expect AMA members to be courageous and proactive in leading and/or aiding their organizations in the fulfillment of the explicit and implicit promises made to those stakeholders. We recognize that every industry sector and marketing subdiscipline (e.g., marketing research, e-commerce, Internet selling, direct marketing, and advertising) has its own specific ethical issues that require policies and commentary. An array of such codes can be accessed through links on the AMA Web site. Consistent with the principle of subsidiarity (solving issues at the level where the expertise resides), we encourage all such groups to develop and/or refine their industry and discipline-specific codes of ethics to supplement these guiding ethical norms and values.

CHARTERED INSTITUTE OF PUBLIC RELATIONS CODE OF CONDUCT (UK)[7]

Principles

1. Members of the Chartered Institute of Public Relations agree to:

- maintain the highest standards of professional endeavour, integrity, confidentiality, financial propriety and personal conduct;
- deal honestly and fairly in business with employers, employees, clients, fellow professionals, other professions and the public;

- respect, in their dealings with other people, the legal and regulatory frameworks and codes of all countries where they practise;
- uphold the reputation of, and do nothing that would bring into disrepute, the public relations profession or the Chartered Institute of Public Relations;
- respect and abide by this Code and related Notes of Guidance issued by the Chartered Institute of Public Relations and ensure that others who are accountable to them (e.g. subordinates and sub-contractors) do the same;
- encourage professional training and development among members of the profession in order to raise and maintain professional standards generally.

Putting the principles into practice
2. Examples of good public relations practice include:

Integrity and honesty

- Ensuring that clients, employers, employees, colleagues and fellow professionals are fully informed about the nature of representation, what can be delivered and achieved, and what other parties must do in order to enable the desired result.
- Never deliberately concealing the practitioner's role as representative of a client or employer, even if the client or employer remains anonymous: e.g. by promoting a cause in the guise of a disinterested party or member of the public.
- Checking the reliability and accuracy of information before dissemination.
- Supporting the CIPR Principles by bringing to the attention of the CIPR examples of malpractice and unprofessional conduct.

Capacity, capability and competence

- Delivering work competently: that is, in a timely, cost-effective, appropriate and thoughtful manner, according to the actual or implied contract; applying due professional judgement and experience; taking necessary steps to resolve problems; and ensuring that clients and other interested parties are informed, advised and consulted as necessary.
- Being aware of the limitations of professional capacity and capability: without limiting realistic scope for development, being willing to accept or delegate only that work for which practitioners are suitably skilled and experienced and which they have the resources to undertake.
- Where appropriate, collaborating on projects to ensure the necessary skill base.

Transparency and avoiding conflicts of interest

- Disclosing to employers, clients or potential clients any financial interest in a supplier being recommended or engaged.

- Declaring conflicts of interest (or circumstances which may give rise to them) in writing to clients, potential clients and employers as soon as they arise.
- Ensuring that services provided are costed, delivered and accounted for in a manner that conforms to accepted business practice and ethics.

Confidentiality

- Safeguarding confidences, e.g. of present and former clients and employers.
- Never using confidential and 'insider' information to the disadvantage or prejudice of others, e.g. clients and employers, or to self-advantage of any kind.
- Not disclosing confidential information unless specific permission has been granted or if required or covered by law.

Interpreting the Code
3. In the interpretation of this code, the Laws of the Land shall apply. With that proviso, the code will be implemented according to the decision at the time of the Professional Practices Committee.

Maintaining professional standards
CIPR Members are encouraged to
a) raise and maintain their own professional standards by, for example:

- identifying and closing professional skills gaps through the Institute's Continuing Professional Development programme;
- participating in the work of the Institute through the committee structure, special interest and vocational groups, training and networking events;
- evaluating the practice of public relations through use of recognised tools and other quality management and quality assurance systems (e.g. ISO standards);
- constantly striving to improve the quality of business performance;
- sharing information on good practice with Members and, equally, referring perceived examples of poor practice to the Institute.

b) raise the professional standards of other public relations practitioners to the level of CIPR Members by, for example:

- offering work experience to students interested in pursuing a career in public relations;
- encouraging employees and colleagues to join and support the CIPR;
- specifying a preference for CIPR applicants for staff positions advertised.

c) spread awareness of the CIPR's role as guardian of standards for the public relations profession by, for example:

- displaying the CIPR designatory letters on business stationery;
- referring to the CIPR Code of Conduct in every contract.

SOCIETY OF PROFESSIONAL JOURNALISTS CODE OF ETHICS[8]

Preamble
Members of the Society of Professional Journalists believe that public enlightenment is the forerunner of justice and the foundation of democracy. Ethical journalism strives to ensure the free exchange of information that is accurate, fair and thorough. An ethical journalist acts with integrity.

The Society declares these four principles as the foundation of ethical journalism and encourages their use in its practice by all people in all media.

Seek Truth and Report It
Ethical journalism should be accurate and fair. Journalists should be honest and courageous in gathering, reporting and interpreting information.

Journalists should:

- Take responsibility for the accuracy of their work. Verify information before releasing it. Use original sources whenever possible.
- Remember that neither speed nor format excuses inaccuracy.
- Provide context. Take special care not to misrepresent or oversimplify in promoting, previewing or summarizing a story.
- Gather, update and correct information throughout the life of a news story.
- Be cautious when making promises, but keep the promises they make.
- Identify sources clearly. The public is entitled to as much information as possible to judge the reliability and motivations of sources.
- Consider sources' motives before promising anonymity. Reserve anonymity for sources who may face danger, retribution or other harm, and have information that cannot be obtained elsewhere. Explain why anonymity was granted.
- Diligently seek subjects of news coverage to allow them to respond to criticism or allegations of wrongdoing.
- Avoid undercover or other surreptitious methods of gathering information unless traditional, open methods will not yield information vital to the public.
- Be vigilant and courageous about holding those with power accountable. Give voice to the voiceless.
- Support the open and civil exchange of views, even views they find repugnant.
- Recognize a special obligation to serve as watchdogs over public affairs and government. Seek to ensure that the public's business is conducted in the open, and that public records are open to all.

- Provide access to source material when it is relevant and appropriate.
- Boldly tell the story of the diversity and magnitude of the human experience. Seek sources whose voices we seldom hear.
- Avoid stereotyping. Journalists should examine the ways their values and experiences may shape their reporting.
- Label advocacy and commentary.
- Never deliberately distort facts or context, including visual information. Clearly label illustrations and re-enactments.
- Never plagiarize. Always attribute.

Minimize Harm
Ethical journalism treats sources, subjects, colleagues and members of the public as human beings deserving of respect.

Journalists should:

- Balance the public's need for information against potential harm or discomfort. Pursuit of the news is not a license for arrogance or undue intrusiveness.
- Show compassion for those who may be affected by news coverage. Use heightened sensitivity when dealing with juveniles, victims of sex crimes, and sources or subjects who are inexperienced or unable to give consent. Consider cultural differences in approach and treatment.
- Recognize that legal access to information differs from an ethical justification to publish or broadcast.
- Realize that private people have a greater right to control information about themselves than public figures and others who seek power, influence or attention. Weigh the consequences of publishing or broadcasting personal information.
- Avoid pandering to lurid curiosity, even if others do.
- Balance a suspect's right to a fair trial with the public's right to know. Consider the implications of identifying criminal suspects before they face legal charges.
- Consider the long-term implications of the extended reach and permanence of publication. Provide updated and more complete information as appropriate.

Act Independently
The highest and primary obligation of ethical journalism is to serve the public.

Journalists should:

- Avoid conflicts of interest, real or perceived. Disclose unavoidable conflicts.
- Refuse gifts, favors, fees, free travel and special treatment, and avoid political and other outside activities that may compromise integrity or impartiality, or may damage credibility.

- Be wary of sources offering information for favors or money; do not pay for access to news. Identify content provided by outside sources, whether paid or not.
- Deny favored treatment to advertisers, donors or any other special interests, and resist internal and external pressure to influence coverage.
- Distinguish news from advertising and shun hybrids that blur the lines between the two. Prominently label sponsored content.

Be Accountable and Transparent
Ethical journalism means taking responsibility for one's work and explaining one's decisions to the public.

Journalists should:

- Explain ethical choices and processes to audiences. Encourage a civil dialogue with the public about journalistic practices, coverage and news content.
- Respond quickly to questions about accuracy, clarity and fairness.
- Acknowledge mistakes and correct them promptly and prominently.
- Explain corrections and clarifications carefully and clearly.
- Expose unethical conduct in journalism, including within their organizations.
- Abide by the same high standards they expect of others.

PUBLIC RELATIONS INSTITUTE OF SOUTHERN AFRICA[9]

Code of Ethics and Professional Standards for the Practice of Public Relations and Communication Management
For members of PRISA—The Institute for Public Relations & Communication Management and its chapters—Public Relations Consultants' Chapter of PRISA (PRCC)
Whenever reference is made to an individual, member or colleague, it applies to both the individual and an entity (consultancy).

Preamble A profession is distinguished by certain characteristics or attributes, including:

- Mastery of a particular intellectual skill through education and training
- Acceptance of duties to a broader society than merely one's clients/employers
- Objectivity
- High standards of conduct and performance

Introduction
The Institute for Public Relations and Communication Management Southern Africa (PRISA) is committed to ethical practices. The level of public support our

members seek, as we serve the public good, means we have taken on a special obligation to operate ethically.

The value of member reputation depends upon the ethical conduct of everyone affiliated with PRISA. We set an example for each other—as well as other professionals—by our pursuit of excellence with exemplary standards of performance, professionalism and ethical conduct.

Emphasis on enforcement of our Code has been eliminated. However, the PRISA Board of Directors retains the right to bar from membership or expel from the Institute, any individual who has been or is sanctioned by the PRISA Disciplinary Committee or government agency or convicted in a Court of Law of an action that is in violation of the Code.

We believe ethical practice is the most important obligation of PRISA members and we will strive at all times to enhance and protect the dignity of the profession.

Declaration of Principles

We base our professional principles on the fundamental value and dignity of the individual. We believe in and support the free exercise of human rights, especially freedom of speech, freedom of assembly and freedom of the media, which are essential to the practice of good public relations.

In serving the interests of clients and employers, we dedicate ourselves to the goals of better communication, mutual understanding and co-operation among diverse individuals, groups and institutions of society. We also subscribe to and support equal opportunity of employment in the public relations and communication profession and lifelong professional development.

We pledge:

- to conduct ourselves professionally, with truth, accuracy, fairness and responsibility to the public and towards our colleagues and to an informed society;
- to improve our individual competence and advance the knowledge and proficiency of the profession through continuing education and research;
- to adhere to the articles of the Code of Ethics and Professional Standards for the Practice of Public Relations and Communication Management in Southern Africa and to adhere to the principles of the Global protocol on Ethics in Public Relations and Communication Management.

Code of Ethics and Professional Standards

1   Definition
Public relations is the management, through communication, of perceptions and strategic relationships between an organisation and its internal and external stakeholders.

2 Professional Conduct

2.1   We shall acknowledge that there is an obligation to protect and enhance the profession.

2.2   We shall keep informed and educated about practices in the profession that ensures ethical conduct.

2.3   We shall actively pursue personal professional development.

2.4   We are committed to ethical practices, preservation of public trust, and the pursuit of communication excellence with powerful standards of performance, professionalism, and ethical conduct.

2.5   We shall accurately define what public relations activities can and cannot accomplish. In the conduct of our professional activities, we shall respect the public interest and the dignity of the individual. It is our responsibility at all times to deal fairly and honestly with our clients or employers, past or present, with our colleagues, media communication and with the public.

2.6   We shall conduct our professional lives in accordance with the public interest. We shall not conduct ourselves in any manner detrimental to the profession of public relations.

2.7   We have a positive duty to maintain integrity and accuracy, as well as generally accepted standards of good taste.

2.8   We shall not knowingly, intentionally or recklessly communicate false or misleading information. It is our obligation to use proper care to avoid doing so inadvertently.

2.9   We shall not guarantee the achievement of specified results beyond our direct control. We shall not negotiate nor agree terms with a prospective employer or client on the basis of payment only contingent upon specific future public relations achievements.

2.10 We shall, when acting for a client or employer, who belongs to a profession, respect the code of ethics of that other profession and shall not knowingly be party to any breach of such a code.

2.11 We shall obey laws and public policies governing our professional activities and will be sensitive to the spirit of all laws and regulations and, should any law or public policy be violated, for whatever reason, act promptly to correct the situation.

2.12 We shall give credit for unique expressions borrowed from others and identify the sources and purposes of all information disseminated to the public.

3 Conduct Towards Clients/Employers

3.1   We shall safeguard the confidences of both present and former clients and employers. We shall not disclose or make use of information given or obtained in confidence from an employer or client, past or present, for personal gain or otherwise, or to the disadvantage or prejudice of such client or employer.

3.2   We shall not represent conflicting or competing interests without the express consent of those involved, given after full disclosure of the facts. We shall not place ourselves in a position where our interests are or may be in conflict with a duty to a client, without full disclosure of such interests to all involved.

3.3   We shall not be party to any activity which seeks to dissemble or mislead by promoting one disguised or undisclosed interest whilst appearing to further another. It is our duty to ensure that the actual interest of any organization with which we may be professionally concerned is adequately declared.

3.4   In the course of our professional services to the employer or client we shall not accept payment either in cash or in kind in connection with these services from another source without the express consent of our employer or client.

4   Conduct Towards Colleagues

4.1   We shall not maliciously injure the professional reputation or practice of another individual engaged in the public relations profession.

4.2   We shall at all times uphold this Code, co-operate with colleagues in doing so and in enforcing decisions on any matter arising from this application.

4.3   Registered individuals who knowingly cause or permit another person or organisation to act in a manner inconsistent with this Code or are party to such an action shall be deemed to be in breach of it.

4.4   If we have reason to believe that another colleague has engaged in practices which may be in breach of this Code, or practices which may be unethical, unfair or illegal, it is our duty to advise the Institute promptly.

4.5   We shall not invite any employee of a client to consider alternative employment.

5   Conduct Towards the Business Environment

5.1   We shall not recommend the use of any organisation in which we have a financial interest, nor make use of its services on behalf of our clients or employers, without declaring our interest.

5.2   In performing professional services for a client or employer we shall not accept fees, commissions or any other consideration from anyone other than the client or employer in connection with those services, without the express consent of the client/employer, given after disclosure of the facts.

5.3   We shall sever relations, as soon as possible, with any organisation or individual if such a relationship requires conduct contrary to this Code.

6   Conduct Towards the Channels of Communication

6.1   We shall not engage in any practice which tends to corrupt the integrity of channels or media of communication.

6.2   We shall identify publicly the name of the client or employer on whose behalf any public communication is made.

7 **Conduct Towards the State**
    7.1   We respect the principles contained in the Constitution of the country in which we are resident.
    7.2   We shall not offer or give any reward to any person holding public office, with intent to further our interests or those of our employer.

8 **Conduct Towards PRISA**
    8.1   We shall at all times respect the dignity and authority of PRISA.
    8.2   We are bound to uphold the annual registration fee levied by PRISA, which fee is payable as determined by the PRISA Board.

9 **Communication**
    9.1   PRISA encourages the widest possible communication about its Code.
    9.2   The PRISA Code of Ethics and Professional Standards for the Practice of Public Relations and Communication Management is freely available to all. Permission is hereby granted to any individual or organisation wishing to copy and incorporate all or part of the PRISA Code into personal and corporate codes, with the understanding that appropriate credit be given to PRISA in any publication of such codes.
    9.3   The Institute's magazine, Communika, publishes periodic articles dealing with ethical issues. At least one session at the annual conference is devoted to ethics. The national office of PRISA through its professional development activities encourages and supports efforts by PRISA student chapter, professional chapters and region to conduct meetings and workshops devoted to the topic of ethics and the PRISA Code. New and renewing members of PRISA sign the following statement as part of their application: "I have read, understand and subscribe to the PRISA Code of Ethics and Professional Standards for Public Relations and Communication Management."

10 **Enforcement**
PRISA fosters compliance with its Code by engaging in global communication campaigns rather than through negative sanctions. However, in keeping with the 2.11 article of the PRISA Code, members of PRISA who are found guilty by the PRISA Disciplinary committee or an appropriate governmental or judicial body of violating laws and public policies governing their professional activities may have their membership terminated by the PRISA board following procedures set forth in the Institute's bylaws.

PRACTICAL CHALLENGES AND OPPORTUNITIES

The prevalence of duty-based ethics is apparent in the above ethical codes. Each of the codes is based on principles that practitioners are expected to follow. All practitioners are moral agents that act on their own will to meet the needs of their clients.

They are expected to perform based on the best interests of their clients and to be good and virtuous insofar as professional relationships are concerned. Throughout each of the codes there is an inherent push to work toward affording for the greater good and toward providing your clients with certain rights. For example, clients have the right to honesty, integrity, and unprejudiced information. As a public relations practitioner, it is important to note that despite the likelihood that you will work for a myriad of different employers and you must maintain loyalty to several different publics, your primary loyalty should always remain, first and foremost, to the public.

In examining the six ethical codes listed above, you will notice that there is also significant overlap between them. Each of the codes mentions some form of truth and/or honesty. They highlight the expectation of transparency despite the fact that the PRSA code of ethics labels this as a free flow of information. They also discuss the importance of independence including responsibility and competence and they promote an element of fairness and accountability.

The codes highlight the reliance on publics and reputation managements as well as the ability to act ethically and to follow personal and organizational principles despite the ever-present push to do otherwise.

The initial challenge that each of these codes faces is the lack of social media implementation. While concepts like honesty, truth, fairness, and transparency can be applied to social media, from an ethics perspective this can get tricky. According to PRSA, real-time content generated through applications such as Snapchat, or streaming video content such as Facebook Live, enable authors to capture events as they happen in an unfiltered, unedited manner—creating both opportunity and risk.[10] Since social media platforms evolve and are dynamic in nature, core concepts from the PRSA Code of Ethics (Code) should guide professionals in their responsible use of social media to best serve their clients, organizations, and the public's interests.

Additionally, depending on the situation, minimizing harm and fulfilling a responsibility to stakeholders or an employer can be difficult. What if the stakeholders are requesting that you do something that will protect the organization but harm the general public? For example, if you are the public relations director for a large city, what happens if the mayor tells you there is an issue with the pipes in that city but asks you to keep the information quiet until he can develop an appropriate course of action? He does not want to panic his residents. You don't have concrete details about the problem with the pipes, but you have overheard discussions of lead in the water. How long do you withhold information? If you remain quiet, you are minimizing harm to the city from an investment standpoint; however, you may be contributing to the harm of thousands of unsuspecting residents. If you speak up, there is a likelihood that irreparable damage could be made to your relationship with your employer and you could potentially be out of work. What do you do?

Professionals voluntarily agree to abide by the code of ethics. There is no governing body to enforce ethical principles and no repercussions aside from harm to one's moral character applied to those who choose not to follow the code. Licensing or certification are not required to practice public relations. Therefore, a public relations practitioner merely agrees to follow the professional code. According to Donald Wright, ethical codes are unenforceable.[11] The Institute for Public Relations states that practitioners often find the code of ethics vague with rudimentary ideas that are not useful in situations they have encountered in their careers.[12] If a difficult situation arises and the practitioner strays from the guidelines of their ethical code, they can still maintain a career in public relations. These reasons highlight why opponents of ethical codes state that they play an insignificant role in keeping practitioners ethical.

However, arguments can be made for the idea that having a theoretical grounding in ethics and training in ethical decision making can assist public relations practitioners in effectively navigating ethical dilemmas. Practitioners who counsel clients from a multitude of backgrounds as well as C-suite executives, stakeholders, and other company representatives require the ability to make ethically defensible decisions. Having an arsenal of ethical theories to draw from as well as the knowledge and expertise in a multitude of ethical codes combined with both educational and personal knowledge can assist a practitioner in not only making a moral decision but in having the ability to explain and defend that decision.

Ethical dilemmas are prevalent in all areas. Learning to navigate them and to work confidently within either a personal or professional code of ethics can assist up-and-coming practitioners in job success. In the coming chapters we will continue to explore the codes of ethics and begin to applying these ethical principles to various case studies.

As we conclude, let's examine a case study that deals directly with the ability to make ethical decisions.

SOLVING THE ETHICAL DILEMMA: CALL OF DUTY

On September 29, 2015, at 10 a.m., Current Event Aggregate (Agg. for short) broke the news of a terrorist attack in Singapore.

The dire situation unfolded in a series of tweets claiming that Singapore was in a state of emergency and that martial law had been declared.[13]

BREAKING NEWS: Unconfirmed reports are coming in of an explosion on the North bank of the Singapore Marina.

—Call of Duty (@CallofDuty) September 29, 2015

The cause of the explosion is unknown, but large plumes of dark smoke have been seen rising from the site.

—Call of Duty (@CallofDuty) September 29, 2015

Drones have been spotted over an area approx. 30 square miles in size, broadcasting messages advising people to stay in their homes.

—Call of Duty (@CallofDuty) September 29, 2015

City Authorities urge the public not to panic, and to not hinder the emergency teams that are converging on the area.

—Call of Duty (@CallofDuty) September 29, 2015

UPDATE: Sources confirm explosion took place at Singapore Research Laboratories belonging to Coalescence Corporation.

—Call of Duty (@CallofDuty) September 29, 2015

Authorities have implemented a no-fly zone in response to the apparent crash of relief VTOLs heading to the scene of the explosion.

—Call of Duty (@CallofDuty) September 29, 2015

Reports are starting to emerge of roadblocks on major thoroughfares, turning back traffic from the scene of the apparent accident.

—Call of Duty (@CallofDuty) September 29, 2015

UPDATE: Singapore Authorities have officially announced a state of emergency and declared martial law.

—Call of Duty (@CallofDuty) September 29, 2015

Shots have been fired at the newly established blockades as citizens attempt to flee the new "Quarantine Zone."

—Call of Duty (@CallofDuty) September 29, 2015

The concern with the above tweets is that this was not an actual news story. Nothing was happening in Singapore. Call of Duty simply used its Twitter feed for a publicity stunt. The company altered its branding, including the name, header image, and profile picture on their Twitter account, to look like an account from an aggregate news network. They then tweeted seemingly random content about fashion and movies. These random tweets were followed with the tweets listed above.

The controversial stunt was designed to provide hints about the plot of the upcoming game *Call of Duty Black Ops III*, which takes place in Singapore in the year 2065, and to essentially create hype about the release. It was not until the very end of their tweet storm that they acknowledged that this attack was not happening:

This was a glimpse into the future fiction of #BlackOps3.

—Call of Duty (@CallofDuty) September 29, 2015

The stunt was not well received. Jason Blundell of Treyarch, the multiplatform software developer behind the *Call of Duty* series and a subsidiary of Activision, provided the following apology. He stressed that the campaign was not meant to elicit fear and that it had been taken out of context. "It was done on our channel, and it

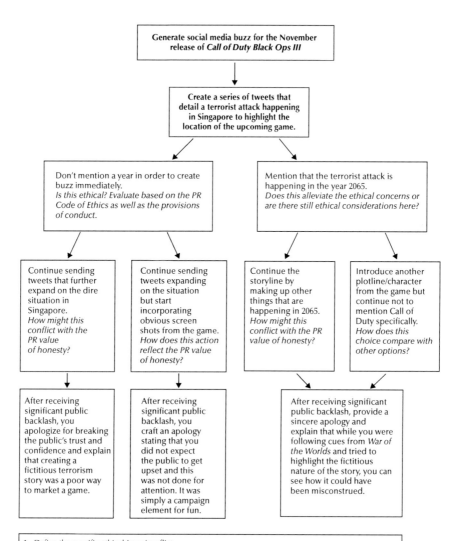

Generate social media buzz for the November release of *Call of Duty Black Ops III*

Create a series of tweets that detail a terrorist attack happening in Singapore to highlight the location of the upcoming game.

Don't mention a year in order to create buzz immediately. *Is this ethical? Evaluate based on the PR Code of Ethics as well as the provisions of conduct.*

Mention that the terrorist attack is happening in the year 2065. *Does this alleviate the ethical concerns or are there still ethical considerations here?*

Continue sending tweets that further expand on the dire situation in Singapore. *How might this conflict with the PR value of honesty?*

Continue sending tweets expanding on the situation but start incorporating obvious screen shots from the game. *How does this action reflect the PR value of honesty?*

Continue the storyline by making up other things that are happening in 2065. *How might this conflict with the PR value of honesty?*

Introduce another plotline/character from the game but continue not to mention Call of Duty specifically. *How does this choice compare with other options?*

After receiving significant public backlash, you apologize for breaking the public's trust and confidence and explain that creating a fictitious terrorism story was a poor way to market a game.

After receiving significant public backlash, you craft an apology stating that you did not expect the public to get upset and this was not done for attention. It was simply a campaign element for fun.

After receiving significant public backlash, provide a sincere apology and explain that while you were following cues from *War of the Worlds* and tried to highlight the fictitious nature of the story, you can see how it could have been misconstrued.

1. Define the specific ethical issue/conflict.
2. Identify internal/external factors (e.g. legal, political, social, economic) that may influence the decision.
3. Identify key values.
4. Identify the parties who will be affected by the decision and define the public relations professional's obligation to each.
5. Select ethical principles to guide the decision-making process.
6. Make a decision and justify it.

The decision guide at the end of chapters 2–8 is based on Kathy Fitzpatrick, "Ethical decision-making guide helps resolve ethical dilemmas," accessed November 2, 2016, http://www.prsa.org/AboutPRSA/Ethics/documents/decisionguide.pdf.

was to talk about the fiction of the world. I think we were as shocked as everybody else when it started blowing up, because essentially we were teeing up ready for a story beat. So again, very sorry for anyone who took it that way. It wasn't meant that way at all—it was supposed to just be getting ready for a campaign element."[14]

Notice the decision tree above limits you to the options you may select for generating social media buzz. The decisions regarding how to constrain or respond to the inevitable fallout from the campaign are provided. These highlight the available options to both demonstrate how the actual campaign was run and to give you an opportunity to think through the crisis that could potentially ensue as a result of these actions.

Take a moment to develop an entirely new/different decision tree with options, including advising a client not to run the campaign and/or to develop a completely new campaign (details of your choosing). Remember to be tactful in your presentation to the client, as it is important to guide them toward the most ethical option while continuing to put the good of the general public at the forefront of your decision-making processes.

II

PUBLIC RELATIONS SOCIETY OF AMERICA'S CODE OF ETHICS

3

Advocacy

As a communicator, how do you feel about taking on the role of advocate?

As a communicator, I've embraced becoming an advocate. In fact, I find advocacy to be a necessity in my position. As part of a public-facing role I will often find myself in situations where I have the opportunity to increase awareness of the company I work for. Working for an insurance company presents many challenges, especially in reputation management. By advocating for my industry and the company I work for, I am able to present the facts and the correct information to help adjust the negative reputation that insurance companies tend to carry.

Discuss the importance of honesty and transparency as it applies to public relations.

Honesty and transparency are largely important in public relations. Luckily for me, I work for a company who prides itself on both honesty and transparency, which is not always the case elsewhere. That doesn't mean I'm not challenged in either area regularly. It is important to practice honesty and transparency in everything we do as public relations professionals because it is our job to present the companies we work for in a positive light. That does not, however, mean hiding or falsifying information to make the company look better than it is. Being honest and transparent also means taking responsibility for mistakes and allowing others the opportunity to see how the company reacts.

What skills are necessary to demonstrate expertise in public relations?
There are many skills necessary to demonstrate expertise in public relations. For young professionals, like myself, it is extremely important to be
aware of these skills and to work toward garnering them. I have found that
excellent written and verbal communication skills are important in all areas
of public relations as well as being able to communicate across all medi-
ums. Creativity, organization, research, event planning, and client relations
are skills my job requires daily.

**Can you provide an example of a time when you had to disagree with what
the client felt was necessary and guide them in another direction?**
In my position, I work on an in-house creative team. I have the pleasure of
working directly with our marketing director on many projects. Sometimes
she and I will disagree with each other. Most recently, I was working on our
social media schedule for the following month. My boss and I discussed the
schedule and she pitched an idea for a specific post. This was a particular
case where I didn't see eye-to-eye with her on the messaging and was forced
to explain to her how it may appear to our audience. She and I discussed our
differing perspectives and those of our audience at length until we agreed on
specific changes in wording. By compromising, we created a successful post
and both of us were satisfied with the messaging. In other similar situations,
she may help me understand her point of view or we may have scrapped
the idea altogether. The key is to stay rational and explain, in a respectful
way, what may work better. In doing so, both sides are able to understand
differing points of view.

How do you balance loyalty to the client and loyalty to society?
Working in-house, I have a loyalty to the company I work for. I enjoy coming to work every day and enjoy the work I do. However, I still have a responsibility to society to communicate with honesty and integrity. There may be
times when mistakes are made and the company is in the spotlight. Although I
am loyal to my company, it is my job to show the public that we take responsibility for such mistakes and are willing to make a bad situation right.

**Can you discuss how you deal with differing opinions or maintain free
expression of ideas?**
In every job and in every industry, departments or teams of employees are
bound to disagree. It comes with the territory. Having multiple ideas and
viewpoints is actually a great thing! Sometimes there are "too many cooks in
the kitchen," but oftentimes one idea is not the best idea. Working on a team
with great synergy means that everyone is respectful of all ideas presented and
the team considers everything. Sometimes we have to deal with negativity or
a coworker who doesn't want to hear our opinion. I deal with this by explaining my position on the idea. Sometimes that person still won't see your point
of view and sometimes you will need to "pick your battles." As long as we're

all working toward the same goal, we are all on the right track. It can be a challenge especially if you are happy with your idea, but sometimes we forget to look at the bigger picture. I do this by asking myself, "Will this benefit the company?" If the answer is yes to any idea presented, then I am willing to compromise. My department has many moving parts and we all wear a lot of hats, so there is a constant free-flow of ideas and information circulating. Although we may disagree from time to time, we challenge ourselves to be the best we can be as a team for the sake of the company. In doing this, we have created an open environment where no idea is a bad idea.

What types of ethical issues are entry-level public relations practitioners likely to encounter?

Ethical issues can arise at any level of tenure. As a young professional, it may be difficult to detect something unethical, so it is important to stay alert. It is our responsibility to use our instincts, our education, and our common sense when dealing with public relations and society. Young professionals are coming into older industries where nothing has been changed for several years, and we must have an understanding of ethics to make changes for the betterment of the company. As an entry-level public relations practitioner it may be tempting to act as an expert when, in reality, you're still learning. This is tempting in all levels of expertise, but as a young professional we may have the need to prove ourselves to the company we work for. Stick to what you know and learn what you don't. It's never a good idea to lie or emphasize a certain skill.

ETHICAL DILEMMA: PREVENTION PROJECT DUNKELFELD

As a society, it is our responsibility to protect the weak and to safeguard those unable to defend themselves. Children are our nation's most precious resource. They require the love, guidance, and care of those around them to mature into functional adults. However, as we have seen multiple times in recent media reports, not all children grow up shielded from harm. With each account, the same questions are always raised. "Why didn't anyone get involved?" or "We, as a society, have to find a way to make this stop."

Molestation or sexual abuse of children is prevalent within our society. According to the Rape, Abuse and Incest National Network (RAINN), "every eight minutes, child protective service substantiates, or finds evidence for, a claim of child sexual abuse."[1] This figure only accounts for the United States. International numbers are similarly abysmal. In England and Wales, part of the United Kingdom, approximately twenty-three thousand child sexual abuse cases were recorded by police in 2012–2013.[2] In South Africa, one in three children will be sexually abused in their lifetime.[3] These numbers are likely to be much higher, as child sexual abuse often goes unreported.[4] Clearly, society is failing these children.

A group in Germany has been running a provocative ad campaign with an unusual target: pedophiles.

lieben sie kinder mehr als ihnen lieb ist?

es gibt hilfe! kostenlos und unter schweigepflicht. institut für sexualmedizin der charité,
telefon: 030/450 529 450, www.kein-taeter-werden.de

mit unterstützung von CHARITÉ

But what if something could be done to protect children from sexual predators? Would you advocate for the implementation of such a program? Prevention Project Dunkelfeld (the "dark field" project) is a program in Germany targeting the identification and treatment of pedophiles. The intense stigma surrounding pedophilia and high percentage of recidivism, 50 to 80 percent, assists in creating the low levels of public support for such programs.[5]

The project launched in 2004 with a media campaign that focused on providing pedophiles an opportunity to receive help. The campaign tagline focused on the idea that not all pedophiles harm children. "You are not guilty because of your sexual desire, but you are responsible for your sexual behavior. There is help! Don't become an offender!"[6] In its outreach to the greater communities, the campaign utilized a number of media channels including print and broadcast. It also targeted heavy traffic locations including movie theaters and billboards. Three years after the project's launch, 808 individuals had inquired about participation.[7] What makes this program both unique and controversial at the same time is that the self-identified pedophile received confidential treatment based on a PIN number; all information remained confidential. Even if the pedophile admitted to assaulting a child, the information was only used to develop a plan to prevent it from happening again. It was not used for criminal prosecution. However, despite the lack of reporting, "studies do show that contemporary cognitive-behavioral treatment does help to reduce rates of sexual re-offending by as much as 40%."[8]

As a public relations practitioner, would you advocate on behalf of this particular program? Could you ethically justify its publicity knowing that you were essentially providing a route for treatment to those who had indeed harmed children? Do the benefits outweigh the consequences of doing nothing? Before offering a final decision, take a moment to look at advocacy and how traditional ethical theories can be utilized to assist practitioners in determining whether a public relations program is ethically sound.

OVERVIEW OF ADVOCACY

In Ancient Greece, successful rhetoricians were paid to strategically use communication to increase understanding and to persuade the public to view social issues; typically, from the same perspectives as those in power. As public relations grew as an industry, many of those initial rhetorical, persuasive devices were utilized by the founders of public relations to continue to manipulate and deceive the public. Despite the fact that Edward Bernays, often touted as PR's founding father, preached a correlation between public relations and social responsibility, early public relations became synonymous with irresponsible and unethical persuasion and advocacy. These suspect practices have created a contentious view of ethical advocacy in public relations that still exists today.

Despite the fact a significant number of scholars contend that ethical persuasion and ethical advocacy are achievable,[9] just as many others disagree.[10] Sociologist Robert Jackall states, "Public relations men and women are simply storytellers with a purpose in the free market place of ideas, advocates of a certain point of view in the court of public opinion."[11] In her book, *Ethics in Public Relations*, Patricia Parsons suggests that the method in which people choose to persuade others to their point of view is what "makes advocacy and persuasion bull's eyes for ethical quagmires."[12]

In fact, many would argue that those same techniques utilized by the ancient Greeks continue to be standard fare for public relations practitioners today. "Despite a few voices to the contrary, public relations practitioners generally and readily accept persuasion and advocacy as their major function."[13] The primary difference between the persuasive advocacy of the late 1800s and the 1900s and present day is that early advocates were solely concerned with advocating for their clients. Current practitioners walk a fine line with obligations to both the public and to their clients.

In the year 2000, the Public Relations Society of America (PRSA) recognized advocacy as one of its six professional values.[14] According to PRSA, as practitioners, "We serve the public interest by acting as responsible advocates for those we represent. We provide a voice in the marketplace of ideas, facts, and viewpoints to aid informed public debate."[15] Scholar Ruth Edgett expands on this notion of advocacy. Advocacy is "the act of publicly representing an individual, organization, or idea with the object of persuading targeted audiences to look favorably on—or accept the point of view of—the individual, the organization, or the idea."[16] Scholar Gerald R. Miller (1989) asserts, "Effective, ethically defensible persuasion and effective, ethically defensible public relations are virtually synonymous."[17]

Since the nature of advocacy is persuasive, Sherry Baker's five baselines for justification in persuasion aptly relate to ethical advocacy.[18] She notes that these models can serve as a way for practitioners to ethically assess their decision making and to justify their actions. Depending on the individual practitioner and/or the organization, advocacy can be motivated by any one of the following models developed by Baker:[19]

1. Self-interest model—Public relations practitioners look out for their own personal interests and make decisions based on personal benefit, regardless of whether it is detrimental to the consumer or society.
2. Entitlement model—Focuses on the legal aspect of ethics. As long as it is permitted by law, the action can be considered ethical. This model protects the public relations practitioner by failing to consider the effects of their actions on society or the utilitarian concept of the greatest good for the greatest number.
3. Enlightened self-interest model—Public relations practitioners will be far more successful if they establish a solid track record of ethical behavior. The focus here is on increasing business or clientele. It is not acting out of goodwill or general concern for others.
4. Social responsibility model—Public relations practitioners have a responsibility to their communities and to society as a whole. Ethics should be based on a responsibility to serve the public as opposed to focusing on personal rights/gains.
5. Kingdom of Ends model—Adapted from Immanuel Kant's categorical imperative of universal law, practitioners should adhere to the same ethical standards that they expect from others.[20]

There has been significant discussion around the idea that a public relations practitioner can effectively serve the dual interests of both their client and the general public. Thomas Bivins developed four possible paradigms for public relations practitioners to consider when keeping both interests in mind:

1. "If every PR practitioner acts in the best interest of their client, then the public interest *will* be served.
2. If, in addition to serving individual interests the practitioner serves public interest causes, the public interest will be served.
3. If a practitioner assures that every individual in need of or desiring their services receives their services, then the public interest will be served.
4. If public relations as a practice improves the quality of debate over issues important to the public, then the public interest will be served."[21]

Bivins addressed the role of a public relations practitioner as both an advocate and a mediator, and suggested that practitioners had an obligation to improve the flow of information, remain transparent, and to encourage debate on issues of importance to the public.[22]

WHY ADVOCACY IS IMPORTANT IN PUBLIC RELATIONS

In their book, *Ethics in Public Relations: Responsible Advocacy*, Fitzpatrick and Bronstein state, "Ethical guideposts for responsible advocacy in public relations in the twenty-first century will include individual accountability, informed decision making, multicultural understanding, relationship building, open communication, dialogue, truth and transparency, and integrity."[23]

Additionally, Ruth Edgett developed ten criteria for desirable advocacy. These criteria provide a way for practitioners to test the ethical advocacy of their campaigns. According to Edgett, "If practitioners meet all of these criteria, they should feel comfortable knowing that, in their advocacy functions, they have met high ethical standards; if they do not meet any of the criteria, they should awaken to the probability that their ethical standards are far too lax."[24]

Ten Criteria for Desirable Advocacy

1. Evaluation—Objectively analyzing the full scope of the issue/situation requiring public relations advocacy and then assessing the needs of both the client and the organization before assuming the role of advocate.
2. Priority—When serving in the role of advocate, the public relations practitioner should serve the interests of the client or organization above those of other publics.
3. Sensitivity—Public relations practitioners must strike a balance between their moral obligation to society and an obligation to best represent the interests of the client.
4. Confidentiality—Practitioners can assure both client and organizational rights to confidentiality on matters that are considered classified such as trade secrets or employee records. Illegal actions or actions that are potentially damaging to society at large are not offered the safe protections.
5. Veracity—PR practitioners are expected to be both truthful and trustworthy.
6. Reversibility—If the situation were reversed, and the practitioner was the recipient of the information as opposed to the communicator, would they feel as though they had been appropriately informed?
7. Validity—All communication on behalf of the client or organization must be based in sound reasoning. In other words, the practitioner is able to defend its stance on particular issues if they come under fire from the public.

8. Visibility—Messaging must be transparent and audiences must have a clear understanding behind the source of their communication.
9. Respect—Acknowledge that audiences have the right to ask questions and to offer diverging thoughts and suggestions on matters that are likely to affect them or lead to information that will assist in decision making.
10. Consent—Communication on behalf of the client or organization is carried out only under conditions to which it can be assumed all parties consent.[25]

APPLICATION OF ETHICAL THEORIES

Several PR scholars have developed ethical decision-making models designed to assist practitioners in making ethically sound decisions. Three of the more commonly touted models are described below. However, it is important to note these three models are not exhaustive. Practitioners can utilize several other models to assist them in arriving at ethical decisions.

The TARES test was developed by Sherry Baker and David Martinson. "The TARES test consists of five principles: Truthfulness (of the message), Authenticity (of the persuader), Respect (for the persuadee), Equity (of the persuasive appeal) and Social Responsibility (for the common good)."[26] Each principle outlines an area of expectation when practitioners are developing persuasive communication campaigns. The TARES test also allows practitioners to justify how their campaign addresses societal value.

The Potter Box model was developed by Ralph Potter of Harvard University and consists of four steps.[27] The steps are to analyze the situation, compare and contrast personal and organizational ethical values, consider applicable ethical principles, and to select loyalties. "This model is one that rests on professionals understanding principles, values and loyalties in order to be able to navigate the ethical choice correctly."[28] Additional application of the Potter Box model can be found in chapter 6.

Bowen's Model for Strategic Decision Making, developed by scholar Shannon Bowen, is grounded in the deontological philosophies of Immanuel Kant. This model "allows issues managers to conduct a thorough, systematic analysis of the ethical aspects of a decision and to understand that decision, and its ramifications, from a multiplicity of perspectives."[29]

"Ethics . . . are not simply a set of rules or a set of 'if–then' statements that will automatically ensure public relations professionals behave ethically. Rather ethics is the art and science of the process used to arrive at a decision, based in a deeper conviction."[30] In order to understand how traditional ethical theories affect modern-day practice, it is imperative to look at each theoretical area—ethics of consequences, ethics of duty, and ethics of character—and examine how each can be applied to ethical dilemmas. Thus far, public relations scholars have not developed a model that guides practitioners in applying varying ethical theories to modern-day dilemmas. The closest model is the Bowens model, but even that model only applies Kantian ethics.

PURE MODEL OF ETHICAL DECISION MAKING

The PURE model of ethical decision making provides practitioners with a method for applying traditional ethical theory to present-day ethical practice. The model affords entry-level practitioners the opportunity to not only see how ethical decisions are grounded in theory but also to better assess their options before making a decision. The model is intentionally simplified to allow entry-level practitioners the opportunity to identify both sides of an issue, apply a multitude of theories, and easily assess outcomes.

The first step of the PURE model of ethical decision making is to follow your personal, organizational, and industry-specific principles. Every individual carries a personal moral code that guides our day-to-day decision-making abilities. Morals may include the golden rule, treating others the way you want to be treated, or something far more basic, such as assisting those who are in need of help.

It is important to note here that there is a significant distinction between morals and ethics. Morality, according to ethicist Scott Rae, "refers to the actual content of right and wrong, and ethics refers to the process of determining right and wrong. In other words, morality deals with moral knowledge and ethics with moral reasoning." The first step of the PURE model of ethical decision making assesses personal moral knowledge because new PR practitioners with limited experience dealing with ethical dilemmas often derive their initial decisions from their morals.

In addition to morals, the first step of the PURE model of ethical decision making analyzes organizational principles. Organizational principles tend to come across as rules—for example, treating clients with respect or making sure that you are being honest with a client about what may be achievable for the campaign. Lastly, industry-specific principles are reviewed. For example, if an organization was dealing with an ethical dilemma regarding evaluation, the Barcelona Principle would call on the practitioner to be transparent and honest in terms of measurement data.

When determining whether a dilemma is ethical, ask yourself whether any personal, organizational, or industry-specific principles have been compromised throughout the campaign. For example, if you are working for a new chain of fast-food restaurants and are charged with the task of building brand recognition, how might you approach helping this brand stand out? Is it important to point out the differences in the grain-fed cattle that your company uses versus the processed meat your competition uses? Is it viable to highlight the health benefits of your company without mentioning any competitors? Would it be appropriate to post infographics on social media directly comparing the calories in your client's food with the calorie count from the competition? Or would you post an infographic that allowed your client's healthy calorie count to stand for itself? Each decision will largely depend on an individual's personal principles as well as organizational and industry standards of operation.

The next step of the PURE model of ethical decision making is to ensure that the selected ethical principles are universal, that is, they can be applied to everyone across the board without exception. This step is grounded in duty-based ethics, or more specifically, Kantian ethics. As mentioned previously, according to Kant's Formula of Universal Law, an individual should "act only on that maxim which you can at the same time will to become a universal law of nature."[31] In other words, individuals are all held to the same standards. Therefore, if a PR practitioner undercuts another agency to get work or uses less-than-ethical means to attain new business, those practices would be deemed acceptable for everyone. Additionally, if a practitioner deceives the general public or the client, it would be perfectly acceptable for the general public to spread malicious lies about the company's business practices through social media or other media outlets.

The third step of this model is to make sure you are valuing the rights of the public as well as your client. Take Martin Shkreli for example. Shkreli is the founder and former CEO of Turing Pharmaceuticals. Turing raised the price on Daraprim, a drug developed to treat infections in AIDS patients, from US$13.50 to US$750 per pill.[32] Upon authorizing this price increase, there was severe backlash from the general public and from many high-profile public organizations including the Infectious Diseases Society of America and HIV Medicine Association.[33] As a result, Shkreli hired a public relations crisis team to assist in justifying the price hike and in calming the public.[34] From the perspective of John Stuart Mill, the government should be able to put regulations in place to protect the public in instances such as this.[35] John Locke, on the other hand, does not believe in morals legislation. Therefore, despite the fact that raising the price on pharmaceutical drugs targets those most vulnerable, Locke is opposed to morals legislation and does not believe that laws should be put in place to uphold the moral convictions held by the majority of society.[36] Analyzing this case from the theoretical perspective using the PURE model, PR practitioners should remain aware of the needs of the public as well as the desires of their client. In this instance, a PR practitioner should have advised their client of the inherent dangers involved in targeting those in desperate need of medical assistance, especially at a time when consumers are expecting organizations to be socially conscious and responsible. As a result, Mark Baum, CEO of Imprimis Pharmaceuticals, developed a replacement for Daraprim as part of a corporate program titled Imprimis Cares and sold the medication for $1 per pill.[37] While Turing is a glaring example of corporate greed, Imprimis plays the role of public health advocate and de facto public hero.

The fourth and final step of the PURE model of ethical decision making is to ensure that the end result can be justified. Utilitarian principles require that public relations practitioners focus on the consequences of their actions.[38] When examining consequences in ethical advocacy, practitioners need to determine if "the ends justified the means." In other words, did the result of the ethical decision justify the persuasive actions supporting it? This final step requires significant consideration in terms of justification. For example, if there was indeed negative backlash from a campaign, would the positive outweigh the negative? Would a loss of some customers justify a company stance on an important social issue? The ends will vary based on the practitioner and the organization's overarching goals.

One can look to the 2016 US presidential election as an example. Republican candidate Donald Trump leveraged inflammatory, anti-Muslim, and anti-immigration

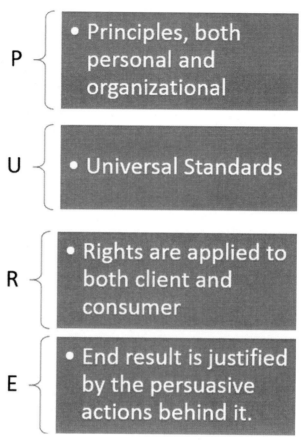

PURE Model of Ethical Decision Making

rhetoric throughout his bid for becoming the next president. His campaign manager, Kellyanne Conway, acted as a strong advocate for Trump, taking a hard line in defense of his policies and consistently confirming his pomposity and ethnocentric viewpoints. Ultimately, an antiliberal, antibusiness stance helped Trump win the presidential election. However, the hostile campaign divided the country in the process. In this example did the end result justify the controversial advocacy supporting the outcome? Depending on the issues you side with, the ends may or may not have justified the means.

STATEMENT ON PUBLICS

When discussing the implementation of any theoretical model, it is imperative to discuss how ethics operate in the public sphere. Anytime an individual attempts to apply a set of universal values we have to ask ourselves if there really is such a thing as a "universal value." In today's society, do we have values that are universal to our communities? Our nations? Our world?

To investigate this idea more fully, we can look to echo chambers. "An echo chamber is a metaphorical description of a situation in which information, ideas, or beliefs are amplified or reinforced by communication and repetition inside a defined system."[39] In other words, how can we apply a model of theoretical analysis, like the PURE model, in a polarized or divided system that simply builds upon existing beliefs?

This is a question of expectation. It forces practitioners to make a concerted effort to identify target publics when applying the PURE model of ethical decision making. As publics differ, they provide competing imperatives. Therefore, when applying a model, we must use our expertise as practitioners to determine whom we are counting as publics, and then within that purview, whom we are counting as target publics. Answering these questions allows practitioners to take a critical stance on where to go with publics and to explain how easily blame can be shifted in situations that go from addressing one's own public to being eclipsed by a company's various publics. An enclave that only looks at itself is open to misinformation.

IMPLICATIONS WITHIN SOCIAL MEDIA

The professionals of social media do not currently have ethical guidelines like the professionals of public relations, marketing, advertising, and journalism. Therefore, it is important to apply the PR code of ethics when making decisions on the social sphere. Public relations practitioners are first and foremost advocates for the organizations that they represent.[40] Social media practitioners should use the same decision-making process in situations on the social sphere as they would in traditional public relations campaigns. Brian Solis, digital analyst, anthropologist, and futurist, who studies the effects of emerging technology on business, marketing, and culture, noted that ethics and the ethical practice of social media bridge the gaps between intentions and desired intentions.[41]

Proponents of social activism maintain that for many nongovernmental organizations (NGOs) or other advocacy groups, social media has the ability to raise awareness to assist supporters in forming collective identities. Clay Shirky maintains that "we are living in the middle of a remarkable increase in our ability to share, to cooperate with one another, and to take collective action, all outside the framework of traditional institutions and organizations."[42] Henry Jenkins expands on this, highlighting the ways in which today's millennials use social media for collective action and have the ability to seamlessly navigate between being socially and culturally active with various types of technology (Facebook, Twitter, YouTube), to being politically and civically engaged utilizing those same platforms.[43]

The ALS Ice Bucket Challenge is a great example of this and began with a golfer named Chris Kennedy.[44] Kennedy was nominated to participate in the Ice Bucket Challenge; however, at the outset, there was not a specific charity affiliated with the challenge. Kennedy selected ALS because a relative was suffering from the disease. He nominated a family member who began utilizing the hashtag #strikeoutALS. In its early days, the challenge was only being passed and promoted between family and friends. After the campaign reached former Boston College baseball player Peter Frates on July 31, 2014, it became universally affiliated with ALS, and it went viral. The challenge was simple. An individual had 24 hours to either dump a bucket of ice water on their heads or donate $100 to ALS. They also needed to challenge three people to further the awareness of the campaign. According to Beth Kanter, over 50 political figures, 200 notable actors and actresses, 200 athletes, and more than 220 musicians, along with thousands of everyday citizens throughout the world, have participated in the challenge.[45] The campaign raised over fifteen million dollars for the ALS Association.[46]

SOLVING THE ETHICAL DILEMMA: PREVENTION PROJECT DUNKELFELD

Now that you have a basis supporting ethical advocacy and have been exposed to some examples of how advocacy can be applied to various public relations campaigns, let's revisit the Prevention Project Dunkelfeld from the beginning of this chapter.

1. Apply Baker's five baselines for justification of persuasion. Based on these principles, is the campaign ethical?
2. Test the campaign against Edgett's ten criteria for desirable advocacy. How many criteria does the campaign meet?
3. Apply the PURE model of ethical decision making. How does the advocacy of this campaign hold up to the principles of traditional ethical theory?
4. If you were the practitioner asked to advocate for this campaign, what would you have done differently?
5. If you were an advocate for a similar campaign in the United States, where we have mandatory reporting rules, how could you persuade pedophiles to seek help even if it could mean they may face criminal prosecution?

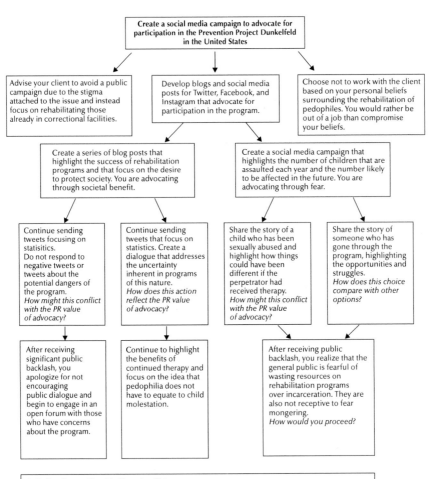

Create a social media campaign to advocate for participation in the Prevention Project Dunkelfeld in the United States

Advise your client to avoid a public campaign due to the stigma attached to the issue and instead focus on rehabilitating those already in correctional facilities.

Develop blogs and social media posts for Twitter, Facebook, and Instagram that advocate for participation in the program.

Choose not to work with the client based on your personal beliefs surrounding the rehabilitation of pedophiles. You would rather be out of a job than compromise your beliefs.

Create a series of blog posts that highlight the success of rehabilitation programs and that focus on the desire to protect society. You are advocating through societal benefit.

Create a social media campaign that highlights the number of children that are assaulted each year and the number likely to be affected in the future. You are advocating through fear.

Continue sending tweets focusing on statisitics.
Do not respond to negative tweets or tweets about the potential dangers of the program. *How might this conflict with the PR value of advocacy?*

Continue sending tweets that focus on statistics. Create a dialogue that addresses the uncertainty inherent in programs of this nature. *How does this action reflect the PR value of advocacy?*

Share the story of a child who has been sexually abused and highlight how things could have been different if the perpetrator had received therapy. *How might this conflict with the PR value of advocacy?*

Share the story of someone who has gone through the program, highlighting the opportunities and struggles. *How does this choice compare with other options?*

After receiving significant public backlash, you apologize for not encouraging public dialogue and begin to engage in an open forum with those who have concerns about the program.

Continue to highlight the benefits of continued therapy and focus on the idea that pedophilia does not have to equate to child molestation.

After receiving public backlash, you realize that the general public is fearful of wasting resources on rehabilitation programs over incarceration. They are also not receptive to fear mongering. *How would you proceed?*

1. Define the specific ethical issue/conflict.
2. Identify internal/external factors (e.g. legal, political, social, economic) that may influence the decision.
3. Identify key values.
4. Identify the parties who will be affected by the decision and define the public relations professional's obligation to each.
5. Select ethical principles to guide the decision-making process.
6. Make a decision and justify it.

4

Honesty

As a communicator, how do you feel about taking on the role of advocate?

I'm more than happy to take on the role as an advocate. In fact, I feel it is a responsibility to future communications professionals to show just how important our jobs are in the world today. Whether on social media, a conference speaker, or mentoring, it is integral to me to inform current and future professionals of the important and defining work we do on a daily basis.

Discuss the importance of honesty and transparency as it applies to public relations.

As individual practitioners, and as an industry, we cannot survive without having trust. We should never put ourselves, or our clients, in a position where you sacrifice the trust you've built. I would rather be last and right, than first and wrong. We also ask clients to be open and transparent. That means, there is no way someone can look at you and not know who you are or what you represent. Being transparent helps immensely if you are in a crisis. CEOs that hide can be seen as keeping something important a secret or looking to not be up-front. Honesty and transparency go a long way into building a foundation of trust.

What skills are necessary to demonstrate expertise in public relations?

Most importantly, we need to be ethical. While not necessarily a skill, it is the foundation of our industry. From there, you need to be a solid writer, effective speaker, and smart thinker. However, one also needs to have the ability to listen and adapt to all situations. Being an expert PR practitioner does not happen overnight. In fact, it takes years to master the craft and you never stop learning.

Can you provide an example of a time when you had to disagree with what the client felt was necessary and guide them in another direction?

I always let clients know that I want to work with them and give them the best possible counsel. One client, an environmental company, wanted to bypass the government regulatory channels and speak directly to an area affected by a contamination. We advised to stay with the regulatory outlets because of potential ways the outreach could appear. One of the company's reps was adamant about speaking to the public. We stated that, in these instances, while we want to be open, we need to be certain that what we say is in step with the government. It took a bit, but, eventually, we were able to convince the client to stick to the plan.

How do you balance loyalty to the client and loyalty to society?

I make a concerted effort to understand my clients, so I never have to cross the line and appear to "sell out." My reputation is very important to me; it's how I build my career and personal brand. I've never had to choose between either. If I did and depending on the situation, I would honor the responsibility to myself and the industry.

Can you discuss how you deal with differing opinions or maintain free expression of ideas?

My experience in the media (my career prior to public relations) gave me a balance to understand others' opinions. During our morning planning meetings, this was often the time to discuss potential stories. There were many times where I would argue for coverage of a certain story, while another producer would disagree. In today's social media world, it's important to understand that people will share their opinions, educated or otherwise. Listening fully, instead of jumping to a conclusion, is a skill that all communicators should work at diligently.

What types of ethical issues are entry-level public relations practitioners likely to encounter?

I believe that social media can present many an ethical issue for entry-level practitioners. Not because social media is bad, but there is still a misunderstanding as to what is right to post and what is wrong. Showing off gifts you received from a client and not stating as such can be a huge issue. Also, being careful to how you present yourself politically could be construed as unethical, depending on the client or what your employer believes.

ETHICAL DILEMMA: FLINT WATER CRISIS

Flint, Michigan, was once a model city bursting with job opportunities and buzzing with life. Fast-forward to the present day and it is clear that the city is beset with high crime rates, a bad reputation, and most recently, contaminated, undrinkable water. The city initially established itself as a player in the timber industry before evolving into "Vehicle City" when General Motors (GM) established its presence in 1947. The Flint River, downtown Flint attractions, several museums, and GM all breathed palpable life into the city. For decades, GM was the backbone of the Flint economy, promoting prosperity and success within the community. However, when GM burdened the city of Flint with over $30 million of debt, the city soon lost much of its appeal. Residents began to leave in an effort to find new opportunities, and as a result crime rates skyrocketed due to economic desperation. In fact, crime rates in Flint remain among the highest in the United States.[1] If things were not bad enough, rumors started to swirl that the Flint River was a prominent outlet for disposing trash, harsh chemicals, and even dead bodies.

When the city declared a financial state of emergency in November 2011, identifying ways to reduce costs was high on the city emergency manager's list. For decades the city of Flint sourced clean drinking water from the city of Detroit, which supplied dozens of systems through SE Michigan from one of the world's most trusted sources of fresh water: Lake Huron. However, rising costs meant that Flint needed to explore an alternative water supply for the community.[2] It was at this point that the Flint city council voted near unanimously (7-1) to disconnect from Detroit's water system and locate an alternative water source: the Flint River.

Flint residents started complaining about the quality of the water almost immediately. They complained that the water smelled and tasted bad, and also appeared dirty. Despite the calls, complaints, and water samples collected from their own taps, Flint residents were assured that the water was safe to drink.

Four months after switching water suppliers, Flint officials announced a boil advisory for all area residents due to increased levels of fecal coliform bacteria in the water. At the time, Michael Prysby, district engineer for the Office of Drinking Water at the Michigan Department of Environmental Quality (MDEQ), said that chlorine would need to be added into the city's water treatment system in an effort to combat the fecal matter.[3] Soon after the boil advisory, General Motors announced that the corporation would stop using water sourced from the Flint River at its manufacturing plant as a result of the high levels of chloride and the potential to create corrosion in their products. Even after a city-wide boil advisory, and the need to add high levels of chlorine just to appropriately sanitize the water, Flint residents were reassured time and again that the water was safe to drink.

Further complicating the situation, city officials announced in January 2015 that the MDEQ issued the city a violation because of the extremely high levels of trihalomethanes in the water—a by-product of the disinfecting process. Flint residents finally received letters warning them of the risks of consuming the water and inform-ing them that measures were being taken by the city and MDEQ to fix the problem.[4]

Recognizing the difficulties that Flint was facing with dangerous levels of bacteria in the water, Detroit officials offered to reconnect Flint to the Detroit water sys-tem—an offer that local Flint officials would ultimately decline. Instead, leaders in Flint continued to divert additional funds to ensure that the water treatment plant was working properly. Despite the continued warnings, residents in Flint were still being told that the water was safe for consumption.

At the request of a concerned parent, LeeAnne Walters, researchers from Virginia Tech tested samples of water from her home and found extremely high levels of lead. Ultimately, this result led to a deeper investigation that identified high levels of lead throughout the Flint water system. Still, after this revelation, residents were told the water was safe to drink.

As each new challenge with the Flint water crisis unfolded and remediation plans were implemented, local government officials and the MDEQ repeatedly assured residents that the water was safe to drink and that all of the identified problems had been appropriately fixed. In late September 2015, researchers at Hurley Medical Center published irrefutable evidence that local children had high levels of lead in their blood. At this point, Flint officials and the MDEQ had no choice but to make a public announcement and address the crisis. Once this information became public knowledge, the Genesee County health officer declared the city of Flint a public health emergency on October 1, 2015, and finally discouraged all residents from drinking the water.[5]

Amid scrutiny and outrage, Michigan Governor Rick Snyder admitted that Flint's water crisis could have been handled better, saying, "In terms of a mistake, what I would say is we found there are probably things that weren't as fully understood when that switch was made."[6]

The situation in Flint represents an example of a public's distrust, disgust, and dissatisfaction with local governments and, in a broader sense, politics. This is the largest environmental and health disaster in Michigan's history. It was exacerbated by the Michigan governor's inability to initiate honest conversations with the public.

OVERVIEW OF HONESTY

The Public Relations Society of America (PRSA) highlights honesty as one of the core values of the public relations profession. PRSA states, "We adhere to the high-est standards of accuracy and truth in advancing the interests of those we represent and in communicating with the public."[7] Open and honest two-way communication should be the foundation of all present-day public relations activities. The idea be-hind two-way symmetric communication was first introduced by Grunig and Hunt in their four models of public relations.[8] These models trace the evolution of the public relations field from its early inception to present day. The four models consist of the press agentry model, the public information model, the two-way asymmetric model, and the two-way symmetric model of communication.[9]

As introduced in the first chapter, press agentry is a one-way communication model that relies primarily on manipulation and deception to persuade or engage the public. As the field began to evolve, the public information model gained traction within the industry and led practitioners away from outright falsehoods as part of standard communication practice to a practice that relied on the delivery of information. This model can also be considered the "I talk, you listen" model. Within the framework of the public information strategy, practitioners shape a story about an organization and deliver the information to the audience. There is no further engagement or room for discussion or questions. The information is delivered and absorbed by the public using one-way communication and is consistent with the magic bullet theory of communication.[10] The third model introduced by Grunig and Hunt, two-way asymmetric communication, focuses on utilizing research to persuade the public. Keep in mind that the research is not conducted to build better relationships or benefit the public at large. It is used solely as a way to make content more persuasive and to better deliver a message. It's all about persuasion designed to trigger a transaction. Grunig and Hunt's final model is two-way symmetric communication. This model most closely resembles the current state of public relations and allows for a higher level of mutual understanding, offering a more balanced approach to consumer-company interactions.[11]

As the field evolved, Scott Cutlip and Allen Center developed a definition of public relations that focused on an honest approach to advocacy and two-way communication. They defined PR as "the planned effort to influence opinion through good character and responsible performance, based upon mutually satisfactory two-way communications."[12] Likewise, Rex Harlow, founder of the American Council on Public Relations, later the Public Relations Society of America, emphasized the importance of dialogic communication and consumer-client relationships. He defines public relations as:

> A distinctive management function which helps to establish and maintain a mutual line of communication, understanding, acceptance and cooperation between an organization and its publics; involves the management of problems or issues; helps management to keep informed on and responsive to public opinion; defines and emphasizes the responsibilities of management to serve the public interest; helps management keep abreast of and effectively utilize change; and uses research and sound ethical communication techniques as its principal tools.[13]

Public relations practitioners should be considered the guardians of truth. Trust is one of the most vital aspects of the relationship between a public relations practitioner and his/her publics and/or organization. Edgett explains, "When the speaker (or communicator) lies, not only has he or she violated the time-honored principle of telling the truth, he or she has broken the implied promise to tell the truth."[14] Jensen expands on this: "The great harms that lying can cause the deceived, the deceiver, and the larger society are many and significant."[15]

In her book, *Lying: Moral Choice in Public and Private Life*, Sissela Bok concluded that when practitioners are attempting to determine whether they should be honest or lie, they should work from the assumption that lying is wrong.[16] She does admit that there are times when being deceptive is acceptable. For example, in American society, many parents lie about mythical creatures including Santa Claus, the Easter Bunny, and the tooth fairy. In these instances, the lies do not cause significant harm to anyone involved. However, when you apply this to most professional situations, there are greater consequences. Bok proposes a "test of publicity" to determine if a lie can be justified.[17] The test assesses the impact of the potential lie on the targeted individuals, the greater society, and the liars themselves. She believes that when the publicity test is applied, the majority of the time the costs of the lie outweigh the benefits.

Additionally, Newsom, VanSlyke Turk, and Kruckeberg aptly summarize Bok's justifications for remaining honest:

1. "Dishonesty leads to lack of trust and cynicism—such as when a reporter later discovers that a PR person has told half-truths resulting in an inaccurate story;
2. Lying is resented by those deceived, even if the deceived are liars themselves;
3. Dishonesty is likely to be discovered, and no climate for credibility can be reestablished;
4. Decisions about when to lie are often made without calculating either alternatives or consequences;
5. A lie always demands another lie to cover it up, and then others to maintain the prevarications; and
6. Lying forces people to act differently from the way they would have behaved if initially told the truth."[18]

Now that you have established a background for the basis of honesty and truth telling, it is important to review some examples of honesty in public relations.

WHY HONESTY IS IMPORTANT IN PUBLIC RELATIONS

Public relations practitioners should have open and honest relationships with their clients. They should act as advocates and be willing to provide the client what they need as opposed to what they want. In other words, clients will likely want you to publicize every company announcement whether it is newsworthy or not. Instead of promising something that is unrealistic, PR practitioners have a duty to explain realistic expectations to their clients. "When a PR pro fundamentally and thoroughly understands what the client is trying to achieve, both parties are positioned for success. When clear expectations are set from the beginning, and both client and PR tell the truth about their capabilities, limitations, and passions, the results of the engagement are desirable."[19]

A blog post written by Lisa Goldsberry of Axia Public Relations discusses some potential examples of unethical behaviors related to dishonesty in public relations. Goldsberry initially cautions against practitioners overselling their capabilities or making false promises to clients;[20] for example, guaranteeing specific attendance at events or media coverage in national publications. A second illustration relates to sidestepping issues measurement.[21] PR practitioners should willingly detail strategic plans and key metrics. A practitioner should never refuse to discuss the specific outlets being pitched or share the detailed organizational plan. Communication should always be transparent. It should be evident that any practitioner who blatantly lies or uses underhanded tactics such as making false or misleading statements to the media is guilty of dishonest, unethical behavior.[22]

In an age when it is easy to locate examples of organizations implementing dishonest public relations methodologies, it is also important to highlight organizations who have demonstrated honesty in their communication with the public. In September 2016, Samsung recalled their Galaxy Note 7 phones because the lithium batteries inside the phones were catching fire and exploding. Rather than trying to lie or work their way out of giving customers a new phone, Samsung confessed to what was happening. The company realized that their product was not functioning the way it was designed to operate. They admitted there was a problem and came up with a solution. Samsung demonstrated care and concern for their customers' safety. This is ideal in the fast-paced world of public relations. From an honesty standpoint, Samsung did exactly what they were expected to do. They put consumer safety above company profit.

While Samsung wasted no time recalling dangerous phones and informing the public about their product's potential dangers, the company did face some criticism for not keeping their social media updated with vital recall information, as well as for initially releasing incorrect information about phones manufactured in Hong Kong.[23] Samsung publicly stated that phones in Hong Kong were not affected by the recall; however, they had to redact that statement one day later. Additionally, in their rush to release information, the company failed to work with the Consumer Product Safety Commission in the coordination of their recall.[24] Duncan Robertson, a portfolio manager at TT International, said, "The battery issue can only be a long-term threat if the company doesn't take the correct steps to restore its brand. We have confidence that they have taken the correct steps so far."[25] By being honest, not side-stepping issues, and quickly correcting inaccurate information, Samsung has paid for this crisis in terms of a costly recall, but fared well in terms of customer loyalty.

THEORETICAL APPLICATION

Nearly all codes of ethics begin with the duty to tell the truth under all conditions. Let's apply the PURE model of ethical decision making to the PRSA ethical value of honesty.

When examining personal and organizational principles, practitioners need to be aware of the long-term costs of dishonesty. The following two cases involve high-profile athletes, Alex Rodriguez and Maria Sharapova, and demonstrate the importance of adhering to the principles of truth and honesty. Alex Rodriguez, the third baseman for Major League Baseball's New York Yankees, was suspended for the entire 2014 baseball season for both his role in the Biogenesis doping scandal and his use of performance-enhancing drugs.[26] "It had been alleged that Rodriguez had been supplied with performance-enhancing drugs by Biogenesis, a South Florida 'anti-aging clinic.' It was further alleged that Rodriguez had actively attempted to interfere with Major League Baseball's investigation of Biogenesis."[27] Rodriguez consistently misled and lied to the public and to investigators about his involvement with steroids. As a result, he permanently tarnished his image and his reputation.

Another widely known athlete, Maria Sharapova, also found herself embroiled in a scandal with performance-enhancing drugs. Sharapova, a top player on the professional tennis tour, began taking the drug mildronate more than ten years prior to this scandal in response to an irregular echocardiogram.[28] The drug was recently added to the list of prohibited substances within the sport; however, Sharapova continued to take it. When she failed a drug test, she admitted to having taken the substance and argued that she had been taking it for a decade prior to its being listed as a banned substance. She was open and honest with the public and the International Tennis Federation. As a result, the International Tennis Federation found that she "did not intend to cheat, but bore responsibility for the positive test."[29] While she was suspended for two years, she did not lose any sponsorships and her reputation has mostly remained untarnished. These cases demonstrate the role that principles of honesty play in reputation management.

When principles become universal, they are applied to everyone across the board. Therefore, if you, as a practitioner, are following dishonest behaviors, this opens the door for others to also be dishonest, and the general trust that individuals have in one another and in organizations disappears. If this were the case, nobody could be trusted and all of the news that you were aware of would have to be researched. It is important to keep in mind that the primary component of relationship building within the field of PR is fundamentally based on trust. You cannot build relationships without some level of trust.

Additionally, honesty plays a significant role in the discussion of rights. When a practitioner lies or misleads the general public, he/she is simply treating the public as a means to an end. The public should be valuable as a stand-alone entity regardless of the benefits they can provide to the practitioner. When the public is lied to, their right to free will is compromised. Individuals will be unable to accurately choose between specific courses of action because they don't have all of the information necessary to make well-informed decisions; they only have part of the story.

Lastly, when looking at whether the ends were justified, we have to delve deeper into the case than simply focusing on lying. Consequentialists will not be satisfied with the logic that as moral human beings we have a duty "not to lie." Consequentialists will want to know the results of the lie. What happened as a result of the deception? Was there social media backlash? Did the media run negative stories revealing the deception and essentially harm your company's credibility? Or did life continue as normal? These questions matter to a consequentialist. Being honest for the sake of society is simply not enough.

IMPLICATIONS WITHIN SOCIAL MEDIA

Take, for example, ghostwriting for bloggers. Is it ethical to write a blog on behalf of an executive and not disclose that the executive was not the blogger? Tiffany Derville Gallicano, Thomas H. Bivins, and Yoon Y. Choo are researchers who conducted surveys with blog readers and found that 60 percent of corporate blog readers expect a CEO blog post to be written by someone else, but only 40 percent agreed that this practice was acceptable.[30]

Ghostwriting is a common practice. As practitioners, though, we must ask ourselves if we are being honest to the readers, our client, and ourselves if we do not disclose that the executive was, in fact, not the writer at all. It should come as no surprise that many great business leaders are poor communicators and speakers. According to Cheryl Conner, collaborating with professional writers is an effective means of extracting excellent advice and knowledge from great leaders.[31] However, when ghostwriting means creating material without the participation of the author the content will represent, or without disclosing the fact that a ghostwriter was used, this is unethical.

Steve Farnsworth of Jolt Communications said, "If someone directly asks you whether you write your posts—or any content with your name on it—you should be honest about the process. In the age of social media, the truth is compulsory. It is important to choose a process you feel comfortable sharing publicly because someone will ask you about it."[32] He uses one of the following scenarios when working with clients:[33]

- "I interview the client to get his thoughts, and then write the piece. Then I have the client review the piece and give feedback.
- I have the client write the first draft and then I edit or rewrite as needed. Then I have the client review and give feedback.
- I have the client bullet-point or outline her thoughts, and then I write the piece and have the client give feedback."

The bottom line is that practitioners should put honesty first. Abiding by the PR code of ethics means that we honor the highest standards of accuracy and truth in advancing the interests of those we represent and in communicating with the public.

IT'S NOT JUST ABOUT HONESTY

By Levick[1]

Jessica Alba's eco-friendly household, baby, and skincare products company, Honest, took another PR hit when the *Wall Street Journal* published a story alleging that it conducted tests with two different independent laboratories and found "a significant amount" of sodium lauryl sulfate (SLS) in its laundry detergent.[2] SLS is one of the chemicals that Honest specifically claims its detergents are "Honestly Made Without" (prior to the *Wall Street Journal* story, the claim was "Honestly Free Of").

This is not the first time that Honest has been under the microscope. Two lawsuits have already been filed, one in California and one in New York, alleging that the company was dishonest with customers about the ingredients and effectiveness of its products.[3] The company has claimed that both suits are baseless.

The real brand and reputation issues for Honest go beyond the obvious challenge of whether or not a company that built its brand literally on the word "honest" is actually lying. It is as much about tone and substance.

In the blog that the company posted on its website after the *Wall Street Journal* story published, Honest said that the *Journal* "falsely claimed our laundry detergent contains Sodium Lauryl Sulfate (SLS)." The blog continues on to provide its readers with a science lesson about the chemical differences between SLS and sodium coco sulfate (SCS); the ingredient the company says it uses in place of SLS.[4]

What Honest is missing is that people aren't interested in the number of carbon atoms in the ingredients or which carbon chains are isolated to make SLS versus SCS. Ideally, the only thing that consumers are interested in understanding is how two independent laboratories both claimed to have found high levels of an ingredient that Honest claims it doesn't use, and specifically what Honest is doing moving forward.

Based on the *Journal* story, there was a lot of confusion in the production and manufacturing process with the detergent manufacturer (Earth Friendly Products, LLC) saying that its chemical supplier (Trichromatic West, Inc.) tests for SLS.

A much better—and increasingly honest—response from the company would have been to state that it would look into the roles and responsibilities of its manufacturer and supplier to ensure that they were both meeting the company's high quality standards, rather than just saying the independent tests were wrong.

Does Honest or anyone in its supply chain conduct its own testing to ensure quality control? If not, will they start doing this now? Is there a way that SCS could create a false positive for SLS? If consumers want to return their detergent because of these findings by the *Journal*, will Honest recall the product? These are some of the issues that the company should have focused on in reacting to the story.

Even if there is not an actual problem (as Honest claims), a company needs to find a way to correct the perception of a problem. Whenever a company finds itself in crisis, it needs to focus on the path forward. That path should never include sticking your head in the sand and pretending nothing is wrong.

---

1. Levick, "It's not just about honesty," *Public Relations and Strategic Communication*, March 23, 2016, accessed January 2, 2017, http://levick.com/blog/brand/not-just-honesty/.

2. Serena Ng, "Laundry detergent from Jessica Alba's Honest Co. contains ingredient it pledged to avoid," *The Wall Street Journal*, March 10, 2016, accessed December 30, 2016, http://www.wsj.com/articles/laundry-detergent-from-jessica-albas-honest-co-contains-ingredient-it-pledged-to-avoid-1457647350?cb=logged0.256154531147331.

3. Lindsay Blakely, "Jessica Alba's Honest Company slapped with second lawsuit," Inc.com, February 18, 2016, accessed January 2, 2017, http://www.inc.com/lindsay-blakely/honest-company-faces-2nd-lawsuit-dishonest-advertising.html.

4. "A message from the Honest Company," *Honestly* (web log), March 10, 2016, accessed January 8, 2016, https://blog.honest.com/a-message-from-the-honest-company/#.

SOLVING THE ETHICAL DILEMMA: FLINT WATER CRISIS

While Governor Snyder retained two PR firms, Finn Partners and Mercury Public Affairs, to assist him in developing messaging and identifying the appropriate media to engage during the Flint water crises, he failed to find a way to connect with the residents of Flint or to rebuild the lost trust amid this crisis. Having honest conversations with the public and treating those affected with fairness and general respect could have significantly decreased the outrage from the public and moved the conversation to one of healing. Unfortunately, these conversations never occurred.

Take a look at the flow chart below. This chart walks through some of the decisions that either occurred or should have occurred in Flint. What are some areas that can be improved upon? What would you have done differently?

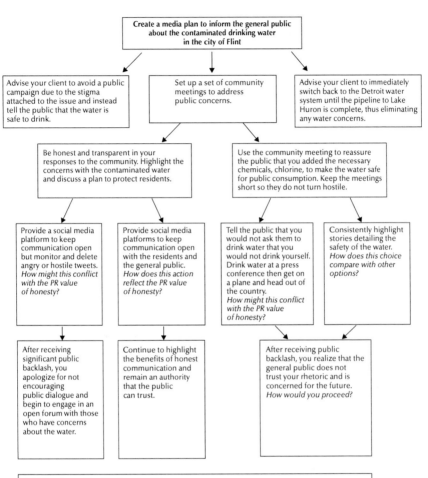

Create a media plan to inform the general public about the contaminated drinking water in the city of Flint

Advise your client to avoid a public campaign due to the stigma attached to the issue and instead tell the public that the water is safe to drink.

Set up a set of community meetings to address public concerns.

Advise your client to immediately switch back to the Detroit water system until the pipeline to Lake Huron is complete, thus eliminating any water concerns.

Be honest and transparent in your responses to the community. Highlight the concerns with the contaminated water and discuss a plan to protect residents.

Use the community meeting to reassure the public that you added the necessary chemicals, chlorine, to make the water safe for public consumption. Keep the meetings short so they do not turn hostile.

Provide a social media platform to keep communication open but monitor and delete angry or hostile tweets. *How might this conflict with the PR value of honesty?*

Provide social media platforms to keep communication open with the residents and the general public. *How does this action reflect the PR value of honesty?*

Tell the public that you would not ask them to drink water that you would not drink yourself. Drink water at a press conference then get on a plane and head out of the country. *How might this conflict with the PR value of honesty?*

Consistently highlight stories detailing the safety of the water. *How does this choice compare with other options?*

After receiving significant public backlash, you apologize for not encouraging public dialogue and begin to engage in an open forum with those who have concerns about the water.

Continue to highlight the benefits of honest communication and remain an authority that the public can trust.

After receiving public backlash, you realize that the general public does not trust your rhetoric and is concerned for the future. *How would you proceed?*

1. Define the specific ethical issue/conflict.
2. Identify internal/external factors (e.g. legal, political, social, economic) that may influence the decision.
3. Identify key values.
4. Identify the parties who will be affected by the decision and define the public relations professional's obligation to each.
5. Select ethical principles to guide the decision-making process.
6. Make a decision and justify it.

5

Expertise

EXPERT ON ETHICS
Jack Pflanz, Development Associate, ACR Health

As a communicator, how do you feel about taking on the role of advocate?
As development and communications associate for a nonprofit health care agency supporting those suffering with chronic diseases including but not limited to AIDS/HIV and local LGBTQ youth, it is vital that I serve not only as an advocate for those that need help in order to raise the funds needed to provide support services, but at the end of the day it makes me feel good about how I spend ten to twelve hours of each day and fifty to sixty hours of each week. Feeling like I make a difference in the lives of youth who face hostility and discrimination every day simply for living their lives their way gives me a tremendous amount of professional and personal satisfaction.

Discuss the importance of honesty and transparency as it applies to public relations.
An important part of working in public relations is building relationships. Beneficial relationships with clients, media, and the public built on trust are in everyone's best interest. A client depends on you to tell them when an idea is worth pursuing, when speaking remarks are effective and truthful, and when they are portraying the best image of themselves and the organization. News media outlets depend on you to provide timely, accurate, honest, and meaningful information. Even if the answer is "I don't know, but I will find out," reporters and journalists appreciate the honesty and effort you make to get them what they need when they need it. The best public relations people serve as an ongoing resource to the media and are called by reporters when they are working on relevant stories because reporters know they can count on you.

What skills are necessary to demonstrate expertise in public relations?

As communicators we cannot expect others to report on our product or service or company or organization if we cannot provide thoughtful, insightful, accurate, and interesting information. It is vital and our responsibility to continually have the latest information or at least know where to get it from. It is also extremely important to be able to foresee questions and concerns that will arise in the future with regard to a topic, an announcement, or a position. The ability to multitask, stay extremely organized, and complete tasks on deadline demonstrates your commitment to excellence in public relations.

Can you provide an example of a time when you had to disagree with what the client felt was necessary and guide them in another direction?

I was asked to design a plan to engage employee involvement in promoting a lifeline phone assistance program around the country with the goal of recruiting more subscribers. After submitting the plan, I was told that there were no available funds in the corporate communications budget to implement it. I felt that the amount needed was minimal and would yield more in profit in the end. I then suggested to my director that I solicit small amounts of budget dollars from several other departments, leveraging the idea that increased profits meant that we all received our year-end bonuses.

How do you balance loyalty to the client and loyalty to society?

It really comes down to honesty and transparency. You have to tell the client exactly how you feel and why if you feel a decision will have a harmful impact to society. You also have to understand that sometimes others are not going to agree with your viewpoints and that you can't win them all, but pick the battles you feel are most worth defending.

Can you discuss how you deal with differing opinions or maintain free expression of ideas?

While I try to see value in all opinions, there are times when it can be extremely difficult. I try to put myself in the other person's position and see things their way and then offer my own opinion. While I do value free expression of ideas, I also believe that it is beneficial to provide feedback on those ideas whether they be positive or negative in a fair, honest, constructive, and peaceful manner.

What types of ethical issues are entry-level public relations practitioners likely to encounter?

I remember early on in my career going through a lot of ethical compliance training. There was a great deal of emphasis on not accepting gifts from outside vendors or media outlets. I had received a piece of clothing representing my favorite sports team from an agency I was working with. I immediately contacted my boss to advise her. She informed me that she had received a food gift from them and was sharing it with the office. She said I could do what I wanted with the sweatshirt, but to please not mention the gift she received to anyone.

ETHICAL DILEMMA: THE WHITE HOUSE

On Saturday, January 21, 2017, Sean Spicer, President Donald Trump's former press secretary, held his first media briefing. This address included a five-minute statement to the press, in which he chastised the media for their understated reports on the number of citizens that attended President Donald Trump's inauguration. "Yesterday, at a time when our nation and the world was watching the peaceful transition of power and, as the President said, the transition and the balance of power from Washington to the citizens of the United States, some members of the media were engaged in deliberately false reporting."[1] Spicer continued, claiming the audience at the inauguration was "the largest audience to ever witness an inauguration, period, both in person and around the globe."[2]

Photos from the inauguration do not support Spicer's claims. According to many news outlets, including CNN, "aerial photos show former President Barack Obama's 2009 inauguration appeared to draw a much larger crowd than the one at Trump's inauguration, while Washington's mass transit ridership and Nielsen television ratings also show Obama's first inauguration was a larger draw."[3]

The New York Times ✓
@nytimes

Comparing the crowds at Donald Trump's and Barack Obama's inaugurations nyti.ms/2j3yaDE

3:57 PM - 20 Jan 2017

↩ ⟲ 12,561 ♥ 14,921

As a result of these statements, Spicer received significant backlash for his media briefing. However, the situation only worsened when Trump's senior advisor, Kellyanne Conway, was confronted on *Meet the Press* the following day about Spicer's claims.

Conway stated, "Sean Spicer, our press secretary, gave alternative facts to that."[4]

Host Chuck Todd responded, "Four of the five facts he uttered were just not true. Look, alternative facts are not facts. They're falsehoods."[5] Todd continued, "Why was it necessary to send out the press secretary on his first day in office to utter a provable falsehood that now calls into question everything the press secretary will say from here on out?"[6]

Conway continued to redirect and failed to ever truly answer the question. "I'll answer it this way: Think about what you just said to your viewers. That's why we feel compelled to go out and clear the air and put alternative facts out there."[7]

OVERVIEW OF EXPERTISE

Public relations practitioners have a unique position within most organizations. They are responsible for building and maintaining trust with C-suite colleagues as well as constructing credible relationships with the general public. According to the PRSA Code of Ethics, public relations practitioners must not only maintain relationships with a variety of different audiences, but they must also utilize their knowledge and expertise for the common good of all involved. "We acquire and responsibly use specialized knowledge and experience. We advance the profession through continued professional development, research, and education. We build mutual understanding, credibility, and relationships among a wide array of institutions and audiences."[8] While it may seem natural to assume that a practitioner would use his/her expertise for the benefit of an organization and its publics, this is easier said than done.

Public relations practitioners often do not have one set of widely accepted practices by which they operate. They are often forced to develop campaigns and to make decisions on a case-by-case basis. During a crisis, decisions often need to be made within minutes with ramifications reverberating through the organization for months, even years. Aristotle noted that the gap between general practical theory and our actual decisions is called practical judgment.[9] "It is far better to think of judgment along 'pragmatic' lines—i.e., as a response to a highly particular problem, a response that reflects and develops character, that calls for imaginative and creative insight, that evolves over time in light of experience and that needs to be considered by a community of inquirers."[10] Public relations practitioners need to develop the ability to make sound judgments reflective of their educational and professional expertise.

Rhonda Breit and Kristin Demetrious identify a set of five characteristics necessary for an occupation to be recognized as professional as opposed to being viewed as a trade or skill.[11]

1. An occupation must be composed of a body of individuals that maintain knowledge or expert skills. Public relations practitioners often have specialized training. *THINK Public Relations*, by Wilcox, Cameron, Reber, and Shin, notes that the six essential qualities necessary for working in public relations are writing skills, research ability, planning expertise, problem-solving ability, business/economics competence, and expertise in social media.[12]
2. Practitioners within the occupation must maintain ongoing education.[13] This could comprise classes taken from traditional brick-and-mortar universities, or continuing education opportunities such as conferences or workshops. Public relations practitioners must remain abreast of new and emerging technologies. Therefore, continuing education is a requirement.
3. The occupation must require some common good beyond profits.[14] According to Schudson and Anderson, all professions need a set of "coherent and consistent attempts to translate scarce resources—special knowledge and skill—into economic and social rewards."[15] Public relations practitioners are charged with using their skills and expertise to benefit the general public.
4. There is a self-governing body designed to reinforce the professional structure.[16] The Public Relations Society of America is the governing body for public relations practitioners across North America. The Chartered Institute of Public Relations is the governing body for public relations practitioners in the United Kingdom. You can review both codes of ethics in chapter 2 as well as several other codes that apply to various parts of the world.
5. The occupation must have a set of rules and/or conventions that it expects practitioners to follow.[17]

Volti further adds dimension to Breit and Demetrious's occupational characteristics by highlighting six *features* necessary for a profession.[18]

1. Professional practice is concentrated on a specialized subject area.
2. Professionals are required to complete specialized training to become experts in their given profession.
3. Professional work is designed to benefit the individual employee and society.
4. Professional roles often afford the capacity to influence the behavior of others.
5. Professions encourage ethical standards of communication both within the profession and with the general public.
6. Professions encourage employees to be independent thinkers/problem solvers and to maintain high levels of autonomy.[19]

It is clear that expertise and professionalism go hand in hand. This means that public relations practitioners need to continually conduct research and use critical thinking when dealing with organizations and their publics in order to maintain credibility as an expert.

WHY EXPERTISE IS IMPORTANT IN PUBLIC RELATIONS

Public relations practitioners often find themselves in situations where their morals and expertise are tested. Some would argue that there is a fine line between moral and immoral ethical activity; the only factor holding PR practitioners in line with an ethical code is a fear of being caught and blackballed from the industry. Others argue that practitioners are ethical because they subscribe to a personal moral code and find value in upholding the principles of the profession. The story of the Ring of Gyges in Book II of Plato's *Republic* addresses this idea. In the Republic, Glaucon, the brother of Plato, believes that morality is a social construction that is not practiced for its own sake, rather practiced out of fear of jeopardizing one's reputation or standing within a community.[20] Therefore, Glaucon asks Socrates to explain how justice and morality are desirable if fear or accountability are not associated with it. Glaucon states that if the repercussions for immoral behavior were eliminated, even moral beings would act in immoral ways, and gives the example of two rings that provide invisibility, stating that if both a moral being and an immoral being are given the rings, they will both eventually engage in immoral behavior.[21]

"Suppose now that there were two such magic rings, and the just put on one of them and the unjust the other; no man can be imagined to be of such an iron nature that he would stand fast in justice."[22] Glaucon believes that if a ring provided both a moral and an immoral person with the opportunity to be invisible, both people would use the invisibility to their advantage and would essentially do things they would not have done if they were visible to others. They essentially gain power over others without accountability. "And this we may truly affirm to be a great proof that a man is just, not willingly or because he thinks that justice is any good to him individually, but of necessity, for wherever any one thinks that he can safely be unjust, there he is unjust."[23]

Socrates argues that being moral and just are their own intrinsic rewards and that with the evolution of morality, individuals are just because they don't want to live with the guilt of an unjust life.[24] This leads us to look at present-day practitioners and the use of expertise to encourage just and moral behavior.

Public relations practitioners demonstrate the highest levels of expertise when they understand their client's corporate social strategy and are working hand in hand with executives at each level of the organization. In this instance, the practitioner has a strong understanding of the organization's target publics and takes a critical stance in regard to how to best reach those publics. Practitioners also need to utilize their expertise to advise C-suite executives. Oftentimes members of an organization's leadership team are not particularly skilled at addressing or contextualizing the needs of polarizing communities. Public relations practitioners need to become adept at not only crafting materials for C-suite executives, but also in vocalizing when things are not going well or when decisions are being made outside the realm of the company's ethical values.

For example, if a leader makes a poor decision, it is up to the public relations practitioner to not only point out the misstep but to assist in correcting the issue. Take the case of Kizzy Clothing. Kizzy Clothing is a network-based marketing company that focuses on selling women's athleisure clothing. Instead of promoting the clothing in brick-and-mortar storefronts, the clothes are sold by sales consultants on social networks like Facebook and Instagram, or at in-home parties. As with any new company, Kizzy has experienced some growing pains. Several lots of the company's signature yoga pants were turning up at home parties with holes in them and, to make matters worse, others were nearly transparent. Company executives addressed the issue with their concerned sales consultants through a video that was later posted online for the general public. In the video, executives tell the consultants that material flaws occur in the fashion industry and if they are able to wear the pants a couple of times, they can simply purchase new yoga pants, essentially implying that the product was disposable. Executives continue by stating if consumers don't like the product, they can certainly shop elsewhere. The communication scolded consultants that requested product changes or that pushed for details on how this problem would be solved.

In this example, the expertise of a PR practitioner would be incredibly valuable to the company. The PR practitioner would not only need to address the ethical missteps of the executives in terms of the way they dismissed their customers and their sales consultants, but also for continuing to produce a product they knew was faulty. It is also the responsibility of the practitioner to identify how the press and the public

---

ENHANCING EXPERTISE

According to Gini Dietrich of the blog *Spin Sucks*, public relations practitioners need to commit to doing five things to enhance their credibility and to highlight their expertise.

- **Check the facts on anything before sharing.** Case in point, a meme was circulating indicating that President Trump copied a portion of his speech from *The Bee Movie*. As much as the public might want this to be true, after researching a bit, it was obvious that this was not true.
- **Educate friends when they post alternative facts or fake news.** In the situation above, correct messaging where appropriate.
- **Have a spine and say no.** Practitioners HAVE to have spines and know how to say no, when asked to do something unethical.
- **Use critical thinking skills.** If something seems false, it probably is. Conduct your due diligence, investigate, and think.
- **Pay for your news.** If you pay for news, the quality of reporting will continue to improve. Consider that, particularly as it relates to public relations.[1]

---

1. "What Alternative Facts Mean to the PR Industry," Public Relations Today, accessed February 11, 2017, http://www.publicrelationstoday.com/edition/daily-ethics-infographics -2017-01-24/?open-article-id=6104081&article-title=what-alternative-facts-mean-to-the-pr -industry&blog-domain=spinsucks.com&blog-title=spin-sucks.

would likely judge the actions of the company and to address any fallout from the release of the video to the public.

Looking further into the case above, put your own expertise to the test.

- How would you advise the C-suite executives?
- Develop messaging that you would deliver to the public to address this situation.
- What channels would you utilize to address this issue? Why did you select these particular channels?

IMPLEMENTATION OF THE PURE MODEL

Let's examine the role of expertise in public relations more thoroughly by looking at a case from the 2016 Summer Olympics involving US Olympic swimmer Ryan Lochte.

Lochte shook up the 2016 Summer Olympics, and it wasn't solely for his swimming. An incident involving Lochte started after a drunken escapade at a Rio gas station.[25] Lochte and three other swimmers claimed that they were robbed at gunpoint. In truth, the swimmers actually vandalized a gas station restroom while intoxicated. The robbery story was used to cover up the use of alcohol. Lochte and his teammates lied to Olympic officials, Brazilian authorities, and the general public about what happened.

Even after the truth was exposed by surveillance camera footage, Lochte continued with his original story. Instead of admitting that he lied and was wrong, he continued to try and cover things up until the eventual truth emerged that he had indeed fabricated the entire story.

Lochte hired publicist Matthew Hiltzik to assist him through his self-made crisis. When Lochte eventually apologized for his actions and false statements in a live television interview, it came across as insincere. He did not apologize for lying to various publics nor did he speak to lessons learned. Instead he said that he was sorry for over exaggerating the story, referencing that it was partly true but slightly fabricated, even though evidence had proven the entire story as fictitious. Lochte never fully owned up to what actually happened that night at the gas station in Rio. Since he never took full responsibility for it, his apology fell on deaf ears.

Of course, when a celebrity or a company hires a publicist/PR team, they should be trained for media interviews. There is little doubt that Lochte was prepped before his television interview; however, his preparation did not translate well on camera.

In terms of applying the PURE model of ethical decision making to this situation, Lochte did not follow the guidelines of the Olympic committee when discussing personal and organizational principles. His immature behavior embarrassed his teammates and his country. The truth behind what Lochte was thinking when he fabricated the robbery story will most likely never be known. When looking at this case from the perspective of Lochte's publicist, Matthew Hiltzik, we can examine the reasons he chose to assist Lochte. Did Hiltzik choose the case solely based on compensation? Did he choose to work with Lochte out of respect for the swimmer? Did he choose to work with Lochte because he felt he deserved a second chance? Personal and professional motivations most certainly come into play when trying to discern personal principles. From an organizational perspective, as long as Hiltzik followed the PRSA Code of Ethics, he likely met his organization's principles for public relations representation.

Lochte, on the other hand, did not fare nearly as well when looking at universal principles. Lochte's unethical and dishonest behavior triggered discontent between himself and his fellow swimmers and caused a great deal of focus to be removed from the Olympic games—actions that are in direct contrast to Kant's Formula of Universal Law. If every athlete behaved in this manner, the communal spirt of the games would not have been achieved.

Lochte also failed to adhere to the third principle of the PURE model of ethical decision making, valuing the rights of publics. Initially, the general public was not able to make an informed decision about this incident due to the lack of information provided. Additionally, Lochte's dishonesty could have affected how members of the public view Rio de Janeiro and how the general public perceives athletes competing in the games. On a much larger stage, his behavior could have affected how other countries view American athletes.

Lastly, were the ends justified? In this case, the ends were not justified by the outcome. Lochte received significant public backlash and loss of personal sponsorships for the deception of multiple publics. He also embarrassed his teammates and his country.

IMPLICATIONS WITHIN SOCIAL MEDIA

Sean Spicer's and Kellyanne Conway's conduct as public relations professionals violates the PR code of ethics. In fact, the outcry and backlash on the social sphere to Spicer and then Conway's introduction of "alternative facts" resulted in the Public Relations Society of America issuing a statement rebuking Conway.

PRSA Statement on "Alternative Facts"

Jane Dvorak, APR, Fellow PRSA, Chair of the Society for 2017, wrote:[26]

> Truth is the foundation of all effective communications. By being truthful, we build and maintain trust with the media and our customers, clients and employees. As professional communicators, we take very seriously our responsibility to communicate with honesty and accuracy.
>
> The Public Relations Society of America, the nation's largest communications association, sets the standard of ethical behavior for our 22,000 members through our Code of Ethics. Encouraging and perpetuating the use of alternative facts by a high-profile spokesperson reflects poorly on all communications professionals.
>
> PRSA strongly objects to any effort to deliberately misrepresent information. Honest, ethical professionals never spin, mislead or alter facts. We applaud our colleagues and professional journalists who work hard to find and report the truth.

By devoting our ethical selves to our core public relations values, adhering to our commitment to sharing our expertise, we can ensure that clients and the public are best served when all relationships between spokespeople, bloggers, social media partners, business partners, and allies are open and transparent.[27]

SOLVING THE ETHICAL DILEMMA: THE WHITE HOUSE

In revisiting the case at the beginning of this chapter, it is evident that both individuals are representing the field of public relations, Spicer as a press secretary and Conway as an advisor. In these roles, it is imperative to reinforce the notion that credible relationships with the general public are paramount to success. Creating language designed to bury factual data and circumvent the truth is not only unethical, but it is also immoral. Both Spicer and Conway broke from the PR code of ethics when they highlighted "alternative facts" as opposed to actual data.

Practitioners should utilize their expertise and advise their clients to develop rhetoric to engage with the general public and to fully highlight their political positions. They should not encourage nor take part in the creation of new word definitions designed to redirect discussions.

Both Spicer and Conway missed key opportunities to not only build relationships, but to educate the president on the importance of picking battles. Not every negative comment necessitates a response. Sometimes it is best to simply let the comment go. Educating the client, in this case, the president of the United States, on the importance of knowing when to speak and knowing when to maintain silence is an important task. Additionally, highlighting the importance of communication between the media and the general public and the potential implications of reporting incorrect data, serve the client and the profession well.

If you served as an advisor to the president of the United States, how would you have handled this situation? Please utilize the decision guide below to work through this case.

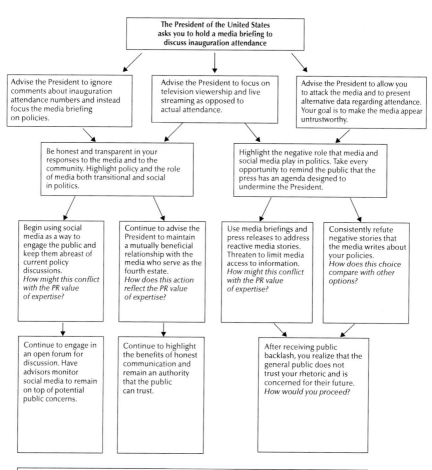

The President of the United States asks you to hold a media briefing to discuss inauguration attendance

Advise the President to ignore comments about inauguration attendance numbers and instead focus the media briefing on policies.

Advise the President to focus on television viewership and live streaming as opposed to actual attendance.

Advise the President to allow you to attack the media and to present alternative data regarding attendance. Your goal is to make the media appear untrustworthy.

Be honest and transparent in your responses to the media and to the community. Highlight policy and the role of media both transitional and social in politics.

Highlight the negative role that media and social media play in politics. Take every opportunity to remind the public that the press has an agenda designed to undermine the President.

Begin using social media as a way to engage the public and keep them abreast of current policy discussions. *How might this conflict with the PR value of expertise?*

Continue to advise the President to maintain a mutually beneficial relationship with the media who serve as the fourth estate. *How does this action reflect the PR value of expertise?*

Use media briefings and press releases to address reactive media stories. Threaten to limit media access to information. *How might this conflict with the PR value of expertise?*

Consistently refute negative stories that the media writes about your policies. *How does this choice compare with other options?*

Continue to engage in an open forum for discussion. Have advisors monitor social media to remain on top of potential public concerns.

Continue to highlight the benefits of honest communication and remain an authority that the public can trust.

After receiving public backlash, you realize that the general public does not trust your rhetoric and is concerned for their future. *How would you proceed?*

1. Define the specific ethical issue/conflict.
2. Identify internal/external factors (e.g. legal, political, social, economic) that may influence the decision.
3. Identify key values.
4. Identify the parties who will be affected by the decision and define the public relations professional's obligation to each.
5. Select ethical principles to guide the decision-making process.
6. Make a decision and justify it.

6

Independence

As a communicator, how do you feel about taking on the role of advocate?

The opportunity to serve as an advocate for clients/products/programs/services that you believe in can be a real privilege, as well as a responsibility. Having the opportunity to bring education, information, or entertainment to the "marketplace of ideas" is one of the most interesting things about being in the PR industry. It is very fulfilling to see your ideas translated into action that positively impacts both your target audiences and the clients you serve.

Discuss the importance of honesty and transparency as it applies to public relations.

To me, this one is a "no-brainer." The ideas/ideals of honesty and transparency should apply to everyone's business ethics, not just those in the public relations field specifically. Lying or covering up inconvenient truths is never the right strategy, in communications or otherwise. A former boss of mine in the PR industry used to often quote Mark Twain . . . "If you tell the truth, you don't have to remember anything."

What skills are necessary to demonstrate expertise in public relations?

To be a PR expert, you need to understand your client's goals and be able to design and implement meaningful media and communications strategies that help them to achieve those goals. There are tangible skills required, like creative and technical writing, research capabilities, big-picture thinking and strategy development abilities, knowledge of how the media works, being adept at multitasking, time management, etc., but that's really only half the battle. Success in the PR field also requires a variety of "soft skills," like the confidence, willingness, and ability to counsel clients who may outrank you in everything from experience to title to salary, a dedication to customer service, a passion for storytelling, tenacity, humility, adaptability . . . and having a sense of humor certainly never hurts!

Can you provide an example of a time when you had to disagree with what the client felt was necessary and guide them in another direction?

It happens quite often that a client will think something they are doing, plan to do, or have done is front-page-above-the-fold kind of news. People have the tendency to fall victim to "tunnel vision" and think that whatever they are planning/implementing is the best, most interesting thing. Most times it is definitely not. In those cases, it is our job, as their PR counselor, to provide expertise and input on why we don't necessarily share their vision, and what instead we recommend as tools and tactics for achieving their goals.

How do you balance loyalty to the client and loyalty to society?

To me those really feel like one and the same thing. What is best for my clients should align with what is in the public's best interest. If we are promoting or publicizing meaningful and worthwhile news/announcements, programs, events, or activities that are helpful, educational, of interest or entertainment value to the public, that should also be positively serving the client behind those initiatives. If ever, however, a client requested that I conduct any PR efforts that somehow were undermining or damaging to society, I would always act in favor of the public. There is no type of client or level of customer loyalty worth sacrificing the well-being of the greater good.

Can you discuss how you deal with differing opinions or maintain free expression of ideas?

Collaboration is a cornerstone of the practice of public relations. As a PR professional, you have to "play nice" with a variety of entities, including clients, media, colleagues, sponsors, and other professional services providers like lawyers, advertising agencies, marketing departments, and more. There are often a lot of cooks in the kitchen! You must be able to differentiate the noise from the quality contributions. If you use as a guide your commitment to what is best for the client, and what is best for your audiences/the public, you rarely can be steered from the right path . . . regardless of how many cats you must herd along the way.

What types of ethical issues are entry-level public relations practitioners likely to encounter?

Although I wish I could say the answer is "none," that unfortunately probably isn't true. It is possible that a new PR pro may at some time be asked/assigned by a client and/or supervisor to implement tactics that may violate the PRSA Code of Ethics. One example might be a request to post an "anonymous" review or response on social media that either promotes the client or diminishes a competitor. If you are working on behalf of a client, you need to be transparent about that relationship . . . always. A young PR pro may also be asked to attend a town hall meeting or other such public gathering, posing as a "concerned community member" as it relates to an issue a client is involved with. This also is a big no-no. You must represent who you are honestly and disclose any relevant connections to the parties involved. Another scenario might involve being asked to leverage friendships or other personal relationships with traditional and/or social media contacts to an unfair advantage for a client.

ETHICAL DILEMMA: TV ANCHOR LESLIE ROBERTS SCANDAL

Can an individual serve as both a professional journalist and as a public relations practitioner and maintain their integrity and ethics in both positions without telling their audiences?

Leslie Roberts was a journalist working for Global News, a division of Global Television Network in Toronto, Canada. Roberts served as a senior news anchor and an executive editor with *Global Toronto* as well as a cohost of the *National Morning Show*.[1] In January 2015, Roberts resigned from his positions after an investigation by the *Toronto Star* uncovered that Roberts was a co-owner of Toronto-based PR firm BuzzPR.[2] Records from the *Toronto Star* highlight several instances where clients of BuzzPR appeared on Global News, often with Roberts interviewing them.[3]

Roberts released a statement saying, "I regret the circumstances, specifically a failure to disclose information, which led to this outcome."[4]

As a reporter, Roberts is charged with providing unbiased information to the general public. While he denies a conflict of interest, others disagree. Roberts stated, "They did not pay me to get on TV. When I sit on the anchor desk I am in journalist mode and nothing comes between me and a story. . . . At no point have I ever, ever crossed the line."[5] However, statements on BuzzPR's website highlighting the strong relationships that the firm has with the local media point to a potential conflict. "The success of our media coverage campaign in Toronto is the result of our strong relationships with select media personnel. . . . Our Media Coverage Toronto services include . . . celebrity and guest speaker appearances/brand ambassadors. . . ."[6]

The roles of journalists and public relations professionals are vastly different. Despite a dedication to public interest and storytelling, journalists are ethically required to provide unbiased reporting, while PR practitioners work to influence public opinion and promote a client's product or service.

Ryerson journalism professor Lisa Taylor is concerned about the reflection this case may have on the way the public views journalism. "What I get concerned about is what it does generally to the vocation of news, where we've already got a bit of crisis of confidence in journalism and it's also really challenging for others at Global who are doing their jobs. . . . but they kind of get tarnished by the same brush."[7]

OVERVIEW OF INDEPENDENCE

The Public Relations Society of America defines independence as "providing objective counsel to those we represent and being accountable for our actions."[8] In other words, public relations practitioners need to uphold the highest levels of ethical standards in both their personal and professional lives in order to guide potential clients. High-profile organizations want public relations practitioners with a proven track record of noteworthy personal and professional branding strategies. A practitioner who is unable to brand himself/herself and to manage that brand would be perceived as unable to effectively manage a corporate brand.

There are several notable examples of cases where a practitioner experienced a personal lapse in judgment that significantly affected their professional standings. Two such cases will be discussed. The first involves a sexist tweet by Pete Codella, and the second, an insensitive and racist tweet by Justine Sacco.

WHY INDEPENDENCE IS IMPORTANT IN PUBLIC RELATIONS

The Tweet Heard 'Round the PRSA International Conference

Theresa Payton, president and CEO of Fortalice Solutions and former White House chief information officer, addressed PRSA and PRSSA members about cybersecurity during a general session of the PRSA International Conference in Indianapolis in October 2016.

In order to draw attention to both the conference and the myriad of attendees, participants were encouraged to tweet and share insights throughout the conference using the hashtag #PRSAICON. They were also urged to live tweet content from various presenters.

journalists don't work to influence like PR

Shortly after Payton's presentation began, the following tweet was posted.

It didn't take long for individuals—PRSA and PRSSA members, men and women—to call Pete Codella out for his sexist messaging.

Stephanie Katcher @happy2... · 12h ⌄
@kardashaaron wow. So not okay.
↩ ⇄ ♥ 1 ✉

Leanne Robinett @leannerobi... · 12h ⌄
.@kardashaaron - PERFECT
example of a women being judged
on her appearance rather than her
thoughts/opinions. This is sad
#PRSSANC #PRSAicon
↩ ⇄ 2 ♥ 25 ✉

Saki Indakwa @sakiindakwa · 12h ⌄
@kardashaaron -I learned a lot from
her. Too bad he was so "distracted."
↩ ⇄ ♥ 6 ✉

WiredPR @WiredPR · 11h ⌄
@kardashaaron Agreed. Super
unnecessary comment. She's

Reply to aaron

🏠 Home   🔔 Notifications   ⚡ Moments   ✉ Messages   👤 Me

WiredPR @WiredPR · 11h ⌄
@kardashaaron Agreed. Super
unnecessary comment. She's
brilliant. Terrific presentation.
#PRSAICON
↩ ⇄ ♥ 4 ✉

Kate Snyder, APR @PiperGold... · 9h ⌄
@kardashaaron Can I 💔 this
comment instead of 🤍ing it?!?
#PRSAICON
↩ ⇄ ♥ 4 ✉

Kate @k_blasco · 3h ⌄
@kardashaaron I really wish @PRSA
could address this because I'm still
upset by this, along with many other
students
↩ ⇄ ♥ 1 ✉

Reply to aaron

🏠 Home   🔔 Notifications   ⚡ Moments   ✉ Messages   👤 Me

Codella, who has a long history in public relations, has received Accreditation in Public Relations (APR) certification from PRSA, which classifies him as an accredited PR professional. APR certification, according to PRSA, "certifies your drive, professionalism, and principles, setting you apart from your peers and positioning you as a leader and mentor in the competitive public relations field."[9]

At the time of the conference, Codella was the director of marketing and communications for the David Eccles School of Business at the University of Utah. He is also a former chapter president of a PRSA chapter in the North Pacific District.

An important responsibility of a PR practitioner is to teach clients how to cope with crisis situations. For clients going through a crisis resulting from an internal mistake, practitioners can encourage the company or individual to own it, apologize, and fix it.

In this instance, Codella did not own the situation, nor did he fix it. Codella could have "stopped the bleeding" by acknowledging the many responses and criticisms his original tweet prompted, or by stating he would vow to avoid making similar statements in the future. He failed to do this. Instead, he defended his tweet. His explanation was that he was giving advice to a fellow speaker and that he viewed his actions as being similar to "someone pulling him aside at a speaking engagement to mention that the vent on his suit jacket was still stitched closed."[10] The problem with Codella's approach is that he offered his advice on Twitter, using an international conference hashtag that connected anyone attending or following the conference. He did not simply speak with Payton.

↩ in reply to @ajrespess

 **Pete Codella, APR**
@codella

.@ajrespess **not, never advocating sexism. making a common sense practical suggestion for public speakers, men & women.** #PRSAicon

Oct 24, 2016, 8:45 AM

As the backlash persisted, Codella eventually apologized.

Justine Sacco's Online Catastrophe

The next case study also involves the use of Twitter; however, in this case, the author did not intend for the tweet to go public. She merely intended to entertain a small group of personal followers.

In 2013, Justine Sacco was the global head of communications for IAC/InterActiveCorp. She was traveling from New York to South Africa. Before she boarded her flight she sent out a tweet to her 170 Twitter followers.

The repercussions of that fateful tweet were swift, and the backlash was immediate. The tweet, intended for her friends and family, was retweeted by Valleywag tech blogger Sam Biddle to his fifteen thousand followers. The tweet went viral.

Responses included:

A tweet from her employer: "IAC on @JustineSacco tweet: This is an outrageous, offensive comment. Employee in question currently unreachable on an intl flight."[11]

Tweet from an angry public. "All I want for Christmas is to see @JustineSacco's face when her plane lands and she checks her inbox/voicemail. #fire"[12]

"Oh man, @justinesacco is going to have the most painful phone-turning-on moment ever when her plane lands."[13]

"We are about to watch this @JustineSacco bitch get fired. In REAL time. Before she even KNOWS she's getting fired."[14]

Not surprisingly, Sacco lost her job and significantly damaged her reputation.[15] Sacco's job was to manage the reputation of her company, yet she was not responsible when it came to her own content. "Justine's name was normally Googled 40 times a month. That month, between December 20–31, Sacco's name was Googled 1,220,000 times."[16]

In an interview after the incident, Sacco explained what she truly meant by her tweet.

> She was flying to South Africa, where she has family. This trip, she explained, made her think about how so many westerners consider HIV/AIDS an "African thing," when of course there is a domestic AIDS epidemic. Her tweet was supposed to mimic—and mock—what an actual racist, ignorant person would say. Ergo, tweeting that thought would be an ironic statement, a joke, the opposite of what it seemed to say.[17]

As public relations practitioners, it is necessary to consistently look at the bigger picture and train clients to do the same. Every instance requiring a tweet, blog post, or social media post to Snapchat or Facebook, or even interviews, should require some reflection on how a practitioner will perceive the content and how the general public will view the content of the messages.

WHEN ETHICAL LAPSES BENEFIT THE CLIENT

It is important to note that not all PR practitioners committing ethical lapses receive negative repercussions. If there were not a perceived benefit to deceit or deception, then it would not be necessary for practitioners to work so diligently to direct clients and maintain integrity. However, even if the initial ethical lapse is not revealed, it is imperative to note that once the general public is aware of the deception, the public's trust is difficult and sometimes impossible to regain.

In a podcast interview on Mixergy, Ryan Holiday, a media strategist for clients including Tucker Max and American Apparel, discusses his book, *Trust Me, I'm Lying: Confessions of a Media Manipulator*, and his processes for media deception. As a media strategist, Holiday is a member of the public relations profession and therefore would be expected to adhere to the PRSA code of ethics. While Holiday provides independent counsel, he finds that deception is more profitable than adherence to ethical standards. Here is an example of one of the ways he garnered publicity for American Apparel.

> We had these photos that we couldn't run for copyright reasons. Essentially, we had done these Halloween costumes with the American Apparel clothes that we couldn't run because they were public figures, like a Lady Gaga costume, let's say, right? And, we're not going to pay Lady Gaga to be able to run that costume. So, I'm sitting there talking to the photographer, and they're like, "Look, we got to throw these away. That really sucks."
>
> So, what I thought was, OK, so these are the sort of rejected, you-can't-see material. This is like the stuff left on the cutting room floor. Well, so, if I went to a blogger and I said, "Look, here's some stuff that wasn't good enough to make our website," they're obviously not going to run that. But, what if I pretended to be someone that stole them from American Apparel, or I pretended to be an employee who "found" them and was giving them away without permission? Now, it's not just a bunch of photos, which are good for content, it's sort of this exclusive news angle.
>
> I know that Gawker loves to run controversial stories about American Apparel. Instead of trying to pitch them another way, which is a fun, lighthearted story, I turned a fun, lighthearted story into a newsy, exclusive sort of taboo story.
>
> It worked really well. From their perspective, it worked really well, too, because it did almost 100,000 page views. It's sort of both laws, right? Because you tell them what they want to hear and then you're also giving them an enormous gift in the sense that they got paid from that so they're not very likely to go, "Hmm. What are the chances of these being real?" because you don't stare a gift horse in the mouth.[18]

Holiday notes that "I created false perceptions through blogs, which led to bad conclusions and wrong decisions—real decisions in the real world that had consequences of real people."[19] He acknowledges the long-term repercussions his decisions had on his clients. While Holiday highlights the benefits of this type of manipulation, he concludes his book by stressing why practitioners and the public in general should fight against it. "Why am I giving away these secrets? Because I'm tired of a world where blogs take indirect bribes, marketers help write the news, reckless journalists spread lies, and no one is accountable for any of it. I'm pulling back the curtain because I don't want anyone else to get blindsided."[20]

Like Holiday, "early public relations practices introduced many ethical concerns because the press agentry approach prevalent back then emphasized hyperbole and sensationalism and often lacked truth."[21] Edward Bernays even called the time period between 1850 and 1905 "the public be damned era."[22] To this day public relations practitioners have to fight the reputation of being considered "spin doctors" and "hacks." PR practitioners are charged with acting ethically in order to provide the best long-term benefits for themselves as experts in the field and for the client that is being represented.

VIRTUE ETHICS AND RESPONSIBILITY

Independence is often associated with the moral principle of responsibility. "To be ethically responsible, one must engage in an external conversation with others and with self."[23] Public relations practitioners are charged with being responsible for their actions and oftentimes for the actions of their organizations. They have morally based obligations and duties to others and to larger ethical, moral, and legal codes, standards, and traditions.[24] The concept of responsibility directly relates to one of the principal approaches used to examine the moral actions of leaders: virtue ethics. Johnson, for example, suggested, "The premise of virtue ethics is simple. Good people (those of high moral character) make good moral choices."[25] To be virtuous, an individual must demonstrate the character traits of honesty, integrity, and morality in their everyday encounters. According to scholars Richard Burnor and Yvonne Raley, one must fulfill several conditions to attain excellence:

- One must *know* what the right thing is
- One must *intend* to do the right thing, because it *is* the right thing
- One's right actions must be the products of one's own "firm and unchangeable character"—one's patterns of behavior must be habitual or second nature.[26]

Public relations practitioners are expected to not only understand what the right thing is, but they are also expected to counsel clients on the proper course of action and to represent themselves accordingly. "Good choices embody and reflect a wide array of habits of human excellence. These excellences include not merely justice and respect (the virtues emphasized in Kantian and utilitarian ethics) but other habits of choice, such as loyalty, caring, moderation, courage and trustworthiness."[27]

ETHICAL DECISION MAKING

Not surprisingly ethical decisions are not always easy to make. There are often several factors, various publics, and distinct consequences for every decision that practitioners are presented with. Nonetheless, as leaders and professionals, PR practitioners are accountable for leading the decision-making process. Additionally, practitioners are often responsible for presenting a coherent, justifiable defense for each ethical action. Ethics scholar Patricia Parsons recommends three defenses for ethical action: principled decisions, precedent decisions, and patron decisions.[28]

Principled decisions are decisions that are made based on traditional philosophical principles. These principles are discussed in chapter 1 and delineated in the ethical theories of utilitarianism, libertarianism, and Kantianism, as well as in virtue ethics or other ethics of care.

Precedent decisions are decisions that are justified based on previous situational outcomes. You look to examples of ethical situations similar to the situation you find yourself in and model the decisions made in those instances.

Patron decisions are decisions that you are unable to make in isolation. Instead, you turn to mentors or those whom you can trust to offer guidance in the situation.

It is important to note that despite the reliance on others for assistance in guiding the decision-making process, the full responsibility for the decision and any outcomes that may occur fall squarely on the shoulders of the PR practitioner.

ETHICAL DECISION-MAKING MODELS

PR practitioners often rely on ethical decision-making models to guide them through decision-making processes. Previous chapters have discussed the PURE model of ethical decision making . As referenced in chapter 3, the Potter Box model was developed by Ralph Potter of Harvard University and consists of four steps.[29] The first step is to thoroughly analyze the situation. The second step is to compare and contrast personal and organizational ethical values. The third step is to consider applicable ethical principles such as utilitarianism, Kantianism, and so on. The fourth step is to select loyalties. Loyalties may be to stakeholders, to the general public, to the organization, and so on.

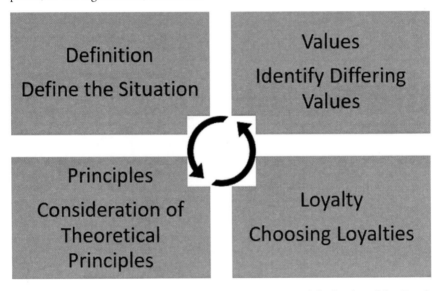

Another model of decision making is the Navran model, developed by Frank Navran. This model consists of a six-step plan and includes PLUS (Policies, Laws, Universal, Self) filters that can be applied at steps 1, 3, and 6.

The six-step process includes:[30]

1. Define the problem—Are there policies, procedures, laws of regulations or individual/group values that apply to this situation?
2. Identify possible solutions.
3. Evaluate the solutions—Are there policies, procedures, laws of regulations or individual/group values that apply to each alternative?
4. Make a decision.
5. Implement the decision.
6. Evaluate the decision/outcomes—Are there policies, procedures, laws of regulations or individual/group values that have been overlooked? Was the decision ethical?

Practitioners would consider the six questions from the model and apply the policies, laws, and individual/group values to steps 1, 3, and 6.

IMPLICATIONS WITHIN SOCIAL MEDIA

Social media created additional challenges for the ethical practice of public relations. Ethical issues such as representatives from companies altering the content of their organization's Wikipedia page to reflect biased content to companies hiring paid bloggers that review and write positive copy on behalf of their products and services, and political candidates hiring individuals to post optimistic comments about them on varying social media platforms are recent issues that have come to the forefront of the ethical conversation.[31] In 2009 the Federal Trade Commission updated its guidelines on endorsements and testimonials to cover social media. They must disclose if a company is paying or giving compensation in any way to a blogger or influencer on any social platform.[32] Staying objective when a client or a manager sees nothing wrong with not disclosing the company paid for a Twitter endorsement or offered free products to a mommy blogger in exchange for a positive review can be tough. The PRSA code of ethics is there to guide practitioners on the social sphere.

SOLVING THE ETHICAL DILEMMA: TV ANCHOR LESLIE ROBERTS SCANDAL

Let's take a moment to revisit the case at the beginning of this chapter dealing with Leslie Roberts. As an individual representing the field of public relations, it is imperative to reinforce the notion that Roberts arguably completes each assignment with the highest level of integrity, and is identified as someone that the public can trust. Leveraging his career as a journalist to promote the clients of his public relations firm is not only unethical, but it calls Roberts's integrity into question. Roberts broke from the PR code of ethics when he decided to misrepresent both the field of journalism by presenting biased content and the profession of public relations by misleading clients in regard to earned media publicity.

Practitioners should be utilizing their independence by acting responsibly in their dealings with the public and by providing sound guidance to those they work alongside and represent. Roberts missed key opportunities to not only divulge his ties to both professions, but also to recuse himself when his business ventures conflicted. Please utilize the decision guide below to work through this case.

1. If you served as an advisor to Leslie Roberts, how would you have handled this situation?
2. Use both the Navran model and the Potter Box to work though this decision.

TOP 10 REASONS FOR EARNING THE APR

As we discuss independence in public relations, we would be remiss to ignore the role that education plays in providing a practitioner with the knowledge and background to provide objective counsel to clients.

In an article for *PRsay*, a public relations and communication blog created by the Public Relations Society of America, Anne W. O'Connell discusses the top ten reasons she earned her Accreditation in Public Relations (APR):[1]

- I now can explain more fully things I knew intuitively (e.g., why writing a news release is not enough).
- I yearned for greater professional accountability. The work we do should have an impact; it should affect behavior and be meaningful.
- I previously had not studied research—qualitative, quantitative, primary, secondary, etc.—and now I am all about research, the foundation for any good PR plan.
- I wanted to be able to demonstrate measurable results to justify the PR function and my position. *Accreditation defines and legitimizes the profession, sets industry/professional standards, and builds accountable ethics and legal knowledge.*
- I desired greater knowledge in preparing an effective public relations plan. *What is a PR plan and why does it matter?*
- I knew there was more to learn about media relations. *Media coverage is an output (not outcome) measure.*
- I once thought of becoming an attorney and now know much about copyright, defamation, SEC filings, Sarbanes-Oxley legislation, and other legal matters. *I've also decided I no longer have a desire to become an attorney!*
- I wanted to be credentialed like other professionals. *The work seems more meaningful and strategic than busy.*
- I wanted the knowledge, skills, and abilities that will allow me to transfer and effectively work in any industry, corporation, or agency.

---

1. "Top 10 Reasons for Earning the APR," *PRSay*, September 28, 2015, accessed February 13, 2017, http://prsay.prsa.org/2015/09/28/top-10-reasons-for-earning-the-apr/.

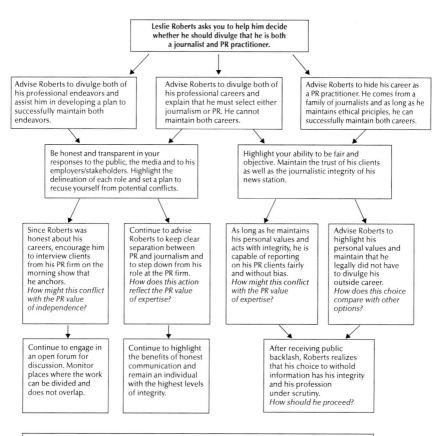

Leslie Roberts asks you to help him decide whether he should divulge that he is both a journalist and PR practitioner.

Advise Roberts to divulge both of his professional endeavors and assist him in developing a plan to successfully maintain both endeavors.

Advise Roberts to divulge both of his professional careers and explain that he must select either journalism or PR. He cannot maintain both careers.

Advise Roberts to hide his career as a PR practitioner. He comes from a family of journalists and as long as he maintains ethical priciples, he can successfully maintain both careers.

Be honest and transparent in your responses to the public, the media and to his employers/stakeholders. Highlight the delineation of each role and set a plan to recuse yourself from potential conflicts.

Highlight your ability to be fair and objective. Maintain the trust of his clients as well as the journalistic integrity of his news station.

Since Roberts was honest about his careers, encourage him to interview clients from his PR firm on the morning show that he anchors. *How might this conflict with the PR value of independence?*

Continue to advise Roberts to keep clear separation between PR and journalism and to step down from his role at the PR firm. *How does this action reflect the PR value of expertise?*

As long as he maintains his personal values and acts with integrity, he is capable of reporting on his PR clients fairly and without bias. *How might this conflict with the PR value of expertise?*

Advise Roberts to highlight his personal values and maintain that he legally did not have to divulge his outside career. *How does this choice compare with other options?*

Continue to engage in an open forum for discussion. Monitor places where the work can be divided and does not overlap.

Continue to highlight the benefits of honest communication and remain an individual with the highest levels of integrity.

After receiving public backlash, Roberts realizes that his choice to withold information has his integrity and his profession under scrutiny. *How should he proceed?*

1. Define the specific ethical issue/conflict.
2. Identify internal/external factors (e.g. legal, political, social, economic) that may influence the decision.
3. Identify key values.
4. Identify the parties who will be affected by the decision and define the public relations professional's obligation to each.
5. Select ethical principles to guide the decision-making process.
6. Make a decision and justify it.

7

Loyalty

situation, I offer my best advice but give them options, given the situation and their budget. We discuss those options and ultimately it is my client's decision. However, with good communication and advice based on the facts and reality of the situation, we generally reach a consensus on the proposed course of action.

How do you balance loyalty to the client and loyalty to society?
I only work for people, organizations, and causes I support or believe have a valid concern.

Can you discuss how you deal with differing opinions or maintain free expression of ideas?
Life is about compromise, and by listening to the differing opinions, we can always find a happy medium.

What types of ethical issues are entry-level public relations practitioners likely to encounter?
It is important to do what you like. As we enter a new industry, it is easy to go where the opportunities are. That's fine. Go where the opportunities are. However, while you are there, find something you enjoy, an issue or industry or area of PR (crisis management, health care, social media, etc.) and develop an expertise in that area—make a name for yourself. Volunteer. Find a cause you are passionate about or connected to, contact their organization, and ask to sit on the PR/marketing committee. Develop a portfolio of experience and work to build your reputation outside of the office.

ETHICAL DILEMMA: PAULA PEDENE, VETERAN WHISTLE-BLOWER

To say that Paula Pedene, APR and PRSA Fellow, has had a long and successful career in public relations is an understatement. Throughout her career, Pedene has earned three Public Relations Society of America Silver Anvil Awards for Institutional Programs, Reputation Management, and Community Outreach—the society's highest honors. Throughout her career, Pedene has been the recipient of more than eighty other awards from government and nongovernment agencies. Additionally, she has created two nonprofit organizations—the Veterans Medical Leadership Council and Honoring Arizona's Veterans—and operates her own PR consultancy firm, Paula Pedene and Associates Inc.[1]

However, even the most seasoned practitioners are confronted with ethical dilemmas. During her time as chief spokeswoman for the Phoenix Veterans Affairs Health Care System (PVAHCS), Pedene became a whistle-blower, exhibiting her loyalty to the veterans that she worked alongside and served. Pedene, along with Sam Foote,

MD, filed a complaint with the Office of the Inspector General citing financial mismanagement of non-VA fee care funds resulting in a multimillion-dollar budget shortfall and a hostile work environment.[2]

According the Department of Veterans Affairs, the non-VA fee care program is designed "to assist veterans who cannot easily receive care at a VA medical facility. This program pays the medical costs of eligible veterans who receive care from non-VA providers when the VA is unable to provide specific treatments or provide treatment economically because of the veteran's geographical inaccessibility."[3] Services can include emergency care and transportation, nonemergency inpatient and outpatient care, as well as some dental procedures.

After a thorough investigation, the Office of the Inspector General substantiated their claims and implemented corrective actions to reduce the risk of any future budget shortfalls.

Shortly after Pedene's initial filing, new leadership was put into place and Pedene was charged with a computer infraction and other alleged misconduct. As a result, she was demoted from her role as public affairs officer, where she had served honorably for eighteen years, and was reassigned as a clerk in the VA library.[4] Despite the demotion, she continued to pursue work on behalf of veterans. She frequently spoke with veterans regarding long wait times and delays in medical care resulting in possible wrongful deaths, as well as mismanagement of hospital resources and a bevy of other patient safety issues. Pedene filed a second complaint with the Office of the Inspector General and as a direct result of her actions, substantial change was implemented.[5]

Pedene was named PRSA's 2015 Professional of the Year. During her acceptance speech she referenced her work with the VA and those that stood beside her. "I did what I needed to do to support Dr. Sam Foote in exposing the unethical practices in the VA wait time scandal. It took enormous efforts on the part of many individuals who stood strong, even when it meant standing alone."[6]

OVERVIEW OF LOYALTY

By definition, loyal means "unswerving in allegiance."[7] When you consider loyalty within public relations, a slightly more poignant definition is realized. Scholar Patricia Parsons defines loyalty as "a constituent to whom the public relations practitioner owes a duty and who in return, places a trust in the practitioner."[8] According to the Public Relations Society of America, loyalty is defined as being "faithful to those we represent, while honoring our obligation to serve the public interest."[9] Public relations practitioners are expected to walk a fine line between meeting the demands of their clients and assuring that the needs of their publics are being accounted for. This is not a simple task. These competing obligations are often a source of contention and the primary basis of several ethical dilemmas.

In order to uphold the ethical value of loyalty, public relations practitioners need to first determine where their loyalties lie. Newsom, Scott, and VanSlyke Turk suggest that public relations practitioners have ethical responsibility to ten different publics, including clients, media, government agencies, educational institutions, information consumers, stockholders and analysts, the community, the organization's competition and critics, and other public relations practitioners.[10] In their book *Public Relations Ethics*, Philip Seib and Kathy Fitzpatrick further narrow the scope of a PR practitioner's ethical duty from ten publics to six publics, including duty to self, duty to client, duty to employer, duty to profession, duty to media, and duty to society.[11] Patricia Parsons narrows the view of publics even further in her text *Ethics in Public Relations* by focusing on four distinct publics: self, employer/client, PR profession, and society.[12]

For purposes of clarification, this text focuses on duties to five publics: self, client, employer, profession, and society. Discussions of media will be included in duty to the profession as social media has become closely tied to the duties of PR practitioners. While deciphering loyalties is an important part of ethical decision making, making a viable effort to respect the interests of all parties is crucial. Fraser Seitel notes that "serving the public interest simply requires public relations professionals to consider the interests of all affected parties and make a committed effort to balance them to the extent possible while avoiding or minimizing harm and respecting all of the persons involved."[13]

To fully understand the challenges inherent in making ethical decisions involving competing duties and loyalties, let's examine a case study and assess the implications on all affected parties.

Imagine that you work for a small public relations firm in California. One of your largest clients is a physician who treats heroin addiction. The doctor, who is also a former heroin addict, has built a thriving practice with various high-profile celebrity clients. She has become a media darling based on her unabashed honesty about her former addiction and her difficult road to success and has amassed a substantial social media following based on her open and honest style. This physician has recently approached you about ghostwriting her blog and makes it clear that she simply does not have time to devote to social media and would like you to write two or three blog posts per week. The general public would think that your client was writing the blogs and was responding to comments, when in actuality you would be researching and creating content, as well as responding to all discussion. How do you respond to the client's request?

As a new practitioner, it is often difficult to discern who should be the priority public. One of the most difficult dilemmas practitioners face involves the conflict between duty to self and loyalty to employer. Let's take a look at the duty to each of the five publics.

Duty to self—The first question that a practitioner should consider is whether you can live with your decision. Would you be comfortable signing over your intellectual property? Are you prepared for the repercussions when the general public finds out that your client is not creating her own content or engaging in direct discussion with her followers? There could be consequences for you as a practitioner due to the high profile of your client. This could affect how you are viewed by other clients.

Duty to client—You have been hired to work on behalf of your client. A large part of this role involves communicating with various publics. Is your ethical duty to blindly do what your client requests of you, or do you offer your public relations expertise to counsel your client on the repercussions of building a career on open and honest communication and then having the public find out that social media outreach has been less than transparent? Simply stated, counseling your client is your ethical duty as a PR practitioner.

Duty to employer—The decisions represented in this case are not made in isolation. Repercussions can affect you, as well as the small PR firm where you are employed. If the client becomes unhappy with either your refusal to ghostwrite or with your contributions (assuming you choose to write on the client's behalf), that displeasure will ultimately reflect on the firm. Discussions with your employer are necessary in this situation. A clear delineation of responsibilities and expectations should be outlined as citing support from your employer and is paramount to mediating a difficult situation with a client. Remember, your employer ultimately signs your paycheck.

Duty to profession—You have a duty to uphold the PRSA code of ethics and to avoid discrediting the PR profession. If your deception is revealed, you could add to the perception that PR practitioners are deceitful and unethical.

Duty to society—How would the public feel if they found out your client was not writing any of her content? Would they feel deceived? Would her credibility be called into question? As a PR practitioner, you are obligated to maintain honest communication with the public and to give the public the opportunity to make decisions based on authentic and genuine content, as opposed to veiled deception.

An appropriate solution in this case might be to counsel your client and have them involved in providing content for the blogs. The content could ultimately be crafted by the PR practitioner or the firm, but the general ideas still derive from the client. Additionally, noting that content contained within the blog is developed by the doctor's team alleviates a lack of transparency. Lastly, insisting that the doctor respond to questions about addiction and treatment will assist in upholding the foundations on which the doctor built her career.

It is important to note that priorities can be altered based on the circumstances. In other words, you may focus on duty to your client in some situations and duty to society in other situations. The whistle-blower case at the beginning of this chapter is a prime example. Paula Pedene focused on her duty and ultimate loyalty to society over her duty and loyalty to her employer.

LOYALTY AND PUBLIC RELATIONS

It is important to understand that each professional code of ethics governing public relations suggests that practitioners should uphold their duty to the public. However, individual codes look at the duty of loyalty in a slightly different way. The PRSA Code of Ethics says, "Protecting and advancing the free flow of accurate and truthful information is essential to serving the public interest and contributing to informed decision making in a democratic society."[14] Several ethical codes focus on honesty and respect for the general public. The Society for Professional Journalists ethical code states, "Ethical journalism treats sources, subjects, colleagues and members of the public as human beings deserving of respect."[15] The Chartered Institute of Public Relations focuses on authenticity and transparency by stating, "Deal honestly and fairly in business with . . . the public."[16] The Public Relations Institute of Southern Africa (PRISA) code addresses loyalty to the public using the most pointed wording. "We shall respect the public interest and the dignity of the individual."[17]

According to ethicist Michael Bayles, "Many of the most interesting, important, and difficult problems of professional ethics concern conflict between a professional's obligations to a client and to others. For a number of reasons, discussions of these problems often appear to sacrifice society's interest to those of individual clients."[18] In order to ensure that decisions are benefiting both the client and society, it is imperative that public relations practitioners utilize the following stages:

1. **Research**—Prior to making recommendations on a potential public relations plan, it is imperative that effective research is completed specifically on the client, the requested situation, and any targeted publics. Additionally, any research should contain outcomes from similar campaigns, whether successful or unsuccessful. Failed campaigns can provide a wealth of information regarding organizational loyalties and their priority publics.
2. **Plan**—Develop a thorough plan that delineates the responsibilities of each team member. Include players from both the public relations firm and from the client's organization. Ensure that each individual understands how to execute their role.
3. **Monitor**—Pay close attention to the social commentary surrounding the campaign and immediately address any negative sentiment.
4. **Strategize**—Always reflect upon the long-term benefits of the campaign and the lasting loyalties of consumers when making decisions. Shortsighted decisions lead to long-term disasters.

DEMANDS OF ETHICAL LOYALTY

Public relations practitioners are often expected to guide organizations in terms of ethical practices. As a point of contact between various publics, stakeholders, and the media, public relations practitioners are charged with shaping an organization's public perception and in maintaining the brand's standard of corporate responsibility. "As the internal conscience of many organizations, the public relations department has become a focal point for the institutionalization of ethical conduct. Increasingly, management has turned to public relations officers to lead the internal ethical charge, to be the keeper of the organizational ethic."[19] Additionally, public relations practitioners are often tasked with remaining loyal to an organization that is struggling. Public relations scholar Kevin Stoker discusses the ebb and flow of organizational performance and the role of a practitioner in helping an organization recuperate while implementing change and fresh ideas.[20] He highlights seven ways to determine the demands of ethical loyalty:[21]

1. **Choose objects worthy of loyalty.** Research and align with organizations that represent the highest levels of ethical principles and practices. In other words, choose to work for organizations that value character, personal responsibility, honesty, and transparency.[22]
2. **Seek truth and listen.** Pay special attention to what is happening within an organization. If you notice product deficiencies or employee unrest, consider asking questions and try to find answers.
3. **Enable voice.** Disassemble the hierarchy and ensure that voices at all levels of the organization and consumers are heard and that C-suite executives acknowledge concerns. This will encourage open discussion and feedback leading to change and improvement.
4. **Serve as a social conscience.** Point out decisions, actions, or communication that might violate the ethical principles of the organization and work to identify solutions to those decisions, actions, or communications.
5. **Bear some of the costs of loyalty.** Recognize that bad decisions are a part of the human condition. Learn from them and move on.
6. **Put authenticity ahead of aesthetics.** Value the inherent importance of loyalty enough to forgo job security for the betterment of the community. Threaten to leave or take legal action if unethical practices continue. Stay true to your word. Think whistle-blowers here.
7. **Show loyalty to loyalty.** If those in power show no willingness to listen, change, or improve the situation, avoid "suffering in silence" and leave the organization.[23]

IMPLICATIONS WITHIN SOCIAL MEDIA

Employees can be the most loyal constituents a brand has. Ethical values can be challenged when companies ask employees to spread the word about a company's good deeds through their social media efforts.[24] This may help build brand awareness, but the employees who engage without disclosing their association violate consumer trust. Public relations professionals have a responsibility to their publics to uphold the PRSA code of ethics while striving for meaningful social media content that fosters trusted relationships and creates value.[25] A time-tested, strategic approach to social media as part of a public relations plan is the only way to help avoid ethical transgressions.

APPLICATION OF THE PURE MODEL

Let's examine loyalty in public relations more thoroughly by considering a case involving the Chevy Tahoe. The public relations team for Chevrolet developed a campaign for the new Chevy Tahoe, including the creation of a website allowing the general public to post their own commercials for the new Tahoe online with music and video clips provided by Chevrolet.[26] The response was huge with more than 30,000 videos submitted within four weeks and 629,000 visitors to the website.[27] Unfortunately, not all of the videos that were created and posted reflected the Chevy Tahoe in a positive light. The company had to then decide how to manage the user-generated content. Should they leave the content up or start censoring content that they deemed inappropriate? The Chevrolet team ultimately decided not to censor the videos and to allow the consumers to completely control the messaging. Let's analyze this decision using the PURE model of ethical decision making.

Personal and organizational principles—This case focuses on organizational principles. In Chevy's case, the company decided not to censor user-generated content and let consumers decide how the brand would be portrayed. The Chevy brand is extremely customer focused, described on its corporate website as "embody[ing] the best of American automobile ingenuity, giving customers the quality they want and the value they need."[28] By choosing not to censor content during this campaign, Chevrolet remained loyal to its principle of respect. The company values its customers enough to give them a voice and to listen to both positive and negative feedback.

Universal principles—The principles here could certainly be applied across the board, but it is unlikely that many other automobile manufacturers would follow suit. Chevy was open and honest in their communication with the public regarding this contest. They provided the public a voice and maintained their commitment to broadcasting that voice regardless of sentiment. This decision expressed loyalty to the company, loyalty to the employer, and loyalty to society.

Rights of publics—Rights in this situation were executed perfectly. The public was able to make an informed decision about the Tahoe based on consumer feedback. Chevrolet chose not to censor in order to guarantee that their messaging was relevant. While they provided the tools, Chevrolet allowed the public to exercise their rights in terms of manipulation of those tools.

Justifiable ends—In this case, the ends justified the means. While Chevrolet was criticized heavily by most media outlets, consumers were pleased that their commercials remained visible to the public throughout the entirety of the campaign.

SOLVING THE ETHICAL DILEMMA: PAULA PEDENE, VETERAN WHISTLE-BLOWER

To conclude this chapter, let's revisit the Paula Pedene case. Pedene demonstrated high levels of loyalty to self and to society throughout her whistle-blowing cases. She also exhibited loyalty to veterans past and present by addressing problems within VA hospitals. Pedene's acts did not go without repercussion. She was demoted from her position as PR spokesperson for the hospital and remained in a hostile work environment. Let's explore the choices Pedene made and the consequences of her actions.

1. Apply the PURE model of ethical decision making to Pedene's decision-making process.
2. Did Pedene's decision benefit the client and society? Utilize the RPMS model of decision making to discuss the publics that Pedene served.

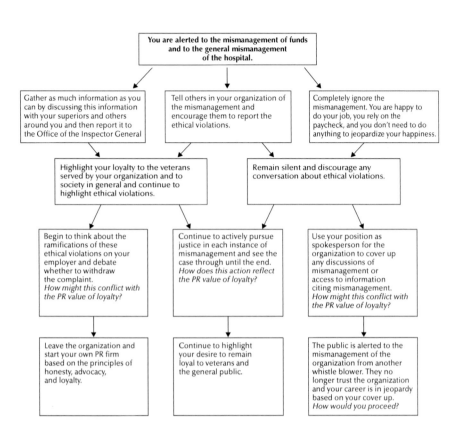

You are alerted to the mismanagement of funds and to the general mismanagement of the hospital.

Gather as much information as you can by discussing this information with your superiors and others around you and then report it to the Office of the Inspector General

Tell others in your organization of the mismanagement and encourage them to report the ethical violations.

Completely ignore the mismanagement. You are happy to do your job, you rely on the paycheck, and you don't need to do anything to jeopardize your happiness.

Highlight your loyalty to the veterans served by your organization and to society in general and continue to highlight ethical violations.

Remain silent and discourage any conversation about ethical violations.

Begin to think about the ramifications of these ethical violations on your employer and debate whether to withdraw the complaint. *How might this conflict with the PR value of loyalty?*

Continue to actively pursue justice in each instance of mismanagement and see the case through until the end. *How does this action reflect the PR value of loyalty?*

Use your position as spokesperson for the organization to cover up any discussions of mismanagement or access to information citing mismanagement. *How might this conflict with the PR value of loyalty?*

Leave the organization and start your own PR firm based on the principles of honesty, advocacy, and loyalty.

Continue to highlight your desire to remain loyal to veterans and the general public.

The public is alerted to the mismanagement of the organization from another whistle blower. They no longer trust the organization and your career is in jeopardy based on your cover up. *How would you proceed?*

1. Define the specific ethical issue/conflict.
2. Identify internal/external factors (e.g. legal, political, social, economic) that may influence the decision.
3. Identify key values.
4. Identify the parties who will be affected by the decision and define the public relations professional's obligation to each.
5. Select ethical principles to guide the decision-making process.
6. Make a decision and justify it.

LOYALTY AND ETHICAL BEHAVIOR

Positive and negative implications of group influence can have an impact on individual behavior. Positive implications can include feelings of belonging, increase in trust, or willingness to sacrifice for the benefit of others. Negative implications can include loss of personal judgment or willingness to engage in damaging unethical behavior for the benefit of the group. Loyalty to an organization has long been blamed for overlooking corporate mismanagement to blatantly ignoring fraud or public corruption. Ethical lapses resulting from abuses of loyalty can be seen in the Enron case or more recently the Flint water crisis, Morgan Stanley's dishonest and unethical business practices, as well as the White House supporting and offering "alternative facts."

In response to research indicating that group loyalty often leads to unethical behavior,[1] Francesca Gino, a professor studying judgment, ethical decision making, and morality at Harvard Business School, and her research colleagues, Angus Hildreth and Max Bazerman, conducted multiple studies focusing on the intersection of loyalty and behavior. "We found loyalty to a group can increase, rather than decrease, honest behavior."[2]

Several studies were conducted in which more than one thousand test subjects were first either divided into groups and administered tests, involved in discussions on ethics, or provided with variegated puzzle games. Half of the groups were asked to take a loyalty oath.[3]

Research findings indicated that test subjects were found to have higher instances of honesty when they were reminded of their loyalty oath before being assigned additional tasks.[4] As an extension to the initial study, participants in the puzzle group were asked to take the loyalty oath and then to grade their puzzle answers. They were given a group incentive of a monetary reward for all answers that were correct.

There was an increased temptation to act unethically based on the loyalty to the group members and the desire to satisfy and impress them. Twenty percent of participants who took a loyalty pledge cheated when scoring their own performance on a set of math puzzles, compared with 44 percent of those who did not take the pledge.[5] Gino stated, "As our research shows, loyalty highlights the importance of ethical principles, bringing people's attention to the fact that behaving ethically is the right course of action."[6]

Discussion:
1. Does loyalty foster ethical behavior or does it reinforce currently maintained ethical beliefs?
2. If there was greater incentive to be unethical, do you believe the results would have been different?
3. Are there actions you believe are *always* ethically wrong? Why or why not?
4. Many organizations have had success utilizing honor codes. Can we translate the same principles from academia and nonprofit into corporate America? Why or why not?

1. Ronald R. Sims, "Linking groupthink to unethical behavior in organizations," *Journal of Business Ethics* 11, no. 9 (1992): doi:10.1007/bf01686345.

2. Will Yakowicz, "How loyalty affects your team's ethics," Inc.com, January 7, 2016, accessed February 28, 2017, http://www.inc.com/will-yakowicz/loyalty-can-improve-moral-judgment.html.

3. Francesca Gino, "If you're loyal to a group, does it compromise your ethics?" *Harvard Business Review*, January 6, 2016, accessed February 18, 2017, https://hbr.org/2016/01/if-youre-loyal-to-a-group-does-it-compromise-your-ethics.

4. Will Yakowicz, "How loyalty affects your team's ethics," Inc.com, January 7, 2016, accessed February 28, 2017, http://www.inc.com/will-yakowicz/loyalty-can-improve-moral-judgment.html.

5. Will Yakowicz, "How loyalty affects your team's ethics," Inc.com, January 7, 2016, accessed March 1, 2017, http://www.inc.com/will-yakowicz/loyalty-can-improve-moral-judgment.html.

6. Francesca Gino, "If you're loyal to a group, does it compromise your ethics?" *Harvard Business Review*, January 6, 2016, accessed February 18, 2017, https://hbr.org/2016/01/if-youre-loyal-to-a-group-does-it-compromise-your-ethics.

8

Fairness

need to be familiar with the different channels of communications that provide opportunities to spread information. It's imperative that we remain objective and strategic in choosing the best way to reach the intended audience. In that vein, we must also be very familiar with the industry with which we're working, which includes the demographics of each audience and competitive landscape.

Can you provide an example of a time when you had to disagree with what the client felt was necessary and guide them in another direction?

Oftentimes, clients who are not as familiar with the role of public relations feel that every happening requires a press release or media outreach. There have been several occasions on which I've had to explain that although press releases are important to public relations and getting information to the public, they are not always the best option. As communicators, we have to be strategic in how we disseminate information and know that not everything qualifies as "news" that media outlets are interested in reporting on in traditional media. This conversation has led to the creation of contributed content, social media content, or even newsletters to the appropriate audiences in lieu of traditional media efforts.

How do you balance loyalty to the client and loyalty to society?

Maintaining transparency as a public relations professional is crucial. While we must remain loyal to sharing the client's story, we are also responsible for doing so honestly and in a way that best serves the public's interest. Unfortunately, PR is not always about sharing positive stories, but rather building meaningful relationships built on integrity and accountability.

Can you discuss how you deal with differing opinions or maintain free expression of ideas?

I think differing opinions within the communications field are extremely valuable because everyone communicates differently. For this reason, it's important to encourage and embrace new ideas to find the best method of communication for each unique situation. Ideally, multiple ideas can be integrated to form all-encompassing communications plans to produce a truly successful campaign. Like anything else, the public relations field can sometimes require a bit of trial and error to better inform future efforts.

What types of ethical issues are entry-level public relations practitioners likely to encounter?

Entry-level PR practitioners may initially encounter issues with loyalty and expertise. As new professionals, it can be easy to compromise our values in order to impress a client or get ahead in the field instead of taking the time required to build expertise and initiate meaningful communication. It's important to remember that our responsibility to the public is as important as our responsibility to the client. Spreading false information or "spinning" stories can damage a practitioner's credibility as much as the organization they are representing, and public trust is difficult to rebuild once it's lost.

ETHICAL DILEMMA: SEAWORLD

SeaWorld Entertainment Incorporated's crisis began in 2013 with the release of a controversial documentary titled *Blackfish*. The emotionally charged documentary explores SeaWorld's treatment of captive killer whales, specifically focusing on a killer whale named Tilikum, and his involvement in the tragic deaths of three individuals, including SeaWorld trainer Dawn Brancheau, while in captivity.[1] The documentary, which was released in select theaters in July 2013 and on CNN in October 2013, portrayed "numerous practices related to orca captivity as unacceptable: SeaWorld's domestic breeding programs; the separation of calves from their mothers; the sizes of the orca environments; and the safety of the trainers themselves."[2] The backlash related to the film was swift and the crisis quickly escalated, not only damaging the reputation of the marine zoological park but also causing substantial declines in revenue and attendance.[3]

Two years after the film's release, SeaWorld began implementing an aggressive rebranding campaign designed to dispel the fervent criticism, negative media headlines, and continually declining attendance. "For SeaWorld, the PR nightmare is much more deep-rooted than the Tilikum tragedy, since the questions raised by *Blackfish* and animal-rights activists challenge the very premise of what the company does: keep orcas in captivity."[4] Therefore, SeaWorld's rebranding campaign centered on shifting the public's focus away from its famous park inhabitants to its conservation and rescue efforts.[5]

In March 2015, SeaWorld launched a Twitter campaign, *Ask SeaWorld*, encouraging the public to ask questions about how the company cares for its animals. However, instead of fielding a series of anticipated questions, SeaWorld found that activists and animal lovers were using the hashtag #askseaworld to highlight the abuses of captive killer whales. Many public relations experts identified the campaign as a social media fail.[6]

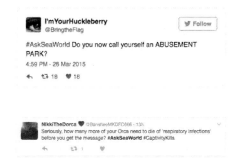

?€v€r€+h¿ng @seekingthenswar · Feb 18
#AskSeaWorld explain to me in what way is this a natural behaviour and what
education is involved? #OpSeaWorld

↩   ⟲   ♡

 Pamela and 2 others follow

KarmenSanDiego @KahrmenSanDiego · Feb 13
Corrupt for profit @SeaWorld never responds to #AskSeaWorld campaign. We
know answers thanks to @Voice_OT_Orcas common sense & #Blackfish

Social Good Karme and 1 other follow

Pam Sullivan @thepamsullivan · Feb 8
#AskSeaworld What would Jesus do?
#EmptyTheTanks
(Flashback 🎬v. @QuornDawg) 😉 #CaptivityKills #Blackfish #Tilikum

↩   ⟲ 5   ♡ 4

John Thomey @JohnThomey · Feb 7
#EnterpriseSM The #AskSeaWorld campaign was a pretty big mistake that left
the brand open to criticism on social in front of millions.

↩   ⟲   ♡

 ♡ - Sylvia - ♡ @Voice4AnimalsNL · · Jan 15
#AskSeaWorld #SeaWorld Are You Listening?! Ringling Bros Will End in May!
You're Next! #Blackfish

OVERVIEW OF FAIRNESS

The final pillar of public relations ethics, fairness, is defined by the Public Relations Society of America as "deal[ing] fairly with clients, employers, competitors, peers, vendors, the media, and the general public. We respect all opinions and support the right of free expression."[7] Merriam-Webster defines fairness as "marked by impartiality and honesty: free from self-interest, prejudice, or favoritism."[8] From an ethical standpoint, fairness is often referenced alongside justice. "While justice has usually been used with reference to a standard of rightness, fairness has often been used with regard to an ability to judge without reference to one's feelings or interests."[9]

In his book, *A Theory of Justice*, John Rawls presents what he labels the *original position*.[10] The original position is designed to be a framework that details the fundamentals necessary to develop a just and fair society. "It is designed to be a fair and impartial point of view that is to be adopted in our reasoning about fundamental principles of justice. In taking up this point of view, we are to imagine ourselves in the position of free and equal persons who jointly agree upon and commit themselves to principles of social and political justice."[11]

The basic argument against the original position highlights that it is not possible to develop a fair society because the individuals enacting the rules ensure that the rules always favor them. These individuals would essentially have unfair bargaining power. For example, regardless of your gender, there is a tendency to enact rules that favor your gender. If you worked in government, you might argue that society needed higher taxes because that would benefit your position. Rawls addressed this with a hypothetical thought experiment labeled the veil of ignorance. According to Rawls, society can be made more fair and just if decision makers are forced to select resolutions with limited knowledge about their place in society.[12]

Behind the veil of ignorance, gender, race, ethnicity, religion, social class, social roles, and sexual orientation would be unknown. Additionally, information regarding physical and mental disabilities and levels of intelligence would be unknown. This veil allows for decisions to truly benefit everyone in society and for social rule to be equitable.

Consider for a moment that a state governor was making decisions for his/her constituents behind the veil of ignorance. These decisions would be made without any knowledge of how the rules would affect not only the governor but his/her immediate family or extended relations. The veil of ignorance essentially forces decisions to be made that affect everyone equally, without benefiting one group over any other.

Rawls is not implying that individuals would forget their place in society, rather he merely highlights that since fairness itself is an idea prone to self-interpretation, if you can eliminate the possibility of self-benefit, the rules would benefit society as a whole.[13]

Rawls believes that a just society could be formed based on two principles resulting from choices made behind the veil of ignorance. The first principle is called the liberty principle. Rawls states, "Each person has the same defeasible claim to a fully adequate scheme of equal liberties, which scheme is comparable with the same scheme of liberties for all."[14] Let's analyze this statement. The basic underlying principle is that individuals enjoy freedom and desire as much freedom as possible. Therefore, Rawls believes that everyone should have a great deal of freedom as long as those freedoms are applied to everyone.[15] In other words, all individuals should have the same freedoms. One example of this principle would be that both men and women should receive the same amount of pay for equal work. Any discrepancy would be unfair and thus unjust. Another example would be that everyone, whether rich or poor, would have access to the same quality of education. Any discrepancy would be unfair and thus unjust.

Rawls also introduces the difference principle, noting, "Social and economic inequalities are to satisfy two conditions: first, they are to be attached to offices and positions open to all under conditions of fair quality of opportunity; and second, they are to be the greatest benefit of the least-advantaged members of society."[16] This second principle examines two things, the first of which is fairness in opportunity. Each person has the same opportunity regardless of background. The second area looks at income disparity, highlighting that there should not be a difference in income and wealth. If there is a difference, taxes would be high enough to level the playing field for those who make significantly less. Rawls states, "Those who have been favored by nature, whoever they are, may gain from their good fortune only on terms that improve the situation of those who have lost out."[17]

Let's take some time to apply the concept of freedom to public relations. The most prevalent example of a discrepancy in terms of fairness in public relations relates to the gender wage gap. According to Elizabeth Toth, "unequal treatment, unequal value, and unequal power are three aspects of the gender balance argument that occur in public relations."[18] According to a Holmes Report, while women comprise 70 percent of the workforce in the public relations industry, they only hold 30 percent of C-suite positions.[19] This discrepancy in both wages and power would be considered unjust by Rawls's standards.

It is important to mention that Rawls's veil of ignorance is not without criticism. Those who disagree with Rawls argue that if you remove all information about individuals, then you also remove the ability for responsible decision making. Opponents of this theory argue that in order to make a responsible decision, an individual requires all of the necessary information and background to make a sensible and balanced choice. Withholding information removes the possibility of objective reasoning.

WHY FAIRNESS IS IMPORTANT IN PUBLIC RELATIONS

In order to demonstrate fairness in public relations, practitioners should respect the opinions of others, allow for the freedom of expression from clients and the general public, and reveal all information necessary for responsible decision making.

Public relations practitioners rarely work in isolation. The public relations profession requires a myriad of partnerships from working with journalists, marketers, and advertisers to collaborating with professional organizations or various publics. Within each of these relationships, practitioners engage in a two-way communication model. Two-way communication is founded on the principle that two parties both send and receive messages simultaneously. Practitioners need to express ideas, but also listen more than they speak. Two-way communication is rooted in mutual respect, often leading to freedom of expression. Clients and the general public feel comfortable expressing ideas.

However, freedom of expression is a two-way street. Practitioners must be comfortable both providing and receiving information. In a social media–driven environment, public relations practitioners want to engage in honest and transparent communication with their publics. This allows the public to share their happiness or displeasure with organizational decisions. From an organizational standpoint, it often assists in keeping abreast of potential negative situations before they develop into crises.

Lastly, practitioners need to disclose any information necessary for responsible decision making. When information is hidden for purposes of deception, the truth always avails itself. The following example highlights the importance of fairness and responsibility in more detail.

Public relations practitioners are trained to simultaneously exhibit and exercise reasonable judgment and take all necessary precautions to ensure that their inherent biases, the boundaries of their proficiency, and the limitations of expertise do not lead to or condone unjust practices. Unfortunately, in the case below, wherein two technology giants are vying for positioning among consumers, a bitter rivalry and a high-profile smear campaign ensues. Despite the fact that the PR code of ethics states that public relations practitioners follow an ethical principle that highlights "promoting healthy and fair competition among professionals and seeks to promote respect and fair competition among ethical practitioners of public relations with no actions that would deliberately undermine a competitor," there are times when practitioners deal unfairly with their competition.[20] The case of Facebook's whisper campaign against Google is one example.

Facebook hired Burson-Marsteller, a global public relations and communications firm, to plant damaging stories in the media claiming that "Google's tool, 'Social Circle,' which lets people with Gmail accounts see information not only about their friends but also about the friends of their friends, which Google calls 'secondary connections,' was rife with privacy concerns."[21] The plan backfired when one of the bloggers that Burson-Marsteller pitched, Chris Soghoian, posted his email exchanges with the PR firm asking him to put his name on an op-ed piece that the firm had drafted. The op-ed highlighted privacy concerns with statements like, "The idea behind the feature [Social Circle] is to scrape and mine social sites from around the web to make connections between people that wouldn't otherwise exist and share that information with people who wouldn't otherwise have access to it. All of this happens without the knowledge, consent or control of the people whose information is being shared."[22]

Michael Arrington, at TechCrunch, severely criticized Facebook for their actions. "By secretly paying a PR firm to pitch bloggers on stories going after Google, even offering to help write those stories and then get them published elsewhere, is . . . offensive, dishonest and cowardly."[23]

Let's analyze the Facebook case based on the PURE model of ethical decision making.

Personal and organizational principles—This case focuses on both personal and organizational principles. In terms of organizational principles, Facebook should never have hired an outside public relations firm to plant stories about Google. If they were truly working under the guise of transparency and privacy concerns, their own PR team should have approached the media. Facebook's principles were called into question because they hired Burson-Marsteller. That being said, Burson-Marsteller also exhibited questionable principles in this case. Instead of advising Facebook to handle this on their own, they worked on behalf of Facebook and tried to hide the involvement of their client. The company did not adhere to standard fairness principles.

According to PRSA, PR practitioners should "promote healthy and fair competition among professionals."[24] They should also "promote respect and fair competition among ethical practitioners of public relations with no actions that would deliberately undermine a competitor."[25] PRSA continues, "Protecting and advancing the free flow of accurate and truthful information is essential to serving the public interest and contributing to informed decision making in a democratic society."[26] Neither Facebook nor Burson-Marsteller was concerned with fair competition or promoting respect.

Universal principles—There is inherent danger in attempting to apply these principles to all PR practitioners or organizations. Facebook and Burson-Marsteller acted unethically. Fairness focuses on dealing justly with competitors and respecting the rights and freedom of expression of both competitors and the general public. Burson-Marsteller attempted to manipulate the media and the general public by planting erroneous stories about Google. If this tactic were to be applied by every organization, the public would not be able to tell the difference between accurate content and creative fiction in regard to an organization's products or services. Additionally, journalistic integrity would be called into question based on the ideas inherent in the op-ed.

Rights of publics—The rights of various groups were completely violated in this case. Media outlets were not given the necessary information to make an informed decision regarding Google and privacy concerns. If Facebook had been transparent about where the information was coming from, this case may have played out differently.

Justifiable ends—In this case, the ends did not justify the means. There is never a justification for outright deception.

IMPLICATIONS WITHIN SOCIAL MEDIA

Social media is a useful and powerful tool that public relations professionals utilize to directly engage consumers. By dealing fairly with clients, competitors, peers, the media, and the general public we work to serve the best interest of each party. Obscuring a relationship that we have with a connection on social media is unethical. This action blurs the lines between a company and their multitiered audiences. Anonymity blurs the ethical boundaries by blending sponsored content into editorial, news, or entertainment content or not revealing an association so as to obscure the identification of the paid, in-kind transactional relationship, competitor status, or opinion-based content.[27] While the practice is not illegal, it flies in the face of the spirit of social media and risks losing consumer trust.

SOLVING THE ETHICAL DILEMMA: SEAWORLD

As Mahatma Gandhi once stated, "The greatness of a nation and its moral progress can be judged by the way its animals are treated."[28] When looking back at the SeaWorld case discussed in the beginning of the chapter, it is crucial that we look at sentientism and how this concept frames the notion of fairness as it applies to animals. Sentientism is "the philosophy that all sentient beings—all beings that feel and can suffer—have intrinsic moral value and rights. Therefore, we are obliged to treat all sentient beings with kindness and compassion, regardless of their external form or level of intelligence."[29] The primary argument here is that since animals feel pleasure and pain, they should be treated as moral agents and therefore should not be held in captivity.

Much of the commentary surrounding SeaWorld involved how unfairly animals were being treated and how the company misrepresented itself as an organization dedicated to animal rescue and conservation, rather than simply chasing a higher bottom line.

- If you were a public relations practitioner employed by SeaWorld, how would you address the #askseaworld crisis?
- Would you have done exactly as SeaWorld did and simply ignore the negative comments on Twitter regarding Tilikum and the captivity of killer whales and instead focus on answering questions about general animal welfare or would you have addressed all comments, both positive and negative?
- How would your response relate back to supporting the freedom of expression and fairness in public relations?

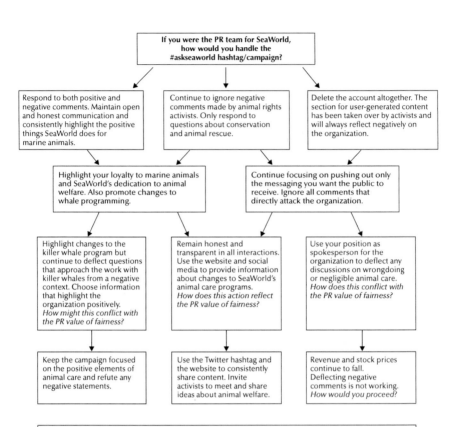

If you were the PR team for SeaWorld, how would you handle the #askseaworld hashtag/campaign?

Respond to both positive and negative comments. Maintain open and honest communication and consistently highlight the positive things SeaWorld does for marine animals.

Continue to ignore negative comments made by animal rights activists. Only respond to questions about conservation and animal rescue.

Delete the account altogether. The section for user-generated content has been taken over by activists and will always reflect negatively on the organization.

Highlight your loyalty to marine animals and SeaWorld's dedication to animal welfare. Also promote changes to whale programming.

Continue focusing on pushing out only the messaging you want the public to receive. Ignore all comments that directly attack the organization.

Highlight changes to the killer whale program but continue to deflect questions that approach the work with killer whales from a negative context. Choose information that highlight the organization positively. *How might this conflict with the PR value of fairness?*

Remain honest and transparent in all interactions. Use the website and social media to provide information about changes to SeaWorld's animal care programs. *How does this action reflect the PR value of fairness?*

Use your position as spokesperson for the organization to deflect any discussions on wrongdoing or negligible animal care. *How does this conflict with the PR value of fairness?*

Keep the campaign focused on the positive elements of animal care and refute any negative statements.

Use the Twitter hashtag and the website to consistently share content. Invite activists to meet and share ideas about animal welfare.

Revenue and stock prices continue to fall. Deflecting negative comments is not working. *How would you proceed?*

1. Define the specific ethical issue/conflict.
2. Identify internal/external factors (e.g. legal, political, social, economic) that may influence the decision.
3. Identify key values.
4. Identify the parties who will be affected by the decision and define the public relations professional's obligation to each.
5. Select ethical principles to guide the decision-making process.
6. Make a decision and justify it.

9

Ethics Matter; Choose Action

This text was designed to provide you with essential tools necessary for making ethically sound public relations decisions. Despite having a sound baseline as an aid, when you are placed in situations where you need to make ethical decisions, you are unlikely to fall back on a textbook; rather, you will likely evaluate and choose among ethical alternatives in a manner consistent with your personal moral codes. As a public relations practitioner, the final decision will always result from your principles. Therefore, ensuring that your actions are ethical according to your genuine moral character, in every aspect of your career, is paramount to your success.

Future practitioners must be able to see beyond themselves and to identify the effects that courses of action have on others. As PR practitioners, our actions have consequences. Whether that is divulging information about potential layoffs or dealing with the news media or general public after an industrial accident that took the lives of several workers, practitioners must keep the needs of various audiences at the forefront of their minds. This requires consistent education as the roles of practitioners are ever changing. A practitioner must maintain cultural knowledge as well as be aware of the current global climate, in addition to remaining abreast of industry standards. This will allow ethical principles to transcend the boundaries of public relations and follow the student into future lines of work.

We have introduced you to a myriad of ethical approaches and numerous decision-making guides to assist you in better understanding how each approach can be applied. There is not one "correct" ethical approach, as each has shortcomings and advantages over one another in certain situations. For example, as mentioned in chapter 1, one of the strengths of utilitarian theory is also its greatest weakness. Individual needs are often ignored in favor of providing collective happiness for all involved. The approach, and the intended application in each ethical situation, will vary based on both individual preference and the situation requiring attention.

There will be times when rules dictate ethical actions. For example, if you are working for an organization that has specific guidelines about confidentiality and are put in a situation that involves divulging confidential information, you may reflect upon these rules to determine your course of action. However, there are likely to be situations where the rules simply do not apply. An example would be the Paula Pedene case discussed back in chapter 7. Despite rules involving confidentiality, Pedene made a conscious choice to focus on the situation at hand and become a whistle-blower, identifying misconduct, instead of remaining silent to uphold an organizational code.

Ethics are ever changing, and as the tools of our trade evolve through social media, we need to remain vigilant in educating ourselves and upcoming practitioners on how to apply ethical theories to those situations. Ethical dilemmas, much like crises, don't follow a consistent pattern. Each dilemma is unique to the circumstances, the organization, and the individuals involved. Therefore, it behooves practitioners to gain experience working through ethical dilemmas. Analyzing sample dilemmas, studying ethical approaches, and utilizing ethical codes can lead to stronger, more confident responses when ethical situations arise. They can also assist in giving new practitioners a solid foundation upon which they can build.

In a world of ongoing dilemmas, it is crucial to develop personal codes to follow. By dissecting the root of one's personal ethics with experiences, influences, and intellectual/emotional ethical systems, a practitioner can better act in future ethical encounters. Our moral principles are shaped and developed as a result of the environments and people that we grow up around. These moral principles change over time as individuals are impacted by events, people, and ideas. Knowing your personal value system can assist in quickly assessing and responding to ethical situations.

Additionally, it is imperative that public relations professionals pay close attention to ethics and their role in ethical decision making before they are required to act upon it. Public relations practitioners should be monitoring social media sentiment for their clients and actively listening to discussions surrounding the brand they are supporting. Despite the fact that public relations practitioners often work in silos, their expertise is harmonized with the knowledge and practical skills of several other departments. Therefore, practitioners need to display and understand ethics in a multitude of frameworks. Organizational culture plays a substantial role in ethical decision making. Cultures that encourage employees to voice their opinions and that offer support to those that go against the status quo are far more likely to support a practitioner educating decision makers or C-suite level executives on ethical lapses than cultures that hinder the delivery of bad news.

The history of public relations has been riddled with examples of deception and mistrust. However, since moving from a one way, I-talk, you-listen model of communication to a two-way model that is genuinely concerned with creating and maintaining mutually beneficial relationships with a multitude of publics, public relations practitioners have been able to reconstruct how the industry is perceived. Now, instead of being seen simply as publicists or spin doctors, public relations practitioners are viewed as liaisons between organizations and their publics and often as the moral compass of their industries. There is still much to be done. Practitioners need to consistently police one another and hold each other accountable. High standards of behavior must be set for the industry and for those we represent.

You have been introduced to several practical decision-making models, including the PURE model of ethical decision making, the Potter Box, and the Navran model. When applying a model, we must use our expertise as practitioners to determine whom we are counting as publics, and then within that purview, whom we are counting as target publics. Answering these questions allows practitioners to take a critical stance on where to go with publics and to explain how easily blame can be shifted in situations that evolve from addressing one's own public to being eclipsed by an organization's various publics. An enclave that only looks at itself is open to misinformation.

This book has been organized based on the Public Relations Society of America's Code of Ethics. It highlights the ethical values of advocacy, honesty, expertise, independence, loyalty, and fairness while also supporting the free flow of information, healthy and fair competition, open communication, safeguarding confidences, conflicts of interests, and enhancing the profession. Professionals voluntarily agree to abide by the code of ethics. There is no governing body to enforce ethical principles and no repercussions aside from harm to one's moral character applied to those who choose not to follow the code. Licensing or certifications are not required to practice public relations; therefore, a public relations practitioner merely agrees to follow the professional code.

All practitioners are moral agents that act on their own will to meet the needs of their clients. They are expected to perform based on the best interests of their clients and to be good and virtuous insofar as professional relationships are concerned. Each of the codes mentions some form of truth and/or honesty. They highlight the expectation of transparency despite the fact that the PRSA code of ethics labels this as a free flow of information. They also discuss the importance of independence, including responsibility and competence, and they promote an element of fairness and accountability.

Having a theoretical grounding in ethics and training in ethical decision making can assist public relations practitioners in effectively navigating ethical dilemmas. Practitioners who counsel clients from a multitude of backgrounds as well as C-suite executives, stakeholders, and other company representatives require the ability to make ethically defensible decisions. Possessing an arsenal of ethical theories to draw from, as well as the knowledge and expertise in a multitude of ethical codes, combined with both educational and personal knowledge can assist a practitioner in not only making a moral decision but in having the ability to explain and defend that decision.

As we look to the future, we must continue this conversation. There are several resources available to practitioners to remain abreast of current communication situations.

WEBSITES

- PRSA—http://www.prsa.org
- Institute for Public Relations—http://www.instituteforpr.org/
- Arthur Page Society—http://www.awpagesociety.com/
- Council of Public Relations Firms—http://prcouncil.net
- Commission on Public Relations Education—http://www.commpred.org
- Issues Management Council—http://issuemanagement.org
- Global Alliance—http://www.globalalliancepr.org
- International Association of Business Communicators—https://www.iabc.com
- National Black Public Relations Association—http://nbprs.org
- Hispanic Public Relations Association—http://www.hpra-usa.org

ACADEMIC AND TRADE JOURNALS

- *Public Relations Review*—https://www.journals.elsevier.com/public-relations -review
- *Public Relations Inquiry*—http://journals.sagepub.com/home/pri
- *Public Relations Tactics*—http://apps.prsa.org/intelligence/Tactics/#.WLRCQm _yvIU
- *The Public Relations Strategist*—https://apps.prsa.org/Intelligence/TheStrate gist/index.html#.WLRCV2_yvIU
- *Ragan's PR Daily*—https://www.prdaily.com/Main/Home.aspx?gclid=CjwKEAi Auc_FBRD7_JCM3NSY92wSJABbVoxB0LIbuOEtGFn52IDhoX5GAta KmejG9vUlhMP7cD3VSBoCnVfw_wcB
- *PR Week*—http://www.prweek.com/us
- *Adweek*—http://www.adweek.com/
- *Advertising Age*—http://adage.com/

BLOGS

- *Edelman's blog 6 A.M.*—https://www.edelman.com/conversations/6-a-m
- *Shift Communications PR Agency*—http://www.shiftcomm.com/blog
- *Spin Sucks*—spinsucks.com
- *Stephen Waddington*—http://wadds.co.uk
- *PRSay*—http://prsay.prsa.org/
- *L2inc*—https://www.l2inc.com/daily
- *Media Village*—https://www.mediavillage.com/
- *The Holmes Report*—http://www.holmesreport.com/

ETHICAL CASE STUDIES FOR CONSIDERATION

The final case studies in this book are award-winning cases from the Arthur W. Page Society's case study competition. They examine the ethical considerations seen in five very different, but ethically challenging situations. As you read, consider the principled implications presented within each of the cases. Think about the PURE model of ethical decision making and consider what you would have done in each situation.

The first case study takes an in-depth look at Apple's stance on consumer privacy. Following the December 2015 San Bernardino shooting, the FBI asked Apple to provide access to the perpetrator's iPhone, forcing Apple to stand its ground on protecting consumer privacy. Agreeing to provide access would jeopardize its consumers' privacy by creating a "back door" into the iPhone, which Apple deemed unacceptable. Apple's decision was met with praise and criticism by the public and other technology companies. Finally, the FBI used a third party to hack the iPhone. Although consumer privacy was eventually compromised, Apple's response set a precedent and started an important dialogue across the business world about customer privacy and security.

The second case study we examined, "An Analysis of Starbucks' Race Together Initiative," launched in the spring of 2015 in response to racial issues in the United States. It was met with backlash. The public was confused as to why a company would address this sensitive social issue. Many considered the initiative a failure. However, Starbucks doubled down and expanded its commitment to the issue. This case study examines how Starbucks attempted to alleviate racial unrest through a broad platform. Although the initial launch was not well received, Starbucks' determination in addressing racial tensions demonstrates its belief in using its resources and scale to influence social change.

America's Railroad® recovered from its worst disaster in nearly thirty years, a May 2015 derailment in the city of Philadelphia that injured hundreds and killed eight. The third case study examines whether Amtrak's actions following train number 188's derailment were enough to regain trust capital to keep its wheels in motion.

The fourth case presented is "The Virtue of Patients: Veterans' Fatal Wait: An Analysis of the U.S. Department of Veterans Affairs' Buildup to and Communication about Its Secret Patient Wait Lists." This case study looks at the historical, organizational, and political factors leading up to the scheduling scandal, how communication regarding the scandal was both handled and responded to, and events that came about as a new leader took charge.

The final case examines the investigation of the 2013 Boston Marathon bombings. During the event two explosions occurred, devastating the city and the entire country. The days leading up to Dzhokhar Tsarnaev's arrest were a blur of posts by various social media outlets. A small portion of information was verified by authorities. However, a large amount of material was false, then published by accredited news outlets. In contrast, the Boston Police Department effectively used social media to communicate with various publics. In a time of ever-advancing technology, tactics like social media shape a response to crisis.

III

AWARD-WINNING CASE
STUDIES FROM THE
ARTHUR W. PAGE SOCIETY
CASE STUDY COMPETITION

Case Study 1

Walking the "Encryption Tightrope"

Getting to the Core of Apple's Privacy and Security Battle with the FBI

Reprinted with permission from the authors, Brooke Lichtman, Jaymie Polet, Bria Smith, and Rubai Soni, and faculty advisor, Matt Ragas, Ph.D., from DePaul University College of Communication. This case study was the Grand Prize recipient of the Arthur W. Page Society 2017 Case Study Competition.

OVERVIEW: TAKING A BITE OUT OF THE APPLE

In December of 2015, a married couple named Syed Rizwan Farook and Tashfeen Malik burst through the doors of Farook's office holiday party in San Bernardino, California. The couple had spent months planning a terrorist attack that came to fruition when they opened fire on Farook's coworkers, killing fourteen and injuring twenty-two. Police were called to the scene, engaging in a gunfight with the perpetrators, killing Farook and Malik. After the incident, investigators searched the couple's home, finding large amounts of ammunition, weapons, and pipe bombs (Mozingo, 2015).

During the investigation, the FBI requested data from Farook's iPhone that might contain valuable information about the attack. Apple provided the data that had been backed up on iCloud; however, Farook had not backed up his phone for several weeks before the attack. Although the FBI had Farook's password-protected phone in their possession, the phone's operating system was set up to automatically erase all local data after too many incorrect password attempts to unlock the phone. Because no one knew Farook's password, this left the FBI with few options for unlocking the phone and accessing the data.

The FBI then turned to Apple again, requesting that the company unlock Farook's phone, specifically asking Apple to create a custom version of iOS for Farook's phone, also known as a "back door" in. This would allow someone to connect an external computer to the phone and unlock the device by "brute force." Apple's CEO, Tim Cook, refused to meet this demand, due to the customer privacy and safety concerns that would arise from the creation of this software.

In a public letter to Apple's customers, Cook called this request "an unprecedented use of the All Writs Act of 1789 to justify an expansion of its authority" (Apple, 2016). Apple appealed the request because it believed that the creation of this "back door" to the iPhone was too dangerous. Apple argued that if it were to create the software for this case, it would be providing a way for hackers to unlock other Apple devices (Crovitz, 2016).

This case is relevant to multiple corporate communication areas including data privacy, government relations, and issues management. Because Apple is such a well-known company, when it declined to decrypt the iPhone, its decision and justification were extremely public and put the company at risk for alienating certain stakeholder groups. As a result, Apple had to figure out how to navigate and explain the ethical and legal ramifications of its decision to all its stakeholders, as its decision was heavily debated within the court of public opinion. Furthermore, this public battle between the FBI and Apple brought the tension between national security and individual and corporations' rights to the forefront. It raised issues of privacy and national security, of freedom of speech, and even foreign policy considerations with respect to repressive regimes and those governments hoping to track journalists' sources. Lastly, this case is an important milestone in the evolution of the digital world and technology. Apple's argument about potential government misuse or criminal appropriation, and the government's counter that the trade-off with privacy in certain cases is needed to fight terrorists, will help decide how all companies balance safety and security in the future against a suspicion about government intrusion into people's daily lives.

COMPANY BACKGROUND: GETTING "SIRI"OUS

History of Apple

Founded by Steve Jobs, Steve Wozniak, and Ronald Wayne in 1976, Apple has been at the forefront of technological innovation for the last four decades. Apple is the world's largest technological company in terms of total assets and the largest information technology company in terms of revenue (Chen, 2015). Since its genesis, Apple has set the standard for functional, innovative, and user-friendly consumer software and electronics. The company has had its ups and downs, including the death of Steve Jobs in 2011. Through it all, one thing that has been consistent is Apple's authority in the technology industry. Apple has been called groundbreaking, brilliant, and a company that leads by example (Bajarin, 2012).

Although Apple has a strict customer privacy policy, the 2016 incident is not the first time the company has faced privacy concerns. The initiation of the iCloud in

2011 caused consumer concern among Apple's customers. Speculations were made that iCloud played a part in the leaking of private celebrity photos. This caused Apple to work on its security issues and protect its customers' privacy (Timberg, 2014). Now Apple has a strong customer privacy policy that it refuses to compromise.

Mission Statement

Apple has never formally published a mission statement; however, the statement found at the bottom of all of its most recent press releases is viewed by many as Apple's version of a mission statement. The statement is as follows:

> Apple revolutionized personal technology with the introduction of the Macintosh in 1984. Today, Apple leads the world in innovation with iPhone, iPad, Mac, Apple Watch and Apple TV. Apple's four software platforms—iOS, macOS, watchOS and tvOS—provide seamless experiences across all Apple devices and empower people with breakthrough services including the App Store, Apple Music, Apple Pay, and iCloud. Apple's 100,000 employees are dedicated to making the best products on earth, and to leaving the world better than we found it.

"Core" Values

Although Apple does not expressly publish a mission statement, it lists six core company values on its website. Each value is discussed in detail, and Apple's site provides multiple examples of how it incorporates its values into everything it does and creates as a company.

Apple's Values:

- **Accessibility**
- **Education**
- **Environment**
- **Inclusion and Diversity**
- **Supplier Responsibility**
- **Privacy:** Apple knows the importance of consumer trust. Privacy is one of Apple's core values, taken into consideration when creating Apple products. Because the company respects its customers' privacy, Apple products have been designed to provide maximum security to its customers' data (Apple Inc., 2016). The software, hardware, and services of an iOS device are built to work together to encrypt data and keep it safe on the iCloud server. Apple does not have a back door for this server, and no one other than Apple has access to this server (Apple Inc., 2016). These stringent security policies are the reason that Syed Farook's iPhone could not be unlocked. The data on Farook's phone had not synchronized with iCloud, and incorrect passcode attempts would have completely erased it.

Corporate Reputation

According to the Arthur W. Page Society, all actions of an organization are a reflection of its defined character. The beliefs and the actions of the company toward its stakeholders help in building its character. The perception of this character is the measure of its reputation. Thus, reputation is the nonfinancial component of a company on which the other financial factors depend (Ragas & Culp, 2014, p. 28). A successful organization with a good reputation is reflected not only by its profits but also by its services toward its stakeholders (Arthur W. Page Society, 2012).

Apple has worked hard to establish and maintain strong relationships and trust with its customers. This effort, combined with Apple's high-quality products, has established a very strong corporate reputation. A poll, conducted by Morning Consult, of 1,935 Americans on February 24 and 25, 2016, showed that 54 percent of respondents trusted Apple with their data and personal information. In the same poll question, Apple was more trusted by respondents than other technology companies, including Uber, Facebook, and Google (O'Neill, 2016). Apple earned a reputation quotient of 83.03 from the 2016 Harris Poll RQ® (Reputation Quotient), which was the second highest reputation score among the general public (Harris Poll, 2016). Finally, Apple has held the number one spot on *Fortune*'s World's Most Admired Companies Top 50 All-Stars list for the past nine years (*Fortune*, 2016).

Corporate Character

A company defines its corporate character on the basis of its "mission, purpose, values, culture, business model, strategy, operations, and brand." This creates a company's brand identity, which is relatable to its customers and is represented consistently through all its communications (Arthur W. Page Society, 2012, p. 5). A company should maintain this corporate character all throughout its hierarchy levels by adhering to its core purpose, values, and culture, leading to a consistent message of corporate character to all the stakeholders.

As indicated by its high reputation rankings, Apple generally communicates its corporate character effectively to its customers. The message is that Apple is innovative, high quality, and trustworthy. These values have created something that many companies want, but few achieve such a high degree of brand loyalty (Smith, 2014). This case served as a high-profile test of Apple's corporate character and reputation during a complex, high-profile situation.

Situation Analysis

Over the years, Apple has become a leader in the technology world. The company is credited with redefining product categories, such as the MP3 player and smartphone, and forging new territory with technological innovation and exceptional design. Each time Apple introduced a new product, both consumers and other tech manufacturers followed, embracing Apple's vision of each new device and the software that accompanied it (Bolluyt, 2015).

Furthermore, Apple and its CEO, Tim Cook, have become more outspoken on their stance regarding societal issues, making Apple and Cook leaders not just in business, but also in terms of corporate social responsibility. After Steve Jobs stepped down as CEO, Cook began making Apple more transparent, publishing an annual report on suppliers and working conditions for more than a million factory workers. Speaking on behalf of Apple, he has also taken aggressive positions on social and legal issues, pushing a once-secretive company into the center spotlight of some highly charged issues (Benner & Perlroth, 2016).

More specifically, privacy has been a priority for Apple and Tim Cook for a long time. At a tech conference in 2010, he said Apple "has always had a very different view of privacy than some of our colleagues in the Valley" (Benner & Perlroth, 2016). Those views on privacy toughened over the years as customers globally began entrusting more personal data to Apple's iPhones and the number of requests from government officials worldwide asking the company to unlock smartphones rose.

After a while, Cook and other Apple executives committed not only to lock up customer data, but to do so in a way that would put the keys into the hands of the customer, not the company. By the time Apple released a new mobile operating system, iOS7, in September 2013, the company was encrypting all third-party data stored on customers' phones by default (Benner & Perlroth, 2016).

Legal Precedence and Implications

Apple's stance on privacy and security comes from a long-held, business-based decision to protect its brand with customers who prize the data protection built into iPhones. In a New York legal dispute with prosecutors in 2015, Apple argued, "forcing Apple to extract data . . . absent clear legal authority to do so, could threaten the trust between Apple and its customers and substantially tarnish the Apple brand" (Harris, 2016).

The 2016 court's order to create a new technological method that would allow government officials to override login safeguards built into Apple's latest phones was completely unprecedented. Not only had something of this magnitude never been requested of a technology company by the US government, no government had ever made a demand of such substance. Furthermore, if Apple obliged to this order, it would have set a legal standard for the US government and other foreign governments to make similar requests of Apple and other technology companies and in future legal cases.

Timeline

- **December 2, 2015:** Shooting occurs in San Bernardino, California, killing fourteen and wounding twenty-two.

- **February 16, 2016:** The Federal Bureau of Investigation (FBI) issues a court order to Apple to unlock the phone of Syed Farook, the terrorist involved in the shooting attacks in San Bernardino (Weise, 2016). Apple responds to the FBI's request by issuing a statement on their website saying they "oppose this order, which has implications far beyond the legal case at hand" (Apple, 2016).
- **February 17, 2016:** Josh Earnest, a spokesperson for the White House, responds to Apple, claiming that the FBI was not asking them to create this backdoor encryption but merely have them open the single phone of the terrorist (Apple vs. FBI, 2016).
- **February 18, 2016:** Apple is told they have until February 26, 2016, to reply to the court order to unlock the phone.
- Twitter founder, Jack Dorsey, tweets from his account in support of Tim Cook, Apple's CEO, on his decision to not unlock the phone. Facebook also releases a statement supporting Apple (Apple vs. FBI, 2016).
- **February 19, 2016:** Donald Trump gives his opinion on the Apple vs. FBI case during a campaign rally in South Carolina. Trump urges his supporters to boycott Apple until they help unlock the phone.
- The Department of Justice files a motion against Apple, asking them to comply with the FBI and unlock the phone (Apple vs. FBI, 2016).
- **February 24, 2016:** Apple CEO Tim Cook is interviewed by ABC's David Muir. Cook speaks of his concerns for safety and privacy involving a backdoor access to the iPhone. Cook reiterates that Apple has cooperated with the FBI but will continue to put its customers' safety first (Apple vs. FBI, 2016).
- **February 25, 2016:** Apple files a motion to vacate the previously issued court order, stating that the FBI is "attempting to expand the use of All Writs Act" (Apple vs. FBI, 2016).
- **February 26, 2016:** Major tech companies, including Google, Facebook, and Twitter, issue statements saying they will file friend of the court briefs in support of Apple (Weise, 2016).
- **February 29, 2016:** Judge James Orenstein of the US District Court of the Eastern District of New York rules against the Department of Justice's request to sidestep a passcode on the iPhone of a criminal involved in a drug case (Apple vs. FBI, 2016).
- **March 1, 2016:** A court hearing labeled "The Encryption Tightrope: Balancing Americans' Security and Privacy" is held in front of the House Judiciary Committee involving representatives from both Apple and the FBI (Tepper, 2016).
- **March 3, 2016:** Seventeen major tech companies publicize their support for Apple in their decision.
- Some big names providing support are Amazon, Facebook, Cisco, Microsoft, Mozilla, Yahoo, and Google (Weise, 2016).
- **March 10, 2016:** The Justice Department replies to Apple's motion to vacate the court order, stating that the FBI's request was "modest," as they only wanted to open the phone of the terrorist and that was it (Weise, 2016).

- **March 15, 2016:** Apple responds to the Justice Department comment, stating that the government is forcing Apple to assist them without having the official authority to do so (Weise, 2016).
- **March 21, 2016:** While at a launch event for the new iPhone SE, CEO Tim Cook speaks out about Apple's stance on privacy with regard to their dispute with the FBI. Cook states, "We owe it to our customers and we owe it to our country. This is an issue that affects all of us and we will not shrink from our responsibility" (Apple vs. FBI, 2016).
- **March 28, 2016:** The Justice Department announces they have unlocked the terrorist's iPhone using a third party. The Justice Department says it will not release how this was accomplished (Weise, 2016).
- **March 29, 2016:** At 4:44 p.m. Pacific time, Judge Sheri Pym withdraws the case against Apple that began on February 16, 2016, and the case comes to an end (Weise, 2016).

RESPONSE: HOW THE (APPLE) PIE WAS SLICED

Public Response

When the news broke, the public immediately began to take sides. The Pew Research Center surveyed the general American public and asked their opinions of the case. The results indicate that, of those surveyed, 51 percent believed Apple should help the FBI unlock the phone, while 38 percent supported Apple's stance of not unlocking the phone (Maniam, 2016). In a national online poll conducted by Reuters/Ipsos, results showed again that the public was pretty divided on whose side to take, with about 45 percent agreeing with Apple's opposition and 35 percent disagreeing.

People also responded online via social media with their opinions about the case and showed up at Apple stores across the country to show support for Apple's stance and protest the FBI's demand.

Lastly, one of the most notable public responses came from Salihin Kondoker, a Muslim man and the husband of one of the San Bernardino shooting victims. Kondoker submitted a letter to the judge in support of Apple's position. In the letter, he says, "I believe privacy is important and Apple should stay firm in their decision. Neither I, nor my wife, want to raise our children in a world where privacy is the tradeoff for security. I believe this case will have a huge impact all over the world" (Kondoker, 2016).

Social Media Response

The story trended on multiple social media channels throughout its duration. Zignal Labs, a social media analytics company, measured and tracked the online chatter at multiple points during the case. Zignal Labs took a twenty-four-hour snapshot of the conversation on Twitter after Tim Cook responded to the court's demand with his public letter. During this time, the case's mention volume averaged around 7,115 mentions an hour, with nearly 172,000 per day. They also created a word cloud to visually represent what people were talking about most in regard to the case (Dietrich, 2016).

News Media Response

News media and blogs around the world immediately began covering the Apple vs. FBI case as soon as the federal court ordered Apple to assist in unlocking the iPhone. Every major news outlet and news blog seemed to be covering the story, including BBC, TechCrunch, the *Washington Post*, *New York Times*, CNBC, NPR, *Time* magazine, *Last Week Tonight with John Oliver*, and *Wired*, to name a few. Steady media coverage continued to analyze the FBI's demand and Apple's response through September 2016, long after the FBI could unlock the iPhone, through an unnamed third party, and after they dropped their demand on March 28, 2016.

Many news outlets remained neutral in their reporting and attempted to explain the nuances of the FBI's demand and why Apple was opposing it. As the case developed, media also reported on who was taking whose side from influential opinion makers, to large corporations, like Amazon, to the 2016 presidential candidates. Multiple news outlets also published op-ed articles with authors siding with either the FBI or Apple and political cartoons depicting the situation.

On February 18, 2016, the *Washington Post* published an op-ed article written by Bruce Schneier, a security technologist and lecturer at the Kennedy School of Government at Harvard University, titled "Why You Should Side with Apple, not the FBI, in the San Bernardino iPhone Case." Finally, many media outlets polled readers to see which party readers sided with to gauge public opinion on topics including privacy rights, security, and government access.

At the start of this incident, Apple CEO Tim Cook did not hold a formal press conference, but rather wrote a personal response to the motion, via a message to Apple customers that was posted on its website, about his stance on the case and explaining why Apple would not create the "back door" the FBI requested of them. At the same time that Apple posted the customer letter, it created an FAQ section on its website that addressed privacy and security questions more in depth (Apple, 2016).

As far as speaking directly with the media, Tim Cook sat down with David Muir from ABC World News for his first exclusive press interview regarding the case. Only a small portion of the interview aired on TV on February 24, 2016. However, the full-length interview was made available online the same day and picked up and shared by multiple news outlets and blogs. On March 10, Tim Cook sat down with *Time*'s Nancy Gibbs and Lev Grossman to discuss Apple's rapidly escalating fight with the FBI over encryption. That interview transcript was made available on *Time*'s website March 17, 2016, and finally, on March 28, 2016, the same day the FBI dropped its demand, *Time* magazine released a cover story about the interview and the case in its entirety. Also just before the court dropped its demand, on March 21,

2016, Apple held a press conference. During the conference, Cook talked about the ongoing conflict with the FBI by saying, "We have a responsibility to protect your data and your privacy. We will not shrink from this responsibility" (Dillet, 2016).

Response from Silicon Valley

Much like the rest of the country, technology companies were divided on the issue. Technology giants Amazon, Box, Cisco Systems, Evernote, Nest, Pinterest, Snapchat, WhatsApp, Yahoo, Mozilla, Dropbox, Facebook, Google, and Microsoft backed Apple, submitting amicus briefs supporting Apple's decision.

On the other end of the issue, tech companies AirBnB, Atlassian PTY Ltd., Automattic Inc., CloudFlare Inc., Ebay Inc., GitHub Inc., Kickstarter PBC, LinkedIn Corporation, MapBox Inc., A Medium Corporation, Meetup Inc., Squarespace Inc., Twilio Inc., Twitter Inc., and Wickr Inc. sided with the government, submitting amicus briefs opposing Apple's decision (Roth, 2016).

Some companies also wrote blog posts and took to social media to express opinions on the controversial topic. For example, Box tweeted about its joint amicus brief.

Although these companies publicly opposed Apple's decision, the briefs voiced the idea that the All Writs Act, under which the government had requested information from Apple, was unbound by legal limits (Deluca, 2016). Ultimately, these opposing companies believe that Apple should have accepted the FBI's request, while still acknowledging that the government could have used a better strategy to request this information.

BUSINESS PERFORMANCE: WILL ONE BAD APPLE SPOIL THE WHOLE BUNCH?

Financial Impact

Prior to the San Bernardino shooting, Apple's stock had been significantly lower than previous years (Thielman, Neate, & Hern, 2016). 2016 was the first year that Apple had seen a significant dip in its stock in years. While this case affected Apple and its customers, many other factors came into play during 2016 that affected Apple's stock price.

According to Apple's second quarter 2016 financial report, quarterly revenue was $50.6 billion, which was down from the prior year's revenue of $58 billion (Apple Reports Second Quarter Results, 2016). Apple briefed investors prior to releasing its quarterly report that revenue and sales would be down. iPhone sales were down from the previous year, and Apple attributed this to no new iPhone releases in 2015 and customers purchasing their phones at that time rather than in 2016. "The total tally for the device was $32.9 billion from 51.2 million phones sold; the previous year Apple brought in $40.3 billion from 61.2 million phones" (Thielman, Neate, &

Hern, 2016). Apple did not make as much money on the iPhone in 2016, resulting in a decline in revenue.

While the sales of the iPhone declined in 2016, there is no clear evidence to indicate that it was directly correlated to the ongoing FBI case. Before the San Bernardino shooting, Apple had been struggling to generate revenue growth in the face of maturing product lines, such as the iPhone.

When the case first began on February 16, 2016, and Tim Cook released his statement online about why Apple would not help, Apple's stock closed the day at $96.64 per share. When the FBI and Apple met on March 1, 2016, to discuss the case in front of the House Judiciary Committee, Apple shares closed at $100.53 per share. This was an increase from February 16 when the case began. On March 29, 2016, the case officially closed after the FBI was able to unlock the phone the day before. On this day, Apple's stock closed at $107.68 per share, its highest close since the case began (Apple Reports Second Quarter Results, 2016).

Throughout the case, Apple's stock continued to rise, further showing that this issue cannot directly correlate to the lower-than-normal stock prices seen in early 2016. This dip could be correlated to a mix of different factors, such as a new iPhone release the year prior, international sales lower than normal, etc. With many factors impacting the company's stock price, we cannot attribute causation to just one. After the case, Apple shares continued to rise (*New York Times*, 2016).

Reputation Impact

Although the iPhone was ultimately unlocked by an unknown third party, the fact that Apple stuck to its core value of privacy in all of its responses throughout the forty-three days strengthens Apple's reputation as a defender of privacy and its claim that strong encryption isn't a security disaster (Grossman, 2016).

Over the past couple of decades, Apple has become one of the most admired and valuable companies in the world. Even though much of the public was split over Apple's decision on whether Apple should comply with the FBI's orders to unlock the iPhone or not, Apple has long ranked among the most reputable companies worldwide (Harris Poll Reputation Quotient, 2016). Reputation rankings for 2017 (post this incident) seem likely to continue this trend.

Looking Ahead: Apple-y Ever After

As we move further into the age of big data, customer data privacy and security will be a challenge for all companies. Cybersecurity, hacks, breaches, and requests from government entities are the new realities that all companies, and by extension all chief communications officers and corporate communication departments must be prepared to address and expertly navigate.

When pushed, Apple reverted to its core principle of privacy to create a strong, clear message on where it stands in this broader discussion. On June 13, 2016, Apple reaffirmed its commitment to encryption by announcing it was applying "differential privacy" research to keep users' information private, a move that bolsters the company's standing as a leader in digital privacy. Executives at Apple's annual developer conference in San Francisco also emphasized the company's commitment to using encryption by default to protect customers' data. Furthermore, privacy researcher Aaron Roth said the move reaffirmed Apple's status as the "clear privacy leader among technology companies today" (Drange, 2016).

REFERENCES: ISN'T THERE AN APP FOR THAT?

Apple Inc. (n.d.). Apple Values. Retrieved from: https://www.apple.com Apple Inc. (2016, May). iOS Security. Retrieved from https://www.apple.com/business/docs/iOS_Secu rity_Guide.pdf.

Apple Inc. (n.d.). Privacy. Retrieved from http://www.apple.com/privacy/government-infor mation-requests/.

Apple Inc. (2016) Supplier Responsibility 2016 Progress Report. Retrieved from http://im ages.apple.com/supplier-responsibility/pdf/Apple_SR_2016_Progress_Report.pdf.

Apple Inc. (2016). Retrieved from https://finance.yahoo.com/chart/AAPL#eyJtdWx0aUNvb G9yTGluZSI6ZmFsc2UsImxpbmVXaWR0aCI6IjIiLCJib2xsaW5nZXJVcHBlckNvbG9 yIjoiI2UyMDA4MSIsImJvbGxpbmdlckxvd2VyQ29sb3IiOiIjOTU1MmZmIiwibWZp TGluZUNvbG9yIjoiIzQ1ZTNmZiIsIm1hY0REaXZlcmdlbmNlQ29sb3IiOiIj ZmY3YjEyIiwibWFjZEE1hY2RDb2xvciI6IiM3ODdkODIiLCJtYWNkU2lnbmFsQ 29sb3IiOiIjMDAwMDAwIiwicnNpTGluZUNvbG9yIjoiI2ZmYjcwMCIsInN0b2NoS0x pbmVDb2xvciI6IiNmZmI3MDAiLCJzdG9jaERMaW5lQ29sb3IiOiIjNDVlM2ZmIi wicmFuZ2UiOiJ5dGQifQ.

Apple Reports Second Quarter Results. (2016, April 26). Retrieved from http://www.apple .com/pr/library/2016/04/26Apple-Reports-Second-Quarter-Results.html.

Apple vs. FBI: A Timeline of the Legal Battle. (2016, March 28). Retrieved from https:// www.graphiq.com/vlp/DW36cJUvtj?utm_source=viz&utm_medium=viz.referral&utm _campaign=viz.ref&utm_viz_id=DW36cJUvtj&utm_pubreferrer=www.foxnews.com/ tech/2016/03/29/fbi-breaks-into-san-bernardino-gunmans-iphone-without-apples-help -ending-court-case.html&vlp_ver=2#0-Apple-vs-FBI-a-Timeline-of-the-Legal-Battle.

Arthur W. Page Society (2012). Building belief: A new model for activating corporate cul ture & authentic advocacy. Retrieved from http://www.awpagesociety.com/wpcontent/ uploads/2012/03/Building-BeliefNew-Model-for- Corp-Comms-2012.pdf.

Bajarin, T. (2012, May 7). 6 Reasons Why Apple Is Successful. Retrieved January 9, 2017, from http://techland.time.com/2012/05/07/six-reasons-why-apple-is-successful/.

Bedford, K. (2016, February 24). Demonstrators rally outside Apple store in Boston [Photo graph found in Boston, MA]. In *Boston Globe*. Retrieved November 20, 2016, from https:// www.bostonglobe.com/metro/2016/02/23/demonstrators-rally-outside-apple-store-bos ton/fyy2bsnMjxuyszSShr9xaP/story.html (originally photographed 2016, February 24).

Benner, K., & Perlroth, N. (2016, February 18). How Tim Cook, in iPhone Battle, Became a Bulwark for Digital Privacy. Retrieved November 20, 2016, from http://www.nytimes .com/2016/02/19/technology/how-tim-cook-became-a-bulwark-for-digital-privacy.html.

Bolluyt, J. (2015, June 20). Apple: 5 Ways It's Gone from Industry Leader to Follower. Retrieved November 20, 2016, from http://www.cheatsheet.com/technology/apple/apple -5-ways-its- gone-from-industry-leader-to-follower.html/?a=viewall.

Chen, L. (2015, May 11). The World's Largest Tech Companies: Apple Beats Samsung, Microsoft, Google. Retrieved October 17, 2016, from http://www.forbes.com/sites/liyan chen/2015/05/11/the-worlds-largest-tech-companies-apple-beats-samsung-microsoft -google/#77efae0c415a.

Coldewey, D. (2016, April 15). Apple tells NY judge FBI has "utterly failed" to prove it needs help unlocking iPhones. Retrieved November 6, 2016, from https://techcrunch.com/ 2016/04/15/apple-tells-ny-judge-fbi-has-utterly-failed-to-prove-it-needs-help-unlocking -iphones/.

Cook, T. (2016, February 16). A Message to Our Customers [Letter written February 16, 2016 to Apple Customers]. In Apple. Retrieved November 6, 2016, from http://www .apple.com/customer-letter/.

Cook, T. (2016, February 24). Exclusive: Apple CEO Tim Cook Sits Down With David Muir (Extended Interview) [Interview by D. Muir]. In ABC News. Retrieved November 6, 2016, from http://abcnews.go.com/WNT/video/exclusive-apple-ceo-tim-cook-sits-david -muir-37174976; Cook, T. (2016, March 17). Here's the Full Transcript of *Time*'s Interview with Apple CEO Tim Cook [Interview by N. Gibbs & L. Grossman]. In *Time*. Retrieved November 6, 2016, from http://time.com/4261796/tim-cook-transcript/.

Crovitz, L. G. (2016, February 19). The FBI vs. Apple—WSJ—http://www.wsj.com/articles/ the-fbi-vs-apple-1455840721. Retrieved November 6, 2016, from http://grabpage.info/t/ www.wsj.com/articles/the-fbi-vs-apple-1455840721.

Customer Letter—FAQ—Apple. (2016, February 16). Retrieved November 6, 2016, from http://www.apple.com/customer-letter/answers/.

Deluca, M. (2016, March 3). Tech vs. the Feds: Apple Allies Rally in Flurry of New Court Filings. Retrieved November 6, 2016, from http://www.nbcnews.com/tech/tech-news/ apple-allies-expected-form-ranks-flurry-court-filings-n530987.

Dietrich, G. (2016, March 10). Privacy, Security, Transparency, and Crisis Management. Retrieved November 20, 2016, from http://explore.zignallabs.com/h/i/222559635-privacy -security-transparency-and-crisis-management/239301.

Dillet, R. (2016, March 21). Apple's Tim Cook on iPhone unlocking case: "We will not shrink from this responsibility." Retrieved November 6, 2016, from https://techcrunch .com/2016/03/21/apples-tim-cook-on-iphone-unlocking-case-we-will-not-shrink-from -this-responsibility/.

Drange, M. (2016, June 13). Apple Reaffirms Commitment to Encryption. Retrieved November 21, 2016, from http://www.forbes.com/sites/mattdrange/2016/06/13/apple-to -strengthen-privacy/#b8292b36b075.

Encryption: *Last Week Tonight with John Oliver* [Television series episode]. (2016, March 13). In *Last Week Tonight with John Oliver*. New York City, NY: HBO.

Facebook and Industry Peers Support Apple in Amicus Brief. Facebook Newsroom. (2016, March 3). Retrieved November 20, 2016, from http://newsroom.fb.com/news/h/facebook -and-industry-peers-support-apple-in-amicus-brief/.

Fiegerman, S. (2016, October 25). Apple's annual sales fall for first time since 2001— Oct. 25, 2016—http://money.cnn.com/2016/10/25/technology/apple-earnings-decline/ index.html. Retrieved November 20, 2016, from http://grabpage.info/t/money.cnn.com/ 2016/10/25/technology/apple-earnings-decline/index.html.

Finkle, J. (2016, February 24). Solid support for Apple in iPhone encryption fight: Poll. Retrieved November 6, 2016, from Solid support for Apple in iPhone encryption fight: poll.

Goldman, D. (2016, February 16). Tim Cook says the FBI wants Apple to "hack" your iPhone. Retrieved November 20, 2016, from http://money.cnn.com/2016/02/17/technology/fbi-apple-hack-iphone/index.html.

Grossman, L. (2016, March 28). Inside Apple CEO Tim Cook's Fight with the FBI. *Time*, 187(11). Retrieved November 6, 2016, from http://time.com/4262480/tim-cook-apple-fbi-2/.

Harris, Shane. "Apple Unlocked IPhones for the Feds 70 Times Before." The Daily Beast. The Daily Beast Company, February 17, 2016. Web. November 20, 2016.

Harris Poll. (2016, February) The Harris Poll Releases Annual Reputation Rankings for the 100 Most Visible Companies in the U.S. Retrieved from http://www.theharrispoll.com/business/Reputation-Rankings-Most-Visible-Companies.html.

Hughes, G. (2016, February 22). Social Media's Response to Apple vs. the FBI. Retrieved November 20, 2016, from http://www.convinceandconvert.com/realtime-today/social-medias-response-to-apple-vs-the-fbi/.

Isaac, M. (2016, February 17). Explaining Apple's Fight with the F.B.I.—*The New York Times*. Retrieved November 6, 2016, from http://www.nytimes.com/2016/02/18/technology/explaining-apples-fight-with-the-fbi.html.

Kharpal, A. (2016, March 29). Apple vs. FBI: All you need to know. Retrieved November 6, 2016, from http://www.cnbc.com/2016/03/29/apple-vs-fbi-all-you-need-to-know.html.

Kokalitcheva, K. (2016, March 22). Apple's Fight with the FBI Isn't Keeping People from Wanting an iPhone. Retrieved November 20, 2016, from http://fortune.com/2016/03/22/poll-apple-fbi-iphone/.

Kondoker, S. (n.d.). [Letter to Honorable Judge Sheri Pym]. In Apple. Retrieved November 20, 2016, from http://images.apple.com/pr/pdf/Letter_from_Salihin_Kondoker.pdf.

La Monica, P. (2016, February 24). Apple's stock has worms but FBI isn't one of them. Retrieved November 20, 2016, from http://money.cnn.com/2016/02/24/investing/apple-stock-fbi-iphone/index.htm.

Lee, D. (2016, February 18). Apple v the FBI—a plain English guide. Retrieved November 6, 2016, from http://www.bbc.com/news/technology-35601035.

Madigan, M. (2016, March 22). Amazon, Box, Cisco, Dropbox, Evernote, Facebook, Google . . . Retrieved November 6, 2016, from http://images.apple.com/pr/pdf/Amazon_Cisco_Dropbox_Evernote_Facebook_Google_Micros oft_Mozilla_Nest_Pinterest_Slack_Snapchat_WhatsApp_and_Yahoo.pdf.

Maniam, S. (2016, February 22). More Support for Justice Department Than for Apple in Dispute Over Unlocking iPhone. Retrieved November 20, 2016, from http://www.people-press.org/2016/02/22/more-support-for-justice-department-than-for-apple-in-dispute-over-unlocking-iphone/.

Mozingo, J. (2015, December 9). San Bernardino Shooting Update. Retrieved November 6, 2016, from http://www.latimes.com/local/lanow/la-me-ln-san-bernardino-shooting-live-updates-htmlstory.html.

Newseum: San Bernardino Shooting. (2015, December 3). Retrieved from http://www.newseum.org/todaysfrontpages/?tfp_display=archive-summary.

O'Neill, P. H. (2016, February 26). Americans trust Apple but remain divided on unlocking iPhone for FBI, new poll finds. Retrieved November 6, 2016, from http://www.dailydot.com/layer8/apple-tim-cook-fbi-iphone-unlock-encryption-morning-consult-poll/.

Ragas, M. W., & Culp, R. (2014). *Business essentials for strategic communicators: Creating shared value for the organization and its stakeholders.* New York: Palgrave Macmillan.

Raza, O. (2016, February 29). [Apple Arm Wrestling FBI]. Retrieved November 13, 2016, from http://www.technewstoday.com/28776-apple-vs-fbi-national-security-justice-or -mass-surveillance/.

Roth, J. C. (2016, March 3). Retrieved November 6, 2016, from http://images.apple.com/ pr/pdf/Airbnb_Atlassian_Automattic_CloudFlare_eBay_GitHub_Kickstarter_LinkedIn _Mapbox_Medium_Meetup_Reddit_Square_Squarespace_Twilio_Twitter_and_ Wickr.pdf.

Schneier, B. (2016, February 18). Why you should side with Apple, not the FBI, in the San Bernardino iPhone case [Editorial]. *Washington Post.* Retrieved November 6, 2016, from https://www.washingtonpost.com/posteverything/wp/2016/02/18/why-you-should-side -with-apple-not-the-fbi-in-the-san-bernardino-iphone-case/.

Selyukh, A. (2016, March 29). Apple vs. the FBI: The Unanswered Questions and Unsettled Issues. Retrieved November 6, 2016, from http://www.npr.org/sections/alltechconsid ered/2016/03/29/472141323/apple-vs-the-fbi-the-unanswered-questions-and-unsettled -issues.

Smith, D. (2014, July 14). Loyalty to Apple's iPhone Is Strongest of Any Phone, and It's Getting Stronger. Retrieved November 6, 2016, from http://www.businessinsider.com/ chart-of-the-day-iphone-owners-are-more-loyal-than-ever-2014-7.

Taking a bite at the Apple. (2016, February 27). *The Economist.* Retrieved November 6, 2016, from http://www.economist.com/news/science-and-technology/21693564-fbis-legal-bat tle-maker-iphones-escalation.

Tepper, F. (2016, February 20). Apple vs. the FBI: Everything you need to know. Retrieved from https://techcrunch.com/timeline/a-timeline-of-apples-iphone-unlocking-fight-with -the-fbi/slide/18/.

Thielman, S., Neate, R., & Hern, A. (2016). Decline in iPhone sales leads to first revenue decline in 13 years for Apple. Retrieved November 20, 2016, from https://www.theguardian .com/technology/2016/apr/26/apple-iphone-first-revenue-decline-13-years.

Timberg, C. (2014, November 4). Apple users raise privacy concerns after hard-drive files uploaded to servers. Retrieved November 6, 2016, from https://www.theguardian.com/ technology/2014/nov/04/apple-data-privacy-icloud.

Weise, E. (2016, March 30). Apple v FBI timeline: 43 days that rocked tech. Retrieved from http://www.usatoday.com/story/tech/news/2016/03/15/apple-v-fbi-timeline/81827400/.

Welch, C. (2016, February 24). Watch Tim Cook's full 30-minute interview on Apple's fight with the FBI. Retrieved November 6, 2016, from http://www.theverge.com/2016/ 2/24/11110802/apple-tim-cook-full-interview-fbi-iphone-encryption.

The World's Most Admired Companies for 2016. (2016). Retrieved November 6, 2016, from http://fortune.com/worlds-most-admired-companies/.

Zetter, K. (2016, February 19). DoJ Files Motion to Force Apple to Hack iPhone in San Bernardino Case. Retrieved November 6, 2016, from https://www.wired.com/2016/02/ doj-files-motion-to-compel-apple-to-cooperate-in-san-bernardino-case/.

Case Study 2

Fatal Derailment

Is Amtrak's Reputation Riding on Its Response to the Wreck of Train 188?

Reprinted with permission from the author, Stacey Hajdak, under the direction of faculty advisor Dr. Laurence Mussio, Ph.D., Syracuse University S.I. Newhouse School of Public Communication. This case study was the second-prize recipient of the Arthur W. Page Society 2016 Case Study Competition.

> *I know what a tremendous trust the public places in us, and we will do everything we can to prove that we're worthy of that trust.*
>
> —Amtrak President and CEO Joe Boardman

HISTORY OF AMTRAK/INDUSTRY BACKGROUND

The National Railroad Passenger Corporation, branded as Amtrak, was enacted by Congress in 1970 and began operations a year later, providing intercity passenger train service in forty-three states (Amtrak, 2013). Amtrak was created to take over services that had been operated by private railroad companies at a net loss of millions of dollars for a number of years (Amtrak, 2014a). Straddling both public and private sectors, Amtrak is a federally chartered corporation, with the federal government as majority stockholder. Amtrak's board is appointed by the president of the United States and confirmed by the US Senate. Amtrak is operated as a for-profit company rather than a public authority (2014a).

Amtrak, a hybrid of "America" and "track" (2014a), now operates more than 300 daily trains on 21,300 miles of track that connect 500 destinations in 46 states, the District of Columbia, and three Canadian provinces. In fiscal year 2014, Amtrak served nearly 31 million passengers and had $2.189 billion in revenue, which covered 93 percent of its operating costs, up 4 percent from 2013 (Amtrak, 2014b). A portion of that revenue comes from capital funding through the states the railway serves. The deficit, $226 million in fiscal year 2014, is covered by federal funding streams (2014b). The organization employs more than 20,000 people.

Three goals—safety and security, customer focus, and financial excellence—guide Amtrak's business practices in the transportation marketplace. These pillars are emphasized in materials across Amtrak's information portfolio such as annual reports and its strategic plan.

Most railroads in the United States transport freight. Today, Amtrak remains the country's only intracity passenger system.

ISSUE

On May 12, 2015, at 9:21 p.m., northbound Amtrak train number 188 entered the Frankford Junction curve just past 30th Street Station in Philadelphia, Pennsylvania (National Transportation Safety Board, 2015a). As the train entered the curve, data indicates the engineer activated the emergency brakes. In seconds, the locomotive and all seven passenger cars derailed. Of the approximately 250 passengers and eight Amtrak employees on board, eight passengers were killed and more than 200 others were transported to area hospitals. According to the National Transportation Safety Board (NTSB) (2015a), the train was traveling at 106 mph in a 50-mph zone, a finding that immediately began raising questions and conjecture about the cause of the derailment and the engineer's culpability. NTSB investigators preliminarily examined the train's braking systems, signals, and track geometry, without any significant findings (NTSB, 2015a). Police questioned engineer Brandon Bostian at his hospital bedside the day after the derailment (Lubrano, 2015). Bostian had sustained a concussion and had no recollection of the crash. The NTSB characterized him as being very cooperative with investigators. His lawyers noted the engineer took a blood test to rule out drugs or alcohol as a cause (CNN, 2015).

The NTSB also examined the engineer's cell phone and related records. On June 10, the NTSB reported the engineer was not on his cell phone during the time leading up to the fatal crash. "Analysis of the phone records does not indicate that any calls, texts, or data usage occurred during the time the engineer was operating the train. Amtrak's records confirm that the engineer did not access the train's Wi-Fi system while he was operating the locomotive" (2015b).

Early reports in the media indicated the locomotive's windshield had been damaged and speculated about whether the damage was caused by some type of weapon. The NTSB, with assistance from the FBI, confirmed the windshield was damaged. The FBI quickly reported it found no evidence that windshield damage was caused by a firearm or projectile (NTSB, 2015a), but social and mainstream media had already been flooded with speculation surrounding foul play.

Another potential cause entered into the conversation just hours following the crash: a lack of positive train control (PTC) on the stretch of track where train 188 was traveling. PTC technology can control a train's movements automatically to prevent collisions and derailments caused by excessive speed (Amtrak, 2010). In 2008, Congress mandated PTC installations on portions of the country's rail network by December 2015, including the Northeast Corridor (NEC), where train 188 crashed. In 2010, Amtrak touted it would install PTC on all tracks in the NEC ahead of schedule, by the end of 2012. The implementation is still incomplete. This commitment, however, is consistent with the reputation dimension of vision and leadership, and illustrated Boardman's clear vision for Amtrak's future (Fombrun & van Riel, 2004). NTSB lead investigator Robert Sumwalt told the media the day after the crash, "We feel that had such a system been installed in this section of the track, this accident would not have occurred" (Mouawad, 2015). Speaking with CNN May 14, Amtrak CEO Joe Boardman bluntly agreed, adding, "That's what I've been saying for a long period of time." The NTSB characterized passenger trains lacking PTC as "one human error away from an accident" (Mouawad, 2015).

Challenges to installing PTC include interoperability between train systems, retrofitting the equipment on required freight and passenger trains, and the requisite funding estimated at a total $10 billion for all the nation's railroad systems (Mouawad, 2015). Amtrak has spent over $110 million since 2008 to install PTC (Amtrak, 2015b). Boardman pointed out during testimony before the House Transportation and Infrastructure Committee June 2 that funding has not been an issue when it comes to implementing PTC (House Transportation and Infrastructure Committee, 2015), though generally, an equity investment in the NEC is necessary to ensure infrastructure integrity and capacity.

Nearly 30 years separate the crash of train 188 and Amtrak's last fatal derailment on the NEC route. As for its safety record, from 2000 to 2014, the total annual accident rate per million passenger miles fell from 4.1 to 1.7, and annual derailments fell from 80 to 28. The overall count of Amtrak accidents decreased from 148 incidents in 2000 to 67 in 2014 (Amtrak, 2015b).

STAKEHOLDER NETWORK

A complex network of stakeholders was involved in rescue, recovery, and investigation efforts: Congress, the Federal Railroad Administration (the Department of Transportation's railroad policy arm), the National Transportation Safety Board investigating the incident, Amtrak, Philadelphia Police Department, Philadelphia Office of Emergency Management, Philadelphia Fire Department, Red Cross, local hospitals, several union organizations, the injured, victims and their families, Amtrak's employees, and even travelers who assisted other victims the night of the crash.

TIMELINE

Tuesday, May 12

9:21 p.m. Train 188 derails in Philadelphia.

10:18 p.m. Amtrak's first train 188–related tweet acknowledges the derailment.

11:13 p.m. Amtrak's first Facebook post includes service cancellation and emergency hotline.

11:13 p.m. Amtrak tweets that injuries are reported, service suspended.

11:40 p.m. Amtrak shares its emergency hotline number for the first time on Twitter.

11:40 p.m. The first press conference takes place, with Philadelphia Mayor Michael Nutter as spokesperson confirming at least five individuals deceased. "It is an absolutely disastrous mess." Philadelphia Office of Emergency Management puts out family assistance center information (CNN, 2015).

11:41 p.m. Philadelphia Office of Emergency Management sends its first of about a dozen train 188–related tweets, first passing on Amtrak's hotline information and then throughout the night and on Wednesday, passing on information about the family assistance center and thanking responders.

Wednesday, May 13

1:44 a.m. Amtrak tweets expression of empathy, announces family assistance center information (linked to Amtrak blog site).

2:45 a.m. Amtrak's second Facebook post echoes its earlier tweet. May 13 was the last time the company posted to its Facebook page until May 25, when it recognized Memorial Day.

Wednesday, May 13 2:45am

We are deeply saddened by the loss of life from Amtrak Northeast Regional Train 188 that derailed north of Philadelphia Tuesday evening. We ask the news media to be respectful of our customers, our employees, and their families.

There were approximately 238 passengers and 5 crew members on board. Individuals with questions about their friends and family on this train should call the Amtrak Incident Hotline 800-523-9101. Amtrak has also established a Family Assistance Center to work closely with family and friends of individuals on the train. Local emergency responders are on the scene and an investigation is ongoing.

On Wednesday, May 13, modified Amtrak service will be provided between Washington and Philadelphia, Harrisburg and Philadelphia, and New York and Boston. There will be no Amtrak service between New York and Philadelphia, but New Jersey Transit will honor Amtrak tickets between New York City and Trenton.

Other Amtrak Service between New York and Albany-Rensselaer; New Haven and Springfield, Mass., and other points will operate.

Additional updates will be provided when available.

Wednesday, May 13, daytime

In addition to setting up a family assistance center in Philadelphia to inform and reunite family and passengers, Amtrak reminds employees who need counseling to contact its employee assistance program. A pair of tweets reiterates Amtrak's expression of empathy, updates its community on service interruption, and notes it will not be commenting on the investigation.

Philadelphia Mayor Michael Nutter calls the engineer "reckless," telling CNN (2015), "I don't know what was going on with him. I don't know what was going on in the cab, but there's really no excuse that can be offered, literally, unless he had a heart attack."

Thursday, May 14

The next communication from Amtrak comes directly from CEO Joe Boardman. The tweet leads readers to the official Amtrak blog.

Although delayed more than twenty-four hours after the tragedy, the message conveys empathy and contrition and takes full responsibility for the tragedy. Mr. Boardman also speaks at a May 14 press conference, along with the Pennsylvania governor and Philadelphia mayor. It is the first time he publicly speaks on the tragedy.

Also May 14, investigators release findings that while the train should have decelerated as it approached the Frankford curve, it accelerated for unexplained reasons (CNN, 2015).

Tuesday, May 17

Amtrak announces service to NEC is fully restored.

Wednesday, June 10

The NTSB announces it has determined the engineer was not using his cell phone surrounding the crash.

Friday, July 10

Amtrak decides against fighting lawsuits that seek compensation for victims and admits the train was speeding (Nixon, 2015). Amtrak spokeswoman Christina Leeds notes, "From the beginning, Amtrak has taken responsibility for this tragic incident, covering initial medical costs, transportation and lodging for passengers and their families." These admissions of liability demonstrate consistency with accountability the company pledged just a day after the crash, a key rule of engagement in the reputation realm (Fombrun & van Riel, 2004). They are in response to the first of several dozen lawsuits filed following the accident.

STAKEHOLDER REACTIONS

Among passengers on train 188 were elected officials and journalists traveling between cities that are home to major political and news hubs, adding speedy access to the high profile of the event throughout traditional and social media spaces.

Former U.S. Representative Patrick Murphy, now an anchor on MSNBC's *Taking the Hill*, tweeted that he was aboard the train but alright about five minutes after the crash. Several minutes later he posted a photo from inside his train. News organizations like the *New York Daily News*, CBS, ABC, *USA Today*, the *Philadelphia Inquirer*, United Press International, the *Washington Post*, and Reuters were requesting permission to use his photo. Murphy returned as an Amtrak customer six days after the crash and tweeted his thanks to the café car worker who helped him and others that night. Amtrak responded in a tweet that they would pass on his gratitude to the worker.

Politico magazine reporter Josh Gotbaum was also riding on train 188 (Gotbaum, 2015). Like Murphy, he lauded police, fire, and EMTs, as well as Good Samaritans who were injured themselves yet helping others. Gotbaum's account of Amtrak's performance the night of the crash was not positive.

> I have no professional view about what caused the derailment or who's responsible for it—Whether the engineer or Amtrak was or was not negligent is a question for lawyers, courts, the National Transportation Safety Board and the FBI. My focus is: "What happened after the derailment? Who was prepared and who was not? Who stepped in and who did not?" Disasters don't follow a schedule, so you can't plan them. But you can plan a response to them. Sometimes the response can be the difference between life and death; sometimes it just helps limit the pain and trauma. Unfortunately, that's a lesson Amtrak evidently never bothered to learn. The railroad's efforts at almost every stage were weak, uncoordinated and late. Amtrak's failure is all the more remarkable because, in a night filled with tragedy, the rest of the emergency response worked—and worked well.

Gotbaum observed that Amtrak seemed to have no response plans, nor did it seem to have trained employees. An employee who was responsible for transporting discharged passengers from Gotbaum's hospital back to 30th Street Station would not answer his group's questions. A form he had to fill out had just been developed that night, and did not include fields for information on lost luggage. Once home, and six days after the crash, he still had difficulty getting through to a customer service representative who was able to answer questions about whether his medical expenses would be reimbursed or provide information on lost luggage and specifically medications. This reporter's frustrations were clear in his story, and point to the magnitude of Fombrun and van Riel's (2004) consistency principle.

> Amtrak's CEO published a letter claiming the railroad "took full responsibility" for the tragedy and implying that Amtrak was doing everything it possibly could to help its pas-

sengers. Such a public relations tactic might have been plausible were there any evidence that Amtrak's management actually took responsibility. Instead, at each level, Amtrak employees seemed to say, "I'm doing my job. You're someone else's responsibility."

The principle of consistency suggests best-regarded companies "coach employees and partners to communicate harmonious messages" (p. 218). Gotbaum also commented on a lack of notification about the family assistance center.

> The Amtrak CEO letter and Amtrak's public relations advisers trumpeted to the public that Amtrak had set up a family assistance center in Philadelphia (which we did in New York after 9/11). However, they neglected to tell us passengers about it. (Perhaps they didn't want us to point out that many of us don't live in Philadelphia.)

Both Murphy and Gotbaum's experiences tie into the employee component of the corporate reputation index (Cravens, Oliver & Ramamoorti, 2003), in which corporate strategy, financial strength, culture, governance, and other dimensions are captured and measured. "Employees are the means by which a corporate reputation is created. Through the actions of all employees, at the senior management and lower levels, the public derives an image of the corporation" (p. 205). In a letter to employees in his monthly publication, Boardman reminded his workforce to continue demonstrating to riders that Amtrak's services are safe and secure. "Everything we do should set the right example so our customers continue to trust Amtrak as a safe way to travel" (Amtrak, 2015e).

The *New York Times* editorial board (2015) took the position that Congress needed to act to more adequately fund the safety and infrastructure of Amtrak, citing a ridership increase of seven million passengers since 2005. "To thrive, a national railway has to be fully supported as a vital government service" (Editorial board, 2015). This key influencer chose to highlight a strategic long-term issue rather than take aim at the specific accident that led to the attention.

Mayor Nutter, a significant influencer locally and main spokesperson during the crisis, was, at first, supportive of Amtrak. But as daylight broke, his tone became much more adversarial, saying there was no acceptable excuse for the tragedy short of the engineer suffering a heart attack.

Another gauge of stakeholder reaction can be found in ridership data (2015d). Amtrak stated in its May 2015 performance report that the derailment had a "significant adverse impact on May's ridership and revenue performance" (2015d, p. 18). May ridership in the NEC was 16 percent below budget and 13 percent below May 2014 numbers. Northeast Regional ticket revenues were 19 percent below budget and 13 percent below last year's May figures. Prior to the derailment, Northeast Regional ridership was trending up 5 percent from last year and ticket revenues in May were trending up 7 percent. June data is not yet available. Only time will tell if this crisis is reflected in Amtrak's future ridership and revenue.

DISCUSSION

It is indisputable that this crash was a tragedy. We can use several lenses through which to judge Amtrak's performance during this crisis. The first is Fombrun and van Riel's Reputation Quotient®, which captures six determinants or dimensions most people associate with a company whose reputation they hold in high regard: social responsibility, emotional appeal, products and services, workplace environment, financial performance, and vision and leadership (2004).

Another reputation doctrine also stems from Fombrun and van Riel (2004), which they characterize as principles or "key ingredients for building star-quality reputations" (p. 86). The principles are: be visible, be transparent, be distinctive, be consistent, and be authentic.

Arguably, the most important determinant in Amtrak regaining some of its reputation capital is that it immediately took full responsibility and exhibited authenticity in its decision not to contest any of the lawsuits coming its way. Perhaps Amtrak could have improved in the area of leadership and visibility. The absence of Mr. Boardman was palpable on May 13, especially when so many other interviews were granted with NTSB officials, city officials, etc. Considering the volumes of print and broadcast coverage running the day after the crash, Amtrak leadership should have made the effort to be more visible early on. The same finding also applies to social media—Amtrak took up very little space in that medium, especially considering the volumes of activity happening by the minute.

DISCUSSION QUESTIONS

1. If you were Mr. Boardman's chief communications officer and were conducting an after-action review with him on Amtrak's communication efforts, what would you advise him to do differently should there be another disaster? What would you say Amtrak should sustain as a practice?
2. Imagine that positive train control installation is now complete. Considering the May disaster, what recommendations will you make to Mr. Boardman about your communication plan regarding the completion of the mandate?
3. Discuss which of the Page Principles Amtrak most strongly exhibited. Which could it have done better at? Why?
4. What is your plan for helping Amtrak determine the sentiment of its key stakeholders and recover its reputation capital following the crisis?
5. Amtrak's chief counsel has advised you and the CEO against speaking publicly following the crash. What is your response?

REFERENCES

Amtrak. (2010). Amtrak positive train control on the fast track. News release. Retrieved July 20, 2015, from http://www.amtrak.com/ccurl/234/107/ATK-10-040%20Amtrak%20 and%20Positive%20Train%20Control,0.pdf.

Amtrak. (2013). Annual Report, Fiscal Year 2013. Retrieved June 10, 2015, from http://www .amtrak.com/ccurl/1000/237/Amtrak-Annual-Report-2013.pdf.

Amtrak. (2014a). National Fact Sheet: FY 2013. Retrieved June 10, 2015, from http://www .amtrak.com/ccurl/826/406/Amtrak-National-Fact-Sheet-FY2013-rev.pdf.

Amtrak. (2014b). Amtrak delivers strong FY 2014 financial results [Press release]. Retrieved June 15, 2015, from http://www.amtrak.com/ccurl/160/780/Amtrak-FY14-Financial-Re sults-ATK-14-107.pdf.

Amtrak. (2015a). A message from president and CEO Joe Boardman on train 188. The of-ficial blog of Amtrak. Retrieved June 16, 2015, from http://blog.amtrak.com/2015/05/ message-president-ceo-joe-boardman-train-188/.

Amtrak. (2015b). Our commitment to passengers and employees: Safety and positive train control. The official blog of Amtrak. Retrieved July 19, 2015, from http://blog.amtrak .com/2015/05/commitment-passengers-employees-safety-positive-train-control/.

Amtrak. (2105c). The official blog of Amtrak. Retrieved July 19, 2015, http://blog.amtrak .com/?s=188.

Amtrak. (2015d). Monthly performance report for May 2015. Retrieved July 22, 2015, from http://www.amtrak.com/ccurl/721/24/Amtrak-Monthly-Performance-Report-May-2015 .pdf.

Amtrak. (2015e). Amtrak Ink: A monthly publication for and by Amtrak employees. May/ June edition.

Bever, Lindsey. (2015, May 13). Journalists and politicians on Amtrak train tweet from crash site. *Washington Post.* Retrieved July 18, 2015, from http://www.washingtonpost.com/ news/morning-mix/wp/2015/05/13/journalists-and-politicians-on-amtrak-crash-train -tweet-from-scene/.

Botelho, Greg & Ford, Dana. (2015, May 14) Amtrak crash: Video shows train speeding up before derailment. CNN. Retrieved July 20, 2015, from http://www.cnn.com/2015/05/14/ us/philadelphia-amtrak-train-derailment/.

Cravens, K., Oliver, E. G., & Ramamoorti, S. (2003). The reputation index: Measuring and managing corporate reputation. *European Management Journal*, 21(2), 201–212.

Editorial Board. (2015, May 13). Amtrak needs help. *The New York Times.* Retrieved July 22, 2015, from http://www.nytimes.com/2015/05/14/opinion/amtrak-needs-help.html?_r=0.

Fombrun, C. J., & Van Riel, C. B. (2004). *Fame & fortune: How successful companies build winning reputations.* FT Press.

Gotbaum, Joshua. (2015, May 20). How Amtrak failed the victims of train 188: A survi-vor's tale (The crash was a tragedy. Amtrak's response was a disaster). *Politico.* Retrieved July 11, 2015, from http://www.politico.com/magazine/story/2015/05/amtrak-188-survi vor-118123.html#.VaFLoF9Vikp.

House Transportation and Infrastructure Committee. (2015). Oversight of the Amtrak Ac-cident in Philadelphia. Retrieved July 22, 2015, from http://transportation.house.gov/ calendar/eventsingle.aspx?EventID=398969.

Lubrano, Alfred. (2015, May 17). The Wreck of Train 188. *Philadelphia Inquirer.* Retrieved June 13, 2015, from http://www.philly.com/philly/news/The_wreck_of_Train_No_188.html.

Mouawad, Jad. (2015, May 13). Technology That Could Have Prevented Amtrak Derailment Was Absent. *The New York Times*. Retrieved July 20, 2015, from http://www.nytimes.com/2015/05/14/us/technology-that-could-have-prevented-amtrak-derailment-was-absent.html?_r=0.

National Transportation Safety Board. (2015a). Preliminary report: Railroad DCA15MR010. Retrieved June 10, 2015, from http://www.ntsb.gov/investigations/AccidentReports/Pages/DCA15MR010_Preliminary. aspx.

National Transportation Safety Board. (2015b). NTSB Issues Second Update on Its Investigation Into the Amtrak Derailment in Philadelphia. Retrieved June 13, 2015, from http://www.ntsb.gov/news/press-releases/Pages/PR20150610.aspx.

Nixon, Ron. (2015, July 10). Amtrak will not fight suits filed in wreck. *The New York Times*. Retrieved July 11, 2015, from http://www.nytimes.com/2015/07/11/us/amtrak-will-not-fight-suits-filed-in-wreck.html?_r=0.

Case Study 3

An Analysis of Starbucks' Race Together Initiative

Reprinted with permission from the authors, Chelsea Michael, Megan Cauley, and Lizmarie Orengo, and faculty advisor, Matt Ragas, Ph.D., from DePaul University College of Communication. This case study was the Grand Prize recipient of the Arthur W. Page Society 2016 Case Study Competition.

OVERVIEW

Following the race-related tragedies in Ferguson, Missouri, and New York City, Howard Schultz, CEO of Starbucks, was deeply saddened by the racial tensions in the United States. He felt his company needed to address the issue and refused to be a silent bystander. Schultz invited Starbucks employees (referred to as partners) to participate in open forums across the nation where they could come together and discuss race issues in the United States. Schultz attended forums in several cities and met with nearly two thousand partners (Solomon, 2015). The response from the forums was overwhelmingly positive. Partners described the meetings as emotionally charged events where they discussed ideas for change. Schultz wanted to share this positive experience with the public. On March 16, 2015, Starbucks released a memo to employees encouraging them to engage customers in a conversation about race by writing the words "Race Together" on their coffee cups.

The initiative was well-intentioned, but when Race Together was introduced to customers it was poorly received. Most people did not want to discuss a topic as complex as race while they rushed to get their morning coffee. The public thought race was an inappropriate topic for a company to address, and the idea was harshly mocked. People took to social media to express their disappointment with Starbucks, and when the writing on the cups stopped a week later, most people thought the initiative had quietly shut down.

However, this was not the case. Starbucks had an entire platform in place to address the issue and was still determined to speak out on race relations. Starbucks' commitment to the initiative, despite the initial backlash, showed the company had strong corporate values and was dedicated to living and activating its corporate character. The company was determined to position itself as a meaningful voice on social issues and to pioneer a new era of corporate activism. In doing so, Starbucks brought an important question to light: Can a corporation influence social change? The following case analyzes whether or not a company like Starbucks can help drive societal change through its actions and communication efforts.

COMPANY BACKGROUND

History of Starbucks

Starbucks is an American coffee company based in Seattle, Washington. It has more than twenty-three thousand stores in seventy countries, making it the largest coffeehouse company in the world (Starbucks, 2015). Founded in 1971, Starbucks originally served as a coffee bean roaster and retailer. The company's owners at the time were three partners who met while attending the University of San Francisco.

In 1987, the three owners sold the Starbucks chain to Howard Schultz. Schultz was born in Brooklyn in 1953 and later moved with his family to the Bayview Housing projects in the Canarsie neighborhood of Brooklyn. Both of his parents worked low-paying jobs, and the family experienced many financial problems. A natural athlete, Schultz earned a scholarship to the University of Northern Michigan, where he graduated with a bachelor's degree in communication. As CEO of Starbucks, Schultz frequently references his humble beginnings and how he uses his past experiences to shape the way he manages the company.

Schultz always had a vision for Starbucks to be more than a coffee chain. While on a trip to Milan, Schultz became transfixed by the coffee culture in Europe and set out to bring the experience back to America. It was on this trip that Schultz decided Starbucks should sell drinks in their stores and not just beans. Schultz later reflected on this trip, saying, "I saw something. Not only the romance of coffee, but a sense of community. And the connection that people had to coffee—the place and one another." Schultz believed Starbucks could grow to become more than a chain, but the "third place" between work and home where people could socialize or unwind (Starbucks, 2015). After taking Starbucks from a small chain in Seattle to a global company, Schultz retired as the company's CEO in 2000.

Return of the Coffee King

During Schultz's eight-year hiatus from the company, Starbucks' financial performance slowed as companies like McDonald's and Dunkin' Donuts expanded within the coffee category. Observing the downward spiral of his former company, Schultz returned in 2008 because he believed Starbucks had drifted away from his original vision and he feared for the company's future (MSNBC Staff, 2008). Schultz vowed to focus on global expansion and a restructuring of the company's management system. Additionally, Schultz wanted to prevent growth from affecting the company's culture and ensure that Starbucks continued operating as if it were a small company and a part of the community. In his book *Onward*, Schultz describes his return to the company and how Starbucks achieved profitability and sustainability without sacrificing humanity during a tough economic period.

Since Schultz's return, Starbucks has made itself known as a company that addresses social issues head-on. The corporation has become vocal on a variety of issues from gun control to gay marriage (Harwell, 2015). These are not topics major companies typically feel comfortable tackling, but Starbucks aspires to build human relationships and act ethically, even when it may be easier and more popular to stay silent.

Corporate Character

The Arthur W. Page Society describes corporate character as the unique identity that distinguishes a company and the characteristics that define its very nature of existence. This identity begins with an enterprise's purpose and values, but it is lived out through a company's strategic business and operating plans (Arthur W. Page Society, 2012). The first step in developing corporate character is to clearly define a company's beliefs. Starbucks has a clear mission statement and values visible on its website and stated below.

Mission

"To inspire and nurture the human spirit—one person, one cup and one neighborhood at a time."

Values

"With our partners, our coffee and our customers at our core, we live these values: Creating a culture of warmth and belonging, where everyone is welcome. Acting with courage, challenging the status quo and finding new ways to grow our company and each other. Being present, connecting with transparency, dignity and respect. Delivering our very best in all we do, holding ourselves accountable for results. We are performance driven, through the lens of humanity. These core beliefs are the cornerstone of Starbucks and used as a clear metric for all business practices across the company."

Corporate Reputation

Companies must develop a strong corporate character if they want to build strong brands and corporate reputations that create trusting relationships with stakeholders.

Corporate reputation refers to the collective judgments of a corporation based on assessments of financial, social, and environmental impacts attributed to the company over a long period of time (Arthur W. Page Society, 2012).

Starbucks has built a bank of trust with its stakeholders, resulting in a strong corporate reputation. The 2015 Harris Poll Reputation Quotient study ranks Starbucks as the thirty-first most reputable US company among the most visible US companies (Harris Poll, 2015). Additionally, Starbucks ranks fifth on the *Fortune* list of World's Most Admired Companies for 2015 and is ranked first within its industry. Starbucks also ranks first on *Fortune*'s list for social responsibility, which is considered a key attribute of the company's reputation (*Fortune*, 2015). Finally, the Reputation Institute shows Starbucks ranked fourth in the RepTrak "governance" division, which assesses stakeholder perceptions of a company as ethical, fair, and transparent (Global RepTrak, 2015).

Timeline of Major Corporate Reputation Events

The following timeline highlights the company's biggest achievements that led to the development and sustainment of this reputation since Schultz's return in 2008.

2008—Howard Schultz returns as chief executive officer and begins the transformation of Starbucks.

- A new mission statement develops: "To inspire and nurture the human spirit—one person, one cup and one neighborhood at a time."
- Launches My Starbucks Idea, Starbucks' first online community.
- Starbucks joins Twitter and Facebook.

2009—Launches My Starbucks Rewards® loyalty program and Starbucks Card mobile payment.

2010—Starbucks expands digital offerings for customers with free unlimited Wi-Fi, Starbucks Digital Network.

2011—Launches first annual Global Month of Service to celebrate the company's fortieth anniversary.

- Opens first Community Stores in Harlem and Crenshaw neighborhoods.
- Launches "Create Jobs for USA" to encourage small-business growth.

2012—Acquires La Boulange® bakery brand to elevate core food offerings.

2013—Strengthens ethical sourcing efforts with coffee farming research and development center in Costa Rica.

- Schultz reinforces company's commitment to marriage equality.
- "Come Together" petition urges US elected leaders to reopen the government.

2014—Launches Starbucks College Achievement Plan with Arizona State University to offer qualifying Starbucks US partners the opportunity to complete a college degree through ASU's online degree program.

- Announces commitment to hiring ten thousand veterans and Starbucks' military spouses by 2018.

2015—Launches "Race Together" initiative.

- Commits to hiring ten thousand opportunity youth by 2018.
- Announces plans to open a store in Ferguson, Missouri, as part of an accelerated program to open stores in fifteen diverse urban communities across the United States.
- Expands Starbucks College Achievement Plan to offer full tuition coverage for all four years of an undergraduate degree for qualifying US Starbucks partners and commits to twenty-five thousand partners graduating by 2025.

Corporate Social Responsibility

Companies are motivated to become socially responsible because their stakeholders expect the company to understand and address the relevant social and community issues related to core values and beliefs. Corporate social responsibility (CSR) is defined as the voluntary actions that a corporation puts in place as it pursues its mission and fulfills obligations to stakeholders, employees, communities, and the environment (Ragas & Culp, 2014). Starbucks defines its CSR efforts as giving back to communities and the environment, treating people with respect and dignity, and serving the world's best coffee (Starbucks, 2015).

Schultz asserts that his company is performance-driven through the lens of humanity and makes every business decision from a socially conscious perspective (Schultz, 2015). Starbucks differs from some corporations because it speaks out on social issues, even when those issues do not directly affect it as a company. By confronting issues like gun control, gay marriage, and, most recently, race, Starbucks is starting a movement that goes beyond traditional CSR. It is actively advocating for social change.

THE CASE FOR RACE

Race Together Initiative

As CEO of Starbucks, Howard Schultz has made himself known not only as a successful entrepreneur, but as a successful social activist as well. He has brought meaning to the relatively new concept of CEO activism by "weighing in on contentious issues without any obvious pretense of raising profits" (Chatterji & Toffel, 2015). Notably, Starbucks does not speak out on issues or financially support causes solely based on an anticipated response from the public, but it reacts to causes based on the corporate values the company already has in place.

Speaking out on race aligns with Starbucks' corporate values. Racial tensions have become an inflammatory issue in the United States surrounding incidents such as the death of Michael Brown in Ferguson, Missouri, and the death of Eric Garner in New York City. Schultz was prepared to have his company address these issues directly. In a Starbucks memo sent on March 16, 2015, Schultz was quoted as saying, "We at Starbucks should be willing to talk about these issues in America. Not to point fingers or to place blame, and not because we have answers, but because staying silent is not who we are" (Starbucks, 2015).

This memo also announced the Starbucks Race Together initiative. Starbucks launched the initiative by inviting its partners to engage in open discussions about race by writing "Race Together" on customers' cups. The memo ended with another quote from Schultz that acknowledged that the initiative is not a solution "but it is an opportunity to begin to reexamine how we can create a more empathetic and inclusive society—one conversation at a time" (Starbucks, 2015).

Public Response

Despite its best intentions, the Race Together initiative was met with harsh criticism and mockery from the public. Starbucks failed to anticipate the backlash it would endure from engaging a topic as sensitive as race. People soon took to social media to express their disapproval. The extensive negative comments drove Corey duBrowa, Starbucks SVP of global communications, to temporarily suspend his Twitter account in fear of personal threats.

The Twitter storm was fierce but blew over quickly because the time frame for the initiative was short. Many believed the campaign had been cut short because of the public's reaction. However, Starbucks maintains that writing "Race Together" on cups lasted for its intended run date, March 16 to March 22, 2015, and only played a small role in the overall Race Together initiative (Ziv, 2015). The act of writing on cups was meant to serve as a jumping-off point in the conversation, and Starbucks claimed it already had a larger plan in place to address the racial divide. Schultz made this clear in an interview with CNBC stating:

> Writing on the cup is a diminutive piece of this issue and it's not going to last long. It was a catalyst to start this. What's going to last long is our company saying that we believe that there is a serious problem in America. We are in almost every community in America, and can we use our stores and our national footprint for good? (Schultz, 2015)

Media Response

The media response was equally critical and labeled the initiative as poorly executed. However, journalists at national publications knew Schultz well enough to question whether this move held more significance than a shortsighted PR stunt. Several publications tried to analyze Starbucks' motive for confronting an issue as complex as race. They helped explain what much of the general public did not realize, that writing on cups was the tip of the iceberg on a much larger initiative. The *Wall Street Journal* published an article titled "Why Starbucks Takes on Social Issues" that examined why Schultz would continue pushing the race discussion despite the backlash. Many other publications, such as *Time, Huffington Post,* and *Fast Company* lauded the overall initiative and praised Schultz's tenacity in combating an issue many other corporations feared to address. Kimberly Cooper of the *Huffington Post* recognized the larger platform behind the campaign, stating, "While Starbucks may have stopped writing 'Race Together' on their drinks, the #RaceTogether initiative is far from over and the ball is in our court to answer their call to action" (Carr, 2015; Yoffie & Cusumano, 2015).

Business Impact

Harsh criticism of the Race Together initiative did not affect Starbucks' sales or stock market performance. In fact, the company's stock price has risen by 20 percent since 2014 and saw a 4 percent jump in April 2015, a month after the March 2015 launch of the Race Together initiative, reaching a record high during its fiscal second quarter. Paul La Monica from CNN Money observes, "Schultz may continue to alienate some people with comments about politics and race. But it doesn't matter for the bottom line. Coffee junkies want their caffeine fix. And so does Wall Street" (La Monica, 2015). Schultz also maintains that performing for his shareholders is top priority: "You have to understand, I spend 90% of my day on Starbucks business—I'm not spending my entire life on the issues of racial inequality, I have a company to run here" (Carr, 2015).

Nonetheless, the safest stance for the bottom line when it comes to social issues such as race is to remain silent. Schultz seems determined to use Starbucks' scale for good, and if he can do so while remaining profitable, he is helping Starbucks redefine the way for-profit public companies can impact social issues.

The New American Dream

With Schultz's guidance, Starbucks is attempting to redefine the way the private sector reacts to social issues. Race Together may have stumbled in its initial execution, but its commitment to the issue seemingly reflects the company's corporate values and belief that the "American Dream should be available to every person in this country, not just a select few" (Starbucks, 2015). Despite the initial negative rollout of Race Together, Schultz doubled down and defended his efforts by further outlining Starbucks' plans to address the issue of race.

In a series of memos after the initial Race Together announcement, Starbucks attempted to support the initiative with action by (1) announcing plans to coproduce content addressing racial issues with *USA Today,* (2) holding open forums across the country to encourage dialogue with police and community leaders, (3) opening stores in fifteen diverse urban communities across the country including Ferguson, Missouri, and (4) hiring ten thousand Opportunity Youth, sixteen- to twenty-four-year-olds who face systemic barriers to jobs and education, by 2018 (Starbucks,

2015). By this time, they also plan to engage with a minimum of one hundred thousand Opportunity Youth. To help reach this goal, Starbucks partnered with different organizations like the Schultz Family Foundation and YouthBuild USA. Together they created a program called Customer Service Excellence Training to help train these young people and find them careers in retail and customer service. The *Wall Street Journal* reports that other major corporations such as Walmart, Microsoft, Lyft, JPMorgan Chase, Taco Bell, Pizza Hut, Macy's, and Alaska Air Group have also pledged to hire one hundred thousand Opportunity Youth (Kieler, 2015).

Starbucks' well-defined corporate character and track record of giving back to its communities is evidence against the idea that Race Together was a public relations stunt jumping on a topical issue. Starbucks is distinguishing itself as a corporation that becomes meaningfully involved in relevant social issues. The company appears to follow its commitments even when the conversation becomes controversial. With this in mind, it is consistent for Starbucks to speak out on race. As argued by Phillip Haid of *Fast Company*, Starbucks is evolving beyond "the outdated view that charities 'do good' and companies make money" (Haid, 2015).

BUSINESS PERFORMANCE

Overview of Earnings

Starbucks is a company that continually executes its mission and values. It has found many ways to get involved with its public and impact society. The company has been able to remain profitable and continue "growing the beans" while involving itself in societal issues. Starbucks' initiatives and market strategies are some of the main reasons for its success. As discussed earlier in the case, during Starbucks' Race Together campaign, the stock increased in value by 4 percent in April 2015 despite criticism from the public and media.

Starbucks' stock rose slightly from Schultz's departure in 2000 and reached a plateau in 2006 before a significant drop over the next year and a half until Schultz's return as CEO in 2008. With Schultz's leadership the company has remained successful with only minor declines in its stock price, from which it has recovered quickly.

Starbucks has taken corporate and financial risks with its CSR initiatives and public relations strategies since its inception. For the past five years, the risks it has taken are working in its favor. The Starbucks Rewards® loyalty program (2009), the Starbucks Digital Network (2010), its Global Month of Service celebration (2011), its farming research in Costa Rica (2013), and the launch of Starbucks' College Achievement Plan (2014) have contributed to Starbucks' business performance and boosted the value of Starbucks stocks for the past five years.

The negative publicity generated by the Race Together initiative has not hurt Starbucks' stock prices. Despite a minor drop in stock prices in August of 2015, the company has consistently reported positive change. Although Starbucks did not implement

Race Together in order to increase revenue, it and other CSR initiatives have helped the company strengthen bonds with stakeholders and increase shareholder value.

A Look Ahead

Some future challenges Starbucks might face could involve an inability to raise prices if coffee bean rates continue to rise and lost revenue against other specialty coffee retailers. Nevertheless, Starbucks anticipates challenges and has a reputation of success in solving tough problems. Starbucks' strategies often involve risks, but the company finds success because of its long-term plans and orientation: "I believe life is a series of near misses. A lot of what we ascribe to luck is not luck at all. It's seizing the day and accepting responsibility for your future. It's seeing what other people don't see and pursuing that vision" (Schultz, 2015).

Starbucks' success seems tied to the CSR efforts and corporate communications strategies they practice. As stated by Starbucks SVP of global communications, Corey duBrowa, "These financial and stock market gains do not seem to have come at the expense of other stakeholders. Starbucks has maintained a strong reputation" (Ragas & Culp, 2014). If Starbucks keeps true to its corporate character, it is poised to be a brand that creates shared value for its stakeholders and outperforms its competitors. Starbucks will likely continue to manage for tomorrow when it comes to its reputation.

THE FUTURE OF CORPORATE SOCIAL RESPONSIBILITY

The Race Continues

As Schultz promised, Starbucks has not retreated from Race Together. The corporation has followed through on its commitment to use its resources to reduce racial tensions in the United States. On November 19, 2015, the company broke ground for its new location in Ferguson, Missouri. The company also partnered with Natalie DuBose of Natalie's Cakes and More. DuBose, whose bakery shop was burned and vandalized during the protests in Ferguson, will sell her desserts at the new Starbucks in Ferguson and eleven other locations. The Ferguson store is set to open in the spring of 2016, and locations in Milwaukee, Phoenix, Chicago, and New York will open within the next year (Stewart, 2015).

Corporate Social Activism

Starbucks has emerged as a pioneer in a new era of corporate social activism, but it is not alone in its belief that corporations can influence social change. Other companies have similarly used their scale for good in attempts to address societal issues. One recent success story is Salesforce, a cloud computing company that announced on March 26, 2015, it would cease all company events in Indiana after the state passed the Religious Freedom Restoration Act, an act that allowed individuals and corporations to legally refuse to do business with same-sex couples (Hesseldahl, 2015). Salesforce CEO Marc Benioff was quoted as saying, "We've made significant investments in Indiana. We run major marketing events and conferences there. We're a major source of income and revenue to the state of Indiana, but we simply cannot support this kind of legislation" (Hesseldahl, 2015).

Other corporations such as Eli Lilly, Levi Strauss, NASCAR, the Indianapolis Motor Speedway, and the Indiana Pacers followed suit to speak out against the law. As businesses became the most compelling opponents of the Religious Freedom Restoration Act, legislators gave in and created necessary revisions to the law. The reaction also caused Georgia and Arkansas to rethink similar laws (Bort, 2015).

Corporate social activism is a novel concept, and companies are just beginning to recognize their ability to influence societal issues through living their corporate character. While it is still a risk for companies to take a stance on controversial "third-rail issues," the potential for businesses to enact change is significant. If progressive companies like Starbucks continue to speak out on issues based on the beliefs of their company even when the issue is not directly tied to financial gain, there could be a major shift in the way the private sector operates in society.

REFERENCES

100,000 Opportunities Press Release (2015, August 4). 100,000 Opportunities Initiative to Kick Off with 29 Companies Expected to Engage at Least 3,000 Opportunity Youth and Make Hundreds of Immediate Job Offers in Chicagoland. Retrieved from http://finance .yahoo.com/news/100-000-opportunities-initiative-kick-160000671.html.

Advertising Specialty Institute (2015, October 30), Howard Schultz's Leadership Mantras. Retrieved from https://www.asicentral.com/news/web-exclusive/october-2015/howard -schultz-s-leadership-mantras/.

Arthur W. Page Society (2012). Building belief: A new model for activating corporate culture & authentic advocacy. Arthur W. Page Society. Retrieved from http://www.awpagesociety .com/wp-content/uploads/2012/03/Building-BeliefNew-Model-for-Corp-Comms-2012.pdf.

Biography.com editors (2015, November 15). Howard Schultz Biography. A&E Television Networks. Retrieved from http://www.biography.com/people/howard-schultz -21166227#support-for-gay-marriage.

Bort, J. (2015, April 7). Salesforce is Investing in Indiana Again, but Will Still Help Employees Relocate. Business Insider. Retrieved from http://www.businessinsider.com/salesforce -will-invest-in-indiana-again-2015-4.

Candea, B. (2014, March 18). Starbucks CEO Defends "Race Together" Campaign on Race Relations. ABC News. Retrieved from http://abcnews.go.com/Business/starbucks-ceo -defends-race-campaign-race-relations/story?id=29738830.

Carr, A. (2015, June 15). The Inside Story of Starbucks's Race Together Campaign, No Foam. *Fast Company*. Retrieved from http://www.fastcompany.com/3046890/the-inside-story-of -starbuckss-race-together-campaign-no-foam.

Chatterji, A., and Toffel, M. (2015, March 24). Starbucks' "Race Together" Campaign and the Upside of CEO Activism. *Harvard Business Review*. Retrieved from https://hbr.org/2015/03/starbucks-race-together-campaign-and-the-upside-of-ceo-activism

DuBrowa, C. (2014, January 6). Personal communication, quoted from Ragas, M. W., & Culp, R. (2014). *Business Essentials for Strategic Communicators*. New York: Palgrave Macmillan.

Fortune (2015, February 19). World's Most Admired Companies 2015. Retrieved from http://fortune.com/worlds-most-admired-companies/google-2/.

Gagen MacDonald. Howard Schultz Founder & CEO Starbucks. Retrieved from https://www.gagenmacdonald.com/lgl-leader/howard-schultz/.

Gonzalez, A. (2015, March 15). Starbucks as citizen: Schultz acts boldly on social, political issues. *Seattle Times*. Retrieved from http://www.seattletimes.com/business/starbucks/starbucks-as-citizen-schultz-goes-bold/

Haid, P. (2015, March 23). Starbucks's Race Together: Why The Naysayers Have It All Wrong. Retrieved from http://www.fastcoexist.com/3044124/starbuckss-race-together-why-the-naysayers-have-it-all-wrong.

Harris Poll (2015, February 4). Regional Grocer Wegmans Unseats Amazon to Claim Top Corporate Reputation Ranking. PR Newswire. Retrieved from http://www.prnewswire.com/news-releases/regional-grocer-wegmans-unseats-amazon-to-claim-top-corporate-reputation-ranking-300030637.html.

Harwell, D. (2015, March 19). Why Starbucks chief Howard Schultz put himself at the center of America's race debate. *Washington Post*. Retrieved from https://www.washingtonpost.com/news/on-leadership/wp/2015/03/19/why-starbucks-chief-howard-schultz-put-himself-at-the-center-of-americas-race-debate/.

Hesseldahl, A. (2015, March 26). Salesforce CEO Benioff Takes Stand Against Indiana Anti-Gay Law. Recode. Retrieved from http://recode.net/2015/03/26/salesforce-ceo-benioff-takes-stand-against-indiana-anti-gay-law/.

Kieler, A. (2015, July 13). Starbucks, 17 Other Companies Partner to Provide "Opportunity Youth" with Jobs, Internships. Retrieved from http://consumerist.com/2015/07/13/starbucks-17-other-companies-partner-to-provide-opportunity-youth-with-jobs-internships/.

La Monica, P. (2015, April 24). Sorry, Starbucks Haters! #RaceTogether hasn't hurt it. CNN. Retrieved from http://money.cnn.com/2015/04/24/investing/starbucks-record-earnings-howard-schultz/index.html?iid=SF_BN_Lead.

MSNBC Staff (2008, January 8). Starbucks Chairman Schultz returning as CEO. NBC News. Retrieved from http://www.nbcnews.com/id/22544023/ns/business-us_business/t/starbucks-chairman-schultz-returning-ceo/#.ViRhlGSrT-k.

NASDAQ (2015, November 15). Starbucks Corp. CNN Money. Retrieved from http://money.cnn.com/quote/chart/chart.html?symb=SBUX.

Ragas, M. W., & Culp, R. (2014). *Business essentials for strategic communicators: Creating shared value for the organization and its stakeholders*. New York: Palgrave Macmillan.

Reputation Institute (June 2015). Global RepTrak 100. Retrieved from https://www.reputationinstitute.com/research/Global-RepTrak-100.

Sanders, S. (2015, March 22). Starbucks Will Stop Putting the Words "Race Together" on Starbucks cups. NPR. Retrieved from http://www.npr.org/sections/thetwo-way/2015/03/22/394710277/starbucks-will-stop-writing-race-together-on-coffee-cups.

Schultz, H. (2015, March 22). A Letter from Howard Schultz to Starbucks Partners Regarding Race Together. Retrieved from https://news.starbucks.com/news/a-letter-from-howard-schultz-to-starbucks-partners-regarding-race-together.

Schultz, H. (2014, November 6). Howard Schultz: Performance Through the Lens of Humanity. CNBC. Retrieved from http://video.cnbc.com/gallery/?video=3000328246.

Schultz, H. (2015, August 13). Howard Schultz: Business Leaders Must Do More. CNBC. Retrieved from http://www.cnbc.com/2015/08/13/starbucks-howard-schultz-business-leaders-must-do-more.html.

Schultz, H. (2015, March 18). Starbucks CEO Speaks to Cramer about Race. CNBC. Retrieved from http://www.cnbc.com/2015/03/18/starbucks-ceo-speaks-out-to-cramer-on-race.html.

Solomon, M. (2015, March 18). Just Because an Idea's Easy to Mock Doesn't Make it Wrong: Starbucks's Race Together Initiative. Retrieved from http://www.forbes.com/sites/micahsolomon/2015/03/18/just-because-an-ideas-easy-to-mock-doesnt-make-it-wrong-starbucks-racetogether-campaign/.

Starbucks Corporation (2015). Starbucks LinkedIn Profile. Retrieved from https://www.linkedin.com/company/2271?trk=hp-feed-company-name.

Starbucks Company Website (2015). Retrieved from http://www.starbucks.com/about-us/company-information.

Starbucks Incorporated (2015, August 4). 29 Companies to Kick Off 100,000 Opportunities Initiative in Chicago. Retrieved from https://news.starbucks.com/news/companies-to-kick-off-100k-opportunities-initiative-in-chicago.

Starbucks Investor Relations (2015). Starbucks 2015 Proxy Statement. Retrieved from http://investor.starbucks.com/phoenix.zhtml?c=99518&p=irol-irhome.

Stewart, M. (2015, November 20). Starbucks Embarks on National Diversity Initiative in Ferguson, Partners with Local Bakery Natalie's Cakes and More. Retrieved from http://www.stlamerican.com/news/local_news/article_1674d4ce-8f92-11e5-a005-db8ec2087fcf.html.

Yoffie, D., and Cusumano, M. (2015, March 18). Starbucks Race Together Initiative is Brilliant. Retrieved from http://time.com/3749221/starbucks-howard-schultz-race-together-initiative/.

Ziv, S. (2015, March 23). Starbucks Ends Phase One of Race Together Initiative After Grande Fail. Newsweek. Retrieved from http://www.newsweek.com/starbucks-ends-phase-one-race-together-initiative-after-grande-fail-316043.

Case Study 4

The Virtue of Patients: Veterans' Fatal Wait

An Analysis of the U.S. Department of Veterans Affairs' Buildup to and Communication about Its Secret Patient Wait Lists

Reprinted with permission from the author, Brenda Middleton, and faculty advisor, J. Suzanne Horsley, Ph.D., from the University of Alabama. This case study was a second-prize recipient of the Arthur W. Page Society 2015 Case Study Competition.

OVERVIEW

The United States Department of Veterans Affairs, in some form or another, has been in existence longer than practically any other government service.[1] Additionally, the veterans' health care system is the largest health provider in the nation.[2] America has fought for its veterans as long as they have fought for America.

Upon further investigation, it becomes clear that the services provided to those who were willing to give their lives for their country have been inconsistent at best. Through the years, corrupt leaders, layers of confusing bureaucracy, lax accountability, and poor standards of care set the stage for scandal. Spring of 2014 brought showers of media coverage about secret wait lists containing thousands of veterans who had been waiting months for appointments. At one health care facility in Arizona, forty veterans died while waiting for care on one such secret wait list.[3] The official records of appointment schedules reflected acceptable wait times. Executives at the dishonest facilities received performance bonuses for exceptional patient care that did not occur.[4] Response to this scandal began with virtual silence from organization officials, and then changed dramatically as federal leadership changed.

This case study examines (1) the historical, organizational, and political factors that led to the scheduling scandal and (2) how communication about the scandal was handled and responded to, both at the peak of the crisis and afterward as a new leader took charge.

171

1. HISTORY

1.1 Veteran Care in America. America's support of its military dates back to 1636. More than a century before a formal nation was established, a law was created in Plymouth Colony that provided support for disabled soldiers who fought against the Pequot Indians.[5] As the country developed, so did its care for those who fought for it. In 1776 the Continental Congress recruited soldiers by providing pensions for those who became disabled.[6] This awarded seriously disabled soldiers with half their pay for the rest of their lives.[7] Additionally, land grants were given to those who served for the war's entirety.[8]

Care expanded again in 1811 when the federal government authorized the first medical facility for veterans.[9] There were approximately 80,000 veterans at the beginning of the Civil War.[10] This number increased by 1.9 million (Confederate soldiers were excluded from veteran services) by the conclusion of the conflict.[11] Veteran benefits were expanded to include services for veteran families in 1862.[12] After World War I, the veteran population expanded by 204,000, and the federal government expanded veteran care to include insurance, disability compensation, and vocational rehabilitation.[13]

In the 1920s veteran benefits were managed by three separate federal agencies: the National Home for Disabled Volunteer Soldiers, the Bureau of Pensions of the Interior Department, and the Veterans Bureau.[14] In 1930, President Herbert Hoover created the Veterans Administration (VA), which consolidated those agencies into one entity.[15] America's participation in World War II significantly increased the number of veterans and services for them.[16] One of these services was the GI Bill, signed in 1944.[17] President Ronald Reagan made the VA a cabinet-level department in 1988 and renamed it the Department of Veterans Affairs; the acronym "VA" was retained.[18]

1.2 Veteran Health Care. Until 1812, veteran benefits consisted mainly of monetary compensation. It was then that the Naval Home in Philadelphia provided federally funded and operated medical care for disabled veterans for the first time.[19] Two more facilities were created by 1855, both located in Washington, DC.[20] With World War I came the establishment of a major system of hospitals for veterans.[21] In 1918, Congress leased hundreds of private hospitals and began building more in order to care for the influx of war veterans.[22]

The Great Depression led to an increase in veterans seeking medical care, especially for tuberculosis.[23] By 1930 there were 54 veteran hospitals.[24] This increased to 125 hospitals just 15 years later.[25] In 1945, WWII came to a close, and General Omar Bradley was named director of the VA.[26] General Bradley faced the challenge of a dramatic increase in returning veterans, many of whom would be seeking medical care.[27] In response, he increased VA staff by over 45,000, established more than 700 new offices, and opened 29 hospitals.[28] Also during this time, there was an increase in amputees, yet a lack of artificial limb options.[29] The VA responded to this need and became a world leader in prosthetics.[30]

In 1952, after the Korean War, there were 541 VA hospitals providing care to 128,000 veterans per day.[31] In reaction to this, the VA reorganized into three divisions: medical, financial, and insurance services. At this time, 2.5 million veterans were seeking some form of medical care each year.[32] Advances in medical treatment allowed for more soldiers to survive the Vietnam War than any previous conflict.[33] Those veterans returned home with new psychological issues as well as medical issues resulting from use of new weapons such as Agent Orange.[34] This, combined with the psychological issues suffered by the 664,000 Gulf War veterans, led to the creation of over 200 counseling service centers by 2005.[35]

In 1991, the medical branch of the VA was renamed the Veterans Health Administration (VHA).[36] As the twenty-first century dawned, so did women's veteran services. The Women Veterans Health Program Office was created in 1997 along with other services focused on females.[37] In 2002, the VA structure was assessed and the CARES project was created.[38] The Capital Asset Realignment for Enhanced Services, a three-year study, resulted in the addition of hundreds of new facilities including hospitals, community clinics, spinal cord injury centers, blind rehabilitation centers, and mental health centers.[39] These facilities were intended to be more modern and better located than those already in existence.[40]

Today, the VHA operates the largest health care system in America, with at least one facility in every state.[41] Its breadth includes approximately 150 hospitals, 126 nursing homes, and 800 outpatient clinics.[42] It is projected that 6.7 million patients will use some service in the VA health care network in 2015.[43]

1.3 US Department of Veterans Affairs (VA) Corruption. President Warren Harding chose his acquaintance, Charles Forbes, to be the first leader of the new Veterans Bureau in 1921.[44] Among other illegal activities, Forbes frivolously spent taxpayer money and embezzled almost $250 million before he was caught and sentenced to two years in prison.[45] As a direct result of this scandal, the VA changed its power structure to include layers of bureaucracy to prevent others from following in Forbes's footsteps.[46]

In 1924 the federal government passed the World War Compensation Act, which promised bonuses for World War I veterans, but then revealed that veterans wouldn't actually begin to receive these payments for twenty years.[47] In the wake of the Great Depression, tens of thousands of destitute and angry veterans marched to Washington, DC, to protest the delay of payment.[48] Federal troops were sent in to remove the protesters, and Congress allowed the VA to pay for the travel expenses of those who would agree to leave.[49] The march did not see immediate success, but payments were made within five years of this immense protest.[50] Another result of the veteran outcry was the passage of the GI Bill. President Franklin Roosevelt passed this bill at the conclusion of World War II in the hopes of doing more to care for veterans after this world war than the last.[51]

Two government reform commissions, first in 1947 then again in 1955, found alarming instances of VA overspending and waste as well as inadequate care for veterans.[52] About 15 years later, another movement for VA reform surfaced.

Marine and decorated Vietnam War veteran Ron Kovic was paralyzed during his second tour in Vietnam.[53] He returned to America for treatment and quickly became disenchanted with the quality of care he received at home.[54] Soon after, he became a frequent lecturer for the Vietnam Veterans Against the War.[55] After another unsatisfactory hospital stint in 1973, he founded the Patients'/Workers Rights Committee that led to the American Veterans Movement.[56] This group led a hunger strike outside the office of the chair of the subcommittee on Veterans Health and Hospitals.

A few weeks later, President Richard Nixon called for a VA operations investigation.[57] VA Director Donald Johnson resigned soon after the investigation was announced.[58] Kovic helped bring veteran issues into the spotlight with his speeches, protests, and with his book, *Born on the Fourth of July*, that was later made into an Academy Award–winning movie starring Tom Cruise.[59]

The spotlight on VA issues continued as one of the country's largest VA facilities, located in Chicago, was subjected to an investigation by the VA Office of Inspector General (OIG) in 1991.[60] The subsequent report stated that the hospital failed to diagnose and/or quickly treat patients. It also performed unnecessary surgeries. All of these instances of neglect and abuse may have led to the untimely deaths of fifteen patients that year.[61] This was the second investigation at this hospital in four years, but despite this, a regional VA office review of the facility in 1990 called it "one of the more sophisticated and productive programs in the Great Lakes Region," according to a 1991 *Chicago Tribune* story by Michael Millenson. The VA secretary at the time said the VA was having serious monitoring issues and that he was pursuing a cleanup of the system.[62]

An audit was performed in 2002 in response to reports of over two hundred thousand veterans waiting six months or more for care.[63] The resulting report by the OIG found that wait lists were overstated due to appointment scheduling documentation errors.[64] The recommendation of this report was that VHA managers needed to more accurately track patients and their wait times.[65] Consequently, a new electronic waiting list, the National Patient Care Database, was introduced to VA medical facilities nationwide in 2003.[66]

One year later, a press release from the Office of the Press Secretary on August 16, 2004, stated, "This year, the list of veterans waiting more than six months for basic medical care, which peaked at 300,000, will be essentially eliminated."[67]

Beginning as early as 2007, the VA received criticism for awarding millions of dollars in bonuses despite a major backlog of disability claims and multiple instances of poor care.[68] CNN reported an audit was performed that stated $24 million in bonuses were awarded to thousands of VA technology employees in 2007 and 2008.[69] Some high-level employees received bonuses as much as $73,000.[70] The issue continued through 2010 when another audit revealed $111 million in retention benefits was paid, against policy, to 16,487 VA employees.[71]

Issues with patient care bubbled to the surface in 2009 when the VA announced that ten thousand veterans in Florida, Georgia, and Tennessee were potentially exposed to infections during colonoscopies as a result of equipment that had not been disinfected properly.[72] Over forty veterans consequently contracted hepatitis or HIV.[73] Two years later nine more veterans contracted hepatitis after receiving dental work at an Ohio VA clinic where the dentist admitted to neglecting to change gloves or wash his hands between patients.[74] Also that year, approximately 40 veterans contracted Legionnaires' disease from a VA hospital in Pennsylvania.[75] Several died as a result of the disease.[76] This outbreak occurred due to a contaminated water source that the hospital had been aware of for several months.[77]

2. THE SECRET WAIT LIST SCANDAL

2.1 Development. The bracketed area within figure 1 shows from 2010 to 2015, there was a steady number of aging Vietnam veterans as well as a steep increase in younger Iraq and Afghanistan veterans.[78] Together, this resulted in an increased overall veteran population. Although this imbalance will level out beginning in 2015, the past few years saw virtually no decline in any veteran groups.

In addition to the increased overall veteran population, there is a rising VA patient population as well. There were 84 million documented outpatient visits in 2012, a 23 percent increase from 2008.[79] Some VA physicians each care for approximately 2,000 patients.[80] This is 800 more per physician than the goal outlined in the Veterans Health Administration handbook.[81] According to the Department of Defense, 24,000 servicemen and women have been wounded in action since commencement of military action in the Middle East.[82] Due to blast injuries, 28 percent of these service members have some degree of brain trauma and are at risk of suffering from mental health impairments such as post-traumatic stress disorder (PTSD).[83] In 2004, the VA responded to the New Freedom Commission on Mental Health by finalizing a five-year Mental Health Strategic Plan, which increased services for and awareness of mental health impairments.[84] Increases in veterans seeking care along with an increase in services provided put a strain on the VA health care system.

Kenneth Kizer was appointed to lead the VA by President Bill Clinton in 1994.[85] He quickly became frustrated by the overwhelming red tape that was still in effect because of the abuse of power committed by Forbes decades earlier.[86] In his mind, if patients were waiting too long for appointments, that information would have to travel up an extensive chain of command before it reached the desk of someone who could make a change.[87] In an attempt to alleviate this issue, Kizer implemented a plan that relied on the theory that statistics could give VA leaders a way to see what was happening on the ground, without the need for middlemen.[88] Kizer reduced VA staffing at the national and regional levels and planned to let the numbers speak for themselves.[89] It is this proposed solution that set the stage for corruption. The numbers-based system that was supposed to alert leaders of problems was instead corrupted to cover up problems.[90]

Since 2005, eighteen incidences of scheduling issues (including long wait times affecting care) were reported by the OIG.[91] Four years ago, a high-ranking VA official issued a memo to all VA medical centers outlining seventeen unethical practices being used to cover up treatment delays.[92] According to this memo and another sent in 2013, these schemes were not acceptable.[93]

In 2009 VA Secretary Eric Shinseki, a Vietnam veteran and the first Asian four-star general, was appointed to lead a major overhaul of the VA.[94] Three guiding principles were adopted to govern the changes: people-centric, results-driven, and forward-looking.[95] Additionally, sixteen major incentives were created.[96] One result of this was a goal for veterans to wait no more than fourteen days for an appointment.[97]

To increase the incentive to implement the fourteen-day standard, leaders of facilities that met this goal were rewarded.[98] Last year, 78 percent of VA senior managers were eligible for bonuses and 100 percent of these managers received evaluation ratings of at least "fully successful."[99]

2.2 Explanation. These apparent successes were actually part of the continuing corrupt management. Scheduling clerks at VA health care facilities across the nation were manipulating the electronic scheduling system to cover up excessive wait times.[100]

This was accomplished by entering patient information into the system to find the next available appointment, sometimes as much as twenty-one months away.[101] The clerk would then inform the patient of this date, take a screen shot, and print the information.[102] The electronic record would then be deleted and the scheduling information would be entered into a separate, secret list and the hard copy would be destroyed.[103] The patient would be moved from the secret list to the official list when the appointment was fourteen days away.[104] This would make it seem that the patient had waited an appropriate amount of time, even though that was not the case.[105]

A VA hospital in Phoenix, Arizona, became the poster child of this scandal. Between 1,400 and 1,600 veterans were on their secret wait list.[106] At least 40 veterans died while waiting for care, some of whom were on this list.[107] Despite this, an administrator at the Phoenix VA hospital received an $8,500 performance bonus in 2014.[108]

Across the nation, 177,000 veterans were waiting at least two months for care, and 93 VA facilities are being investigated as a result.[109] As many as 300 veteran deaths have now been allegedly linked to exorbitant time spent on secret wait lists.[110]

2.3 Timeline

End of 2013

- Credible complaints were made to the Office of Inspector General (OIG) by Dr. Sam Foote, a retired VA physician.[111]

January 2014

- The OIG began an official investigation at the Phoenix VA hospital.[112]

April 2014

- The first hearing regarding the scheduling scandal occurred at the House Veterans' Affairs Committee.[113]

- CNN published an interview with Dr. Foote about the scandal, which brought national attention to the issue.[114]
- Three Phoenix VA leaders were put on administrative leave.[115]

May 2014

- Undersecretary for Health at the VA, Robert Petzel, resigned.[116] While this pleased many, others were unsatisfied because his retirement, scheduled for later this year, had already been announced.[117]
- The OIG began a review of 42 medical facilities.[118]
- On May 21, the House of Representatives passed a bill that gave the VA secretary power to fire senior executives.[119] Previously, federal civil service regulations made it difficult to fire a civil servant.[120]
- On May 30, Secretary Shinseki accepted responsibility for the VA failures and resigned.[121]

June 2014

- The 14-day appointment goal established by Shinseki was removed, and it was announced that there would be no 2014 executive performance bonuses.[122]
- The FBI opened a criminal investigation of the VA scandal. This investigation was centered on, but not limited to, the Phoenix VA hospital.[123]

July 2014

- The Senate confirmed Robert McDonald as the new VA secretary.[124] McDonald was a West Point graduate and served in the Army for five years. Most recently, he was the CEO of Procter & Gamble.[125]

August 2014

- VA Inspector General Richard Griffin reported to the Senate Committee on Veterans' Affairs, stating his office's investigation found "poor quality of care," but the office was "unable to conclusively assert that the absence of timely care caused the death of these veterans."[126]
- President Barack Obama signed the Veterans' Access to Care through Choice, Accountability, and Transparency Act of 2014.[127] This allows veterans who live 40 or more miles away from a VA health facility or who have waited a month or more for care to be seen by a private physician at no cost to the veteran.[128] Additionally, VA staff will be increased by thousands, and 27 new clinics will be opened.[129] This will cost the federal government $16.3 billion.[130]

September 2014

- On September 9, Secretary McDonald reported a VA reform plan to the Senate Committee on Veterans' Affairs.[131]
- On September 17, at a hearing before the House Committee on Veterans' Affairs, Inspector General Griffin backed down from his original claim

that wait times did not cause veteran deaths.[132] When asked point-blank if he agreed that wait lists contributed to the deaths of veterans, Griffin responded affirmatively.[133]

November 2014

- On November 10, Secretary McDonald announced "My VA," the largest reorganization of the VA since its creation.[134]

3. INITIAL RESPONSE

3.1 VA Response. Initially, there was no VA response. Secretary Shinseki gave very few interviews about the topic of VA scheduling issues. One interview, which did not address alleged veteran deaths, was with PBS *NewsHour* and took place in March 2014, a month before the scandal erupted.[135] He gave one interview after the VA patient backlog had gained national attention. This interview was not recorded, but was dictated and published on the Military Times website.[136]

CNN reportedly began investigating the VA patient backlog in November 2013.[137] Despite multiple written and verbal interview requests, Shinseki never responded.[138] One VA spokesperson said comments could not be provided so as not to interfere with the OIG's investigation.[139] Though several written statements from Shinseki were released, he did not give media interviews.[140] Shinseki did testify numerous times in congressional hearings, once where he revealed a raw, emotional side that contrasted with the tone of his polished written statements. He said that if the allegations are true, the fraud and abuse make him "mad as hell."[141]

Other VA leaders echoed Shinseki's silence. After refusing to give any interviews, Arizona administrators agreed to one interview with CNN a week after the initial story broke.[142] In this interview, Sharon Helman said she had no knowledge of any secret wait list.[143] Helman refused any interviews after subsequently being put on administrative leave.[144]

3.2 Public Response. Though there was silence from the VA, virtually everyone else was willing to voice an opinion about the issue. Anger, distrust, and a myriad of other negative reactions came from all across the nation.

According to NPR News, President Obama expressed his thoughts about the VA scheduling scandal, saying, "If these allegations prove to be true, it is dishonorable, it is disgraceful, and I will not tolerate it—period."[145] The president even agreed to discuss it in nontraditional settings such as *Live with Kelly and Michael*.[146] He told ABC hosts Kelly Ripa and Michael Strahan that he was planning to have a serious discussion with Shinseki about his future with the VA.[147]

Members of Congress on Capitol Hill were vocal about their dissatisfaction with the VA as well. According to Matthew Daly in an article published by the Military Times, Democratic Senator Mark Udall said the VA is "suffering from an absence of public leadership and is foundering as a result."[148] Richard Blumenthal, another Democratic senator, spoke out in May calling for the FBI's involvement, saying the OIG did not have the resources to handle this issue.[149] This negative sentiment was felt across party lines as well. According to the same article by Daly, Republican Senator John McCain said, "This has created in our veterans community a crisis of confidence toward the VA."[150]

Veterans groups agreed. The American Legion is an organization with more than 2.4 million veteran members.[151] Its national commander, Michael D. Helm, wrote a letter to President Obama expressing his organization's frustration with the government's lack of action and progress when dealing with the VA issues.[152] In this letter he said:

> Mr. President, I understand that you cannot be held responsible for every act of malfeasance that occurs in the federal government. But let me assure you that if someone on my staff were found to be cooking the books, committing fraud or putting career ambitions ahead of veterans' lives, they wouldn't be transferred or suspended with pay. They would be fired immediately. Our VA employees should be held to the same standard.[153]

He continued on to say that although the American people may have let the VA scandal fall from the forefront of their minds, the American Legion will never forget about the justice and quality of care this country's veterans deserve.[154]

Deputy director of the Veterans of Foreign Wars' (VFW) National Veterans Service Directorate, Ryan M. Gallucci, testified in May before the Senate Veterans' Affairs Committee.[155] He said the VFW is both frustrated and outraged. According to an article on the VFW website, he told the committee, "The allegations are causing veterans and their families to rapidly lose faith and confidence in a system that is supposed to care for them, which is unacceptable."[156] When the VFW reached out to veterans asking for their opinion about the scandal and their own care, hundreds responded.[157] Some were satisfied with their experience, while others reported a clearly overburdened system of care.[158] Almost everyone, however, wanted answers and accountability from the VA.[159]

Younger veterans have also spoken out about their experience with and frustration about waiting for care at VA facilities. Andrew O'Brien, a twenty-six-year-old Army veteran who served in Iraq, told NBC News, "As a young veteran myself, I do not feel as though the world owes me something for what I did. I signed up out of my own free will. But, the one place I do expect appreciation and respect more than anywhere is the VA—and that's the last place you're going to find it."[160] Founder and executive director of Iraq and Afghanistan Veterans of America (IAVA), Paul Rieckhoff, said, "There's an old saying that VA is supposed to stand for veterans' advocate. But too often, it ends up standing for veterans' adversary."[161]

IAVA created a website called thewaitwecarry.org. This is an interactive website that has information about wait times veterans are experiencing across the country.[162] It calls on veterans to share their experience and to use #EndTheVABacklog to get the attention of public officials.[163] The peak of social media discussion of the VA scheduling scandal clearly occurred during the month of May. Other hashtags surrounding the discussion included #SaveOurVets, #VAScandal, and #VASurge.

3.3 Media Response. The media's coverage of the VA scheduling scandal was almost entirely negative. Even before official reports from the OIG or FBI were concluded, news outlets used language that gave the impression there was a clear scandal and veterans undoubtedly died as a result of VA wait times.

Examples include headlines such as "A fatal wait: Veterans languish and die on a VA hospital's secret list"[164] and "Death toll from Veterans Affairs delays, incompetence climbing."[165] Many stories made accusations about where blame for the scandal should fall. Some believed it was Shinseki, some blamed the VA system as a whole, others still pointed to the president. One article attributed blame with the headline "Obama has every reason to fix the VA. Why hasn't he?"[166] Jon Stewart, a comedian who isn't concerned with political correctness, also got in on the VA discussion. In an episode of his television series, *The Daily Show*, he said, "General Shinseki, since you've headed up the VA since 2009, five years into your tenure might be a good time to better convey the anger you say you feel. Your mad as hell face looks a lot like your, oh, we're out of orange juice, face."[167]

When one person called for neutrality in reporting, he was openly criticized. Senator Bernie Sanders, chair of the Senate Committee on Veterans' Affairs, told C-SPAN, "If we're going to do our job in a proper and responsible way, we need to get the facts and not rush to judgment. And one of the concerns I have, to be very honest, is there has been a little bit of a rush to judgment."[168] In response to Sanders's position on the media's response to the VA scheduling scandal, a CNN host asked Sanders, "Is it unfair criticism, Senator, to say that you sound like a lawyer defending the hospital as opposed to a senator trying to make sure the right thing is done?"[169] This question clearly drew a line in the sand between defense of the VA hospital and doing the right thing.

In addition to questionable objectivity of some news sources, there was a debatably unethical delay in coverage of the VA scheduling scandal. CNN reported that it had been investigating the situation since November 2013.[170] Despite its six-month wait, CNN delayed releasing its story until it felt timing was right for maximum impact. CNN was criticized for its large amount of coverage of the missing Malaysian plane, but its arguably excessive coverage could have been a strategic move.[171] "Quite frankly, the plane coverage bought us some of that time," said CNN senior investigative reporter Drew Griffin to Hadas Gold of *Politico*.[172] "Once there was a news hole opening we were ready to go."[173]

This delay in coverage paired with the lack of public discussion of the issue prior to April leads to the conclusion that agenda setting played a role in the overall response of this scandal. People knew there were issues because they (or their loved ones) had experienced the wait times firsthand at VA health care facilities across the country. Despite the large number of people affected, there was virtual silence surrounding the issue until the media put it on the public's agenda. Only after CNN found its "hole" and published its stories did public outrage begin.

4. SECRETARY MCDONALD'S ACTIONS

4.1 Summary. In July of 2014 the Senate confirmed Robert McDonald as the new VA secretary.[174] About a month later, McDonald gave a report on his plan for action to the Senate Committee on Veterans' Affairs.[175] Because of the Phoenix VA's large contributions to this scandal, McDonald specifically reported on actions that had been taken at that facility. There, two top VA executives were replaced and 53 new positions were added.[176] In regard to the Phoenix wait list, 146,596 appointments were completed from May to July, and as of August 15, only 56 veterans remained on the wait list.[177] Thanks to new regulations set forth by the Veterans' Access to Care through Choice, Accountability, and Transparency Act, every person on this waiting list was contacted and scheduled for an appointment at a private physician's office if a timely appointment was not available at the Phoenix VA.[178]

McDonald also reported on actions being taken nationwide. Across the country, 226,000 veterans were contacted to get them off a waiting list, which had decreased in size by 57 percent.[179] Additionally, 975,741 referrals had been made to private physicians, which is approximately 200,000 more than the same time last year.[180] Over 13,000 performance plans were amended, which included the deletion of 14-day appointment goals.[181] Finally, every VA health care facility was scheduled to have a face-to-face audit by September 30.[182]

On November 10, the eve of Veterans' Day, McDonald announced "the largest reorganization of the Department of Veterans Affairs since its establishment. We're calling it 'My VA' because that's what we want veterans to think about it."[183] The VA plans to put a new emphasis on customer service with the appointment of a new chief customer service officer.[184] It also plans to increase its public-private partnerships while decreasing veteran exposure to the overwhelming VA bureaucracy.[185] Currently veterans must navigate 12 different websites to manage their benefits.[186] McDonald seeks to streamline these services into one portal that will then push veterans to the proper place for information and service.[187]

McDonald has stressed transparency and access through actions such as veteran town hall meetings, media interviews with virtually every major news station, appearances at several veteran organization meetings and conventions, and by insisting that people call him by his first name.[188] "Call me Bob, I'm Bob," Secretary McDonald said, as he drew a pyramid to explain his plan that had veterans written at the top and himself at the bottom.[189] He also gave out his personal cell phone number to a room of reporters on live television that has resulted in about 900 calls or text messages.[190]

McDonald echoed Shinseki's "mad as hell" response by saying in a *60 Minutes* interview that he was "incensed" when he read the OIG report detailing the widespread scheduling deceit and the possible fatal results.[191] In a response to calls for disciplinary actions from media and veterans alike, McDonald reported that at least 35 people are already facing such actions, and 1,000 could be next.[192] At the conclusion of 2014, only two senior VA health facility leaders have been fired: Jamel Talton from the central Alabama VA,[193] and most recently and notably, Sharon Helman from the Phoenix VA, who was dismissed on November 24.[194]

When asked during a *60 Minutes* interview who should be fired, McDonald responded by saying anyone who violated our values of integrity, advocacy, respect, and excellence.[195] In order to fire a government manager he has to present the case and get a judge's approval. Even then, the person in question can appeal the ruling, so it is often a long process. McDonald said that is why there are so many on administrative leave right now.[196] Those who need to leave have been removed from day-to-day operations, but it will take some time to remove them from the VA completely.[197]

As the weak links are fired, McDonald seeks to add new VA employees that will help fix the problem. McDonald said he needs to hire 28,000 medical professionals including 2,500 mental health professionals to meet the needs of the current VA population.[198] He admitted this will take time, but has begun to provide VA physicians with raises so their salaries would be more comparable with private positions.[199] "It's gonna take time because every adverse outcome that gets amplified by the media doesn't help me."[200] He admitted the VA has a bad reputation, but stated emphatically that they are changing that reputation.[201] McDonald is personally recruiting physicians. He has made personal visits to employees at top hospitals such as Massachusetts General, as well as medical schools, and has made personal phone calls to physicians he wants on his team.[202]

McDonald had visited 41 VA facilities as of November 2014, and this, he says, is because he "wants to get to the bottom of things."[203] McDonald is using his past managerial and business know-how to implement changes. One obvious spillover from Procter & Gamble to the VA is that he calls veterans "customers."[204] In his mind, the customer always comes first.[205] "We have no hope of taking care of veterans if we don't take care of each other," he told a VA health care facility staff during one of his visits.[206] Sloan Gibson, fellow West Point classmate and McDonald's new number two, visited Phoenix first. He said he saw a system failure, not a failure of the people at the heart of the VA.[207]

McDonald wrote an open letter to veterans and VA employees in November outlining some of the plans to improve the VA and reminding everyone that it will be a long road to recovery.[208] He wrote, "We don't have all the answers right now, and that's why we are reaching out to you for your thoughts. This will be a fair and deliberate process, and we need your help to make sure our decisions are the right ones for our veterans."[209]

One way the VA is reaching out is through the My VA Idea House, a website powered by the VA with the tagline "Let your ideas light the way."[210] The goal of this website is for people to submit ideas to improve the VA.[211] Later, VA employees will vote for the ideas they believe will be most successful.[212] Another is through social media. In July, the VA launched #VetQ, which stands for veterans questions, and is an initiative that hopes to provide information and answers for veterans and their loved ones who have service-related questions.[213] The VA partnered with at least eight veteran organizations to collectively answer questions via social media and curate the conversation on Storify.[214]

According to Ben Kesling of the *Wall Street Journal*, veteran groups are responding well to the new secretary's hands-on, open-door approach to the situation.[215] IAVA executive Paul Rieckhoff told the *New York Times*, "We think [McDonald's plan] is a good step forward, but it is only one of a marathon of steps that are going to be required to turn this around. We'll see over the next few years if he can make it happen."[216] When asked about McDonald's plan for reform, Pete Hegsdeth, leader of Concerned Veterans for America, told the *Washington Examiner*, "It's good to hear [McDonald] talk about it, but he needs to do it."[217]

The public and veteran groups seem cautiously optimistic about the future of the VA and its new leader, who unlike his predecessors, has experience supervising people outside the military.[218] In a stark contrast to previous stories about the VA and its leadership, even the media displays some degree of optimism and trust in McDonald and the future of the VA. Reports of scandal and incompetence have been replaced with headlines such as "Robert McDonald: Cleaning up the VA."[219] Fox News said of Secretary McDonald, "His commitment to the cause is clear and obvious."[220]

McDonald was asked by *60 Minutes* reporter Scott Pelley, "What do you owe these veterans?"[221] Through teary eyes he described the important, sincere, and lasting relationships he formed with those he served with as well as the veterans he has met since.[222] In a statement full of poignancy and no political bravado, he emphatically declared, "This is very personal."[223]

4.2 Analysis of Communication Strategies. McDonald's public relations and communication strategy developed through four distinct steps. First, he made it clear that the VA accepted full responsibility for any and all wrongdoing. Admission of guilt was something the public desired after months of silence from the VA.

Second, he took immediate action. In health care terms, the goal of this step was to "stop the bleeding." With an issue of this magnitude and breadth, a short-term solution could not be the only solution, but McDonald had to show the VA was taking its patients seriously and was ready to act in any way possible.

Third, McDonald conducted research to determine how to proceed. This was the most important and successful element of McDonald's communication strategy. He used a transparent, hands-on approach to research that took the form of both one-way and two-way communication. He used open letters, media interviews, government reports, and veteran meeting appearances to communicate his thoughts and plans to all relevant stakeholders. McDonald then took this one-way communication to the next level by asking for help from others. He opened the door to opinions, advice, and questions from stakeholders through town hall meetings, social media, personal visits to VA health care facilities, and even by giving out his personal cell phone number. McDonald realized that silence is not a way to pause inquiries, but that it is a response in and of itself. Therefore, he spoke up even when he didn't have a simple or easy answer.

Information gathered from the research stage will be used to move into step four, which is to create a long-term solution. Currently, McDonald is working toward this goal as media coverage declines and public outrage wanes. He has successfully established trust in and hope of a better system of care for America's veterans. Only time will tell if he will continue to keep open lines of communication and follow through with his promises of a renewed VA.

5. SUMMARY

The VA has a history of communication crises. Appalling internal communication led to years of corruption and deceit between regional and federal leaders. Communication between the VA and its stakeholders suffered as well. This left veterans frustrated, confused, and most importantly, poorly cared for. In the wake of the scheduling scandal, silence from VA officials fueled the media fire, making matters worse for everyone.

Finally, after the appointment of new VA Secretary Robert McDonald, communication channels opened and tempers began to cool. McDonald used a hands-on approach of personally discussing the matter with virtually anyone who wanted to talk about it, from reporters to physicians to patients.

Veterans and other stakeholders will surely keep an eye on McDonald. It remains to be seen if he can improve the structural integrity of the VA and walk the walk as well as he talks the talk. Thus far, one thing is clear: in a very short time, he has effectively used transparency and honesty to begin to improve the damaged brand image of the US Department of Veterans Affairs.

REFERENCES

1. United States Department of Veterans Affairs (n.d.). VA history. Retrieved from http://www.va.gov/about_va/vahistory.asp.

2. Hicks, Josh (2014). Some key facts about VA's Veterans Health Administration. *Washington Post.*

3. Harper, Jon (2014, April 25, 2014). Congress to probe Phoenix VA system amid outrage over reported 'secret' waiting lists. McClatchy—Tribune Business News.

4. Ure, Laurie (2009). VA workers given millions in bonuses as vets await checks. CNN. Retrieved from http://www.cnn.com/2009/POLITICS/08/22/veterans.affairs.bonuses/.

5–6. United States Department of Veterans Affairs (n.d.). VA history. Retrieved from http://www.va.gov/about_va/vahistory.asp.

7–8. United States Department of Veterans Affairs (n.d.). VA history in brief. Retrieved from http://www.va.gov/opa/publications/archives/docs/history_in_brief.pdf.

9. United States Department of Veterans Affairs (n.d.). VA history. Retrieved from http://www.va.gov/about_va/vahistory.asp.

10–13. United States Department of Veterans Affairs (n.d.). VA history in brief. Retrieved from http://www.va.gov/opa/publications/archives/docs/history_in_brief.pdf.

14–18. United States Department of Veterans Affairs (n.d.). VA history. Retrieved from http://www.va.gov/about_va/vahistory.asp.

19–20. United States Department of Veterans Affairs (n.d.). VA history in brief. Retrieved from http://www.va.gov/opa/publications/archives/docs/history_in_brief.pdf.

21–22. United States Department of Veterans Affairs (n.d.). VA history. Retrieved from http://www.va.gov/about_va/vahistory.asp.

23. United States Department of Veterans Affairs (n.d.). VA history in brief. Retrieved from http://www.va.gov/opa/publications/archives/docs/history_in_brief.pdf.

24–25. United States Department of Veterans Affairs (n.d.). VA history. Retrieved from http://www.va.gov/about_va/vahistory.asp.

26–35. United States Department of Veterans Affairs (n.d.). VA history in brief. Retrieved from http://www.va.gov/opa/publications/archives/docs/history_in_brief.pdf.

36. United States Department of Veterans Affairs (n.d.). VA history. Retrieved from http://www.va.gov/about_va/vahistory.asp.

37–40. United States Department of Veterans Affairs (n.d.). VA history in brief. Retrieved from http://www.va.gov/opa/publications/archives/docs/history_in_brief.pdf.

41–43. Hicks, Josh (2014). Some key facts about VA's Veterans Health Administration. *Washington Post*.

44. Fahrenthold, David A. (2014). How the VA developed its culture of coverups. *Washington Post*. Retrieved from http://www.washingtonpost.com/sf/national/2014/05/30/how-the-va-developed-its-culture-of-coverups/.

45. Ohio History Central (n.d.). Charles Forbes. Retrieved from http://www.ohiohistorycentral.org/w/Charles_Forbes.

46. Fahrenthold, David A. (2014). How the VA developed its culture of coverups. *Washington Post*. Retrieved from http://www.washingtonpost.com/sf/national/2014/05/30/how-the-va-developed-its-culture-of-coverups/.

47. United States Department of Veterans Affairs (n.d.). VA history in brief. Retrieved from http://www.va.gov/opa/publications/archives/docs/history_in_brief.pdf.

48. Pearson, Michael (2014). The VA's troubled history. CNN. Retrieved from http://www.cnn.com/2014/05/23/politics/va-scandals-timeline/.

49–50. United States Department of Veterans Affairs (n.d.). VA history in brief. Retrieved from http://www.va.gov/opa/publications/archives/docs/history_in_brief.pdf.

51. Levine, Murray, & Levine, Adeline Gordon (2011). Who said the government can't do anything right? The World War II GI Bill, the growth of science, and American prosperity. *American Journal of Orthopsychiatry*, 81(2), 149–156. doi:10.1111/j.1939-0025.2011.01082.x.

52. Pearson, Michael (2014). The VA's troubled history. CNN. Retrieved from http://www.cnn.com/2014/05/23/politics/va-scandals-timeline/.

53–56. Gay, Margaret (2011). Ron Kovic. In K. Gay (ed.), *American dissidents: An encyclopedia of activists, subversives, and prisoners of conscience*, volume 1 (pp. 360–361, 362). Santa Barbara, California: ABC-CLIO.

57–58. Pearson, Michael (2014). The VA's troubled history. CNN. Retrieved from http://www.cnn.com/2014/05/23/politics/va-scandals-timeline/.

59. Gay, Margaret (2011). Ron Kovic. In K. Gay (ed.), *American dissidents: An encyclopedia of activists, subversives, and prisoners of conscience*, volume 1 (pp. 360–361, 362). Santa Barbara, California: ABC-CLIO.

60–62. Millenson, Michael L. (1991). North Chicago VA hospital under fire. *Chicago Tribune.* Retrieved from http://articles.chicagotribune.com/1991-03-27/news/9101270620_1 _poor-care-hospital-surgery.

63. Pearson, Michael (2014). The VA's troubled history. CNN. Retrieved from http://www.cnn.com/2014/05/23/politics/va-scandals-timeline/.

64–66. Department of Veterans Affairs Office of Inspector General (2013). Audit of Veterans Health Administration's reported medical care waiting lists. (No. 02-02129-95). Washington, D.C.: VA Office of Inspector General.

67. Office of the Press Secretary (2004). Fact sheet: Honoring our commitment to America's veterans. Retrieved from http://georgewbush-whitehouse.archives.gov/news/re leases/2004/08/20040816-3.html.

68–70. Ure, Laurie (2009). VA workers given millions in bonuses as vets await checks. CNN. Retrieved from http://www.cnn.com/2009/POLITICS/08/22/veterans.affairs.bonuses/.

71. Veterans Affairs Office of Inspector General (2011). Audit of intention incentive of Veterans Health Administration and VA Central Office employees. (No. 10-02887-30). Washington D.C.: VA Office of Inspector General.

72–74. Pearson, Michael (2014). The VA's troubled history. CNN. Retrieved from http://www.cnn.com/2014/05/23/politics/va-scandals-timeline/.

75–77. Black, Nelli, & Griffin, Drew (2012). VA under scrutiny after Legionnaires' cases in Pittsburgh. CNN. Retrieved from http://www.cnn.com/2012/12/13/health/legionnaires -hospital-water/.

78. United States Department of Veterans Affairs (2014). Quick facts-National Center for Veterans Analysis and Statistics. Retrieved from http://www.va.gov/vetdata/Quick_Facts.asp.

79–81. Somashekhar, Sandhya (2014). VA and its systemic health-care problems. *Washington Post.*

82–83. Bascetta, Cynthia A. (2007). DOD and VA health care [electronic resource]: Challenges encountered by injured servicemembers during their recovery process: Testimony before the Subcommittee on National Security and Foreign Affairs, Committee on Oversight and Government Reform, House of Representatives / statement of cynthia A. bascetta Washington, D.C. [U.S. Govt. Accountability Office, 2007].

84. Pincus, Harold Alan, & Watkins, Katherine E. (2011). Veterans Health Administration mental health program evaluation. (Capstone Report). Santa Monica, CA: RAND Corporation.

85–90. Fahrenthold, David A. (2014). How the VA developed its culture of coverups. *Washington Post.* Retrieved from http://www.washingtonpost.com/sf/national/2014/05/30/ how-the-va-developed-its-culture-of-coverups/.

91–93. Hicks, Josh (2014). Some key facts about VA's Veterans Health Administration. *Washington Post.*

94–96. Kesling, Ben, Crittenden, Michael R., & Nelson, Colleen McCain (2014, May 31). Heat stays on VA after exit—Shinseki resigns, but successor faces entrenched health-care problems at agency. *Wall Street Journal.*

97–99. Cohen, Tom, & Decine, Curt (2014). Performance reviews at troubled VA showed no bad senior managers. CNN. Retrieved from http://www.cnn.com/2014/06/20/politics/ va-scandal-bonuses/index.html.

100–105. Bronstein, Scott, & Griffin, Drew (2014). A fatal wait: Veterans languish and die on a VA hospital's secret list. CNN. Retrieved from http://www.cnn.com/2014/04/23/ health/veterans-dying-health-care-delays/.

106–107. Harper, Jon (2014, April 25, 2014). Congress to probe Phoenix VA system amid outrage over reported 'secret' waiting lists. McClatchy—Tribune Business News.

108. Cohen, Tom, & Decine, Curt (2014). Performance reviews at troubled VA showed no bad senior managers. CNN. Retrieved from http://www.cnn.com/2014/06/20/politics/va-scandal-bonuses/index.html.

109. Zoroya, Gregg (2014, August 27). FBI, Justice Department to investigate 93 VA facilities. *USA Today*.

110. Devine, Curt, & Bronstein, Scott (2014). VA inspector general admits wait times contributed to vets' deaths. CNN. Retrieved from http://www.cnn.com/2014/09/17/politics/va-whistleblowers-congressional-hearing/index.html.

111–114. Kesling, Ben (2014, April 25). U.S. news: VA expands a probe of Phoenix hospital. *Wall Street Journal*.

115. The American Legion (2014). Phoenix VA staff placed on leave. Politics & Government Business.

116–117. Kesling, Ben (2014). Senior VA official resigns in wake of allegations; undersecretary for health resigns one day after testifying in front of senate hearing. *Wall Street Journal* (online).

118. Phillips, Erica E. (2014, June 5). Acting VA head makes first public appearance; Sloan Gibson visited Phoenix hospital at center of nationwide scandal. *Wall Street Journal* (online).

119–120. O'Keefe, Ed (2014). What is the VA Accountability Act? *Washington Post*. Retrieved from http://www.washingtonpost.com/blogs/post-politics/wp/2014/05/21/what-is-the-va-accountability-act/.

121. Kesling, Ben, Crittenden, Michael R., & Nelson, Colleen McCain (2014, May 31). Heat stays on VA after exit—Shinseki resigns, but successor faces entrenched health-care problems at agency. *Wall Street Journal*.

122. Phillips, Erica E. (2014, June 5). Acting VA head makes first public appearance; Sloan Gibson visited Phoenix hospital at center of nationwide scandal. *Wall Street Journal* (online).

123. Kesling, Ben (2014, September 8). VA director outlines plan for fixing veterans' health care; Secretary Robert McDonald gives broad goals with few specific details on revamping beleaguered organization. *Wall Street Journal* (online).

124–125. Kesling, Ben (2014, September 8). VA director outlines plan for fixing veterans' health care; Secretary Robert McDonald gives broad goals with few specific details on revamping beleaguered organization. *Wall Street Journal* (online).

126. Department of Veterans Affairs Office of Inspector General (2014). Review of alleged patient deaths, patient wait times, and scheduling practices at the Phoenix VA healthcare system. (No. 14-02603-267). Washington, D.C.: VA Office of Inspector General.

127–130. Daly, Matthew, & Superville, Darlene (2014). Boost for vets' health: Obama signs new law. Associated Press DBA Press Association.

131. McDonald, Robert A. (2014). Statement of the honorable Robert A. McDonald Secretary of Veterans Affairs before the Senate Committee on Veterans' Affairs. Retrieved from http://www.veterans.senate.gov/imo/media/doc/VA%20Testimony%209.9.14.pdf.

132–133. Devine, Curt, & Bronstein, Scott (2014). VA inspector general admits wait times contributed to vets' deaths. CNN. Retrieved from http://www.cnn.com/2014/09/17/politics/va-whistleblowers-congressional-hearing/index.html.

134. Devine, Curt, & Diamond, Jeremy (2014). VA chief announces restructuring, firings. CNN. Retrieved from http://www.cnn.com/2014/11/10/politics/va-reforms-and-restructuring/.

135. Extended interview: VA Secretary Shinseki responds to benefits backlog. (2014). [Video/DVD] http://www.youtube.com/watch?v=gUWdMnFLLpk: PBS NewsHour.

136. Shane, Leo (2014). To veterans: VA is here to care for you. Military Times. Retrieved from http://www.militarytimes.com/article/20140507/BENEFITS04/305070054/Shinseki -veterans-VA-here-care-you.

137. Bronstein, Scott, Griffin, Drew, & Black, Nelli (2014). VA chief Eric Shinseki not talking about delays. CNN. Retrieved from http://www.cnn.com/2014/05/02/politics/ veterans-dying-shinseki-not-talking/.

138–140. Bronstein, Scott, Griffin, Drew, & Black, Nelli (2014). VA chief Eric Shinseki not talking about delays. CNN. Retrieved from http://www.cnn.com/2014/05/02/politics/ veterans-dying-shinseki-not-talking/.

141. Mulrine, Anna (2014). Secretary Shinseki 'mad as hell' over VA deaths, not ready to resign. *Christian Science Monitor*. Retrieved from http://www.csmonitor.com/USA/Mili tary/2014/0515/Secretary-Shinseki-mad-as-hell-over-VA-deaths-not-ready-to-resign-video.

142–144. Bronstein, Scott, Griffin, Drew, & Black, Nelli (2014). VA chief Eric Shinseki not talking about delays. CNN. Retrieved from http://www.cnn.com/2014/05/02/politics/ veterans-dying-shinseki-not-talking/.

145. Liasson, Mara (2014). Politicians on both sides of the aisle outraged over VA scandal. Morning Edition (NPR).

146–147. Miller, Zeke J. (2014). Shinseki removing hospital leadership amid mounting calls for his resignation. Time.com, 1-1.

148–150. Daly, Matthew (2014). Congress grows impatient on inquiry in VA deaths. Military Times. Retrieved from http://www.militarytimes.com/article/20140516/ NEWS05/305160031.

151–154. The American Legion (2014). American Legion national commander slams lack of accountability at VA in letter to President Obama. *Politics & Government Business*, 7.

155–159. Veterans of Foreign Wars (2014). VFW outraged by VA allegations. Retrieved from http://www.vfw.org/News-and-Events/Articles/2014-Articles/VFW-OUTRAGED-BY -VA-ALLEGATIONS/.

160–161. Briggs, Bill (2014). New generation of vets demands a VA for the 21st century. NBC News. Retrieved from http://www.nbcnews.com/storyline/va-hospital-scandal/new -generation-vets-demands-va-21st-century-n104606.

162–163. Iraq and Afghanistan Veterans of America (2014). The wait we carry. Retrieved from www.thewaitwecarry.org.

164. Bronstein, Scott, & Griffin, Drew (2014). A fatal wait: Veterans languish and die on a VA hospital's secret list. CNN. Retrieved from http://www.cnn.com/2014/04/23/health/ veterans-dying-health-care-delays/.

165. Tapscott, Mark (2014). Death toll from veterans affairs delays, incompetence ris- ing. Washington Examiner. Retrieved from http://www.washingtonexaminer.com/death-toll -from-veterans-affairs-delays-incompetence-climbing/article/2548652.

166. Carney, Jordain, & Kaper, Stacy (2014). Obama has every reason to fix the VA. Why hasn't he? *National Journal*. Retrieved from http://www.nationaljournal.com/defense/obama -has-every-reason-to-fix-the-va-why-hasn-t-he-20140514.

167. Liasson, Mara (2014). Politicians on both sides of the aisle outraged over VA scandal. Morning Edition (NPR).

168–169. Parker, Bruch (2014). Sen. Bernie Sanders stuns nation with response to VA scandal. Fox News. Retrieved from http://nation.foxnews.com/2014/05/27/sen-bernie-sanders -stuns-nation-response-va-scandal.

170–173. Gold, Hadas (2014). Anatomy of a veterans affairs scandal. *Politico*. Retrieved from http://www.politico.com/story/2014/05/veterans-administration-scandal-106982.html.

174–182. McDonald, Robert A. (2014). Statement of the honorable Robert A. McDonald Secretary of Veterans Affairs before the Senate Committee on Veterans' Affairs. Retrieved from http://www.veterans.senate.gov/imo/media/doc/VA%20Testimony%209.9.14.pdf.

183. Devine, Curt, & Diamond, Jeremy (2014). VA chief announces restructuring, firings. CNN. Retrieved from http://www.cnn.com/2014/11/10/politics/va-reforms-and -restructuring/.

184–187. Leonard, Kimberly (2014). Massive VA overhaul announced. *US News & World Report*. Retrieved from http://www.usnews.com/news/articles/2014/11/10/robert-mcdonald -announces-massive-va-health-overhaul.

188. Kesling, Ben (2014, September 8). VA director outlines plan for fixing veterans' health care; Secretary Robert McDonald gives broad goals with few specific details on revamping beleaguered organization. *Wall Street Journal* (online).

189–190. Wax-Tibodeaux, Emily (2014). VA secretary: 'We've got to design this organization so it doesn't depend on my cell phone,' *Washington Post*. Retrieved from http://www .washingtonpost.com/blogs/federal-eye/wp/2014/11/14/va-secretary-weve-got-to-design-this -organization-so-it-doesnt-depend-on-my-cellphone/.

191. Pelley, Scott (2014). Robert McDonald: Cleaning up the VA. *60 Minutes*. Retrieved from http://www.cbsnews.com/news/robert-mcdonald-cleaning-up-the-veterans-affairs-hos pitals/.

192. Wax-Tibodeaux, Emily (2014). VA secretary: 'We've got to design this organization so it doesn't depend on my cell phone.' *Washington Post*. Retrieved from http://www .washingtonpost.com/blogs/federal-eye/wp/2014/11/14/va-secretary-weve-got-to-design-this -organization-so-it-doesnt-depend-on-my-cellphone/.

193. Devine, Curt, & Diamond, Jeremy (2014). VA chief announces restructuring, firings. CNN. Retrieved from http://www.cnn.com/2014/11/10/politics/va-reforms-and -restructuring/.

194. Klimas, Jacqueline (2014). VA fires head of Phoenix hospital at center of scandal. *The Washington Times*. Retrieved from http://www.washingtontimes.com/news/2014/nov/24/ va-fires-sharon-helman-head-phoenix-hospital-cente/?page=all.

195–207. Pelley, Scott (2014). Robert McDonald: Cleaning up the VA. *60 Minutes*. Retrieved from http://www.cbsnews.com/news/robert-mcdonald-cleaning-up-the-veterans -affairs-hospitals/.

208–209. Leonard, Kimberly (2014). Massive VA overhaul announced. *US News & World Report*. Retrieved from http://www.usnews.com/news/articles/2014/11/10/robert-mcdonald -announces-massive-va-health-overhaul.

210. United States Department of Veterans Affairs (2014). VA idea house. Retrieved from https://vaideahouse.ideascale.com/.

211–212. Hicks, Josh (2014). VA chief unveils restructuring plan for troubled agency. *Washington Post*. Retrieved from http://www.washingtonpost.com/blogs/federal-eye/ wp/2014/11/10/va-chief-unveils-restructuring-plan-for-troubled-agency/.

213. Veterans of Foreign Wars (2014). VFW is first veterans organization to join VA's #VetQ initiative. Retrieved from http://www.vfw.org/News-and-Events/Articles/2014-Arti cles/VFW-is-First-Veterans-Organization-to-Join-VA%E2%80%99s—VetQ-Initiative/.

214. United States Department of Veterans Affairs (2014). #VetQ day 1—veteran ques tions answered. Retrieved from https://storify.com/DeptVetAffairs/vetq-day-1-veteran-ques tions-answered.

215. Kesling, Ben (2014, September 8). VA director outlines plan for fixing veterans' health care; Secretary Robert McDonald gives broad goals with few specific details on revamp ing beleaguered organization. *Wall Street Journal* (online).

216. Oppel, Richard A. (2014). V.A. creates plans to consolidate services. *The New York Times.* Retrieved from http://www.nytimes.com/2014/11/11/us/va-creates-plans-to-consoli date-services.html?_r=1.

217. Cohen, Kelly (2014). Veterans groups challenging the VA secretary to make good on promises of reform. *Washington Examiner.* Retrieved from http://www.washingtonexaminer .com/article/2555996/.

218. Mickelway, Doug (2014). VA secretary pushes major overhaul, firings at agency. Fox News. Retrieved from http://www.foxnews.com/politics/2014/11/10/va-secretary-pushing -major-shakeup-firings-at-agency/.

219. Pelley, Scott (2014). Robert McDonald: Cleaning up the VA. *60 Minutes.* Retrieved from http://www.cbsnews.com/news/robert-mcdonald-cleaning-up-the-veterans-affairs-hos pitals/.

220. Mickelway, Doug (2014). VA secretary pushes major overhaul, firings at agency. Fox News. Retrieved from http://www.foxnews.com/politics/2014/11/10/va-secretary-pushing -major-shakeup-firings-at-agency/.

221–223. Pelley, Scott (2014). Robert McDonald: Cleaning up the VA. *60 Minutes.* Retrieved from http://www.cbsnews.com/news/robert-mcdonald-cleaning-up-the-veterans -affairs-hospitals/.

Case Study 5

#SocialStrong

The Effect of Social Media on the Boston Marathon Bombing

Reprinted with permission from the author, Lexie Broyton, and faculty advisor, Alexander V. Laskin, Ph.D., professor of strategic communication at Quinnipiac University. This case study was the third-prize recipient of the Arthur W. Page Society 2014 Case Study Competition.

OVERVIEW

The devastating Boston Marathon bombings that occurred in April 2013 have forever changed the way social media is viewed. The actions taken in the search for and apprehension of the Tsarnaev brothers gave the public and professionals within communications an in-depth look at the current state of media presence and influences.[1] Many companies decided to halt all social media updates out of respect for the events that occurred. However, news sources continued to search for the latest updates of information.[2] In many cases, the most bountiful resource for news was posted on various social media outlets.

The use of social media outlets during the incident resulted in both positive and negative outcomes affecting the media, authorities, and the general public. Traditional media outlets made extensive use of Twitter and other social media to report the story. In one instance, the *New York Post* ran a front-page photo of two teenagers adjacent to the headline "Bag Men," thereby implying they had a connection to the backpack bombs; the image was taken from a crowdsourcing site.[3] Websites such as Reddit used crowdsourcing where members collectively sifted through images of the bombing scene. These well-meaning people incorrectly accused innocent bystanders whose lives are forever affected.[4] In some cases, Twitter reported misinformation either accidentally or maliciously; then, the information spread on a global plat-form.[5] For example, some untrue stories were circulated, such as conspiracy theories.[6]

Yet in other instances, social media was used very effectively. The Boston Police Department's use of Twitter was arguably one of the most poignant actions amidst all of the noise. The department used social media both cautiously and power-fully to get information out to the public and the media.[7] During a time when cell phone reception was blocked due to the concern of detonating subsequent bombs, Commissioner Ed Davis decided social media was the best route to take in terms of communication tactics.[8] Their approach was a carefully calibrated "command-and-control" use of social media with a selective sharing of timely and factual information to counter media rumors, in turn, reassuring the public while simultaneously protecting the location of investigating officers in a fast-moving and unpredictable environment.[9]

Cheryl Fiandaca, bureau chief of public information, assumed the role of running the department's Twitter feed, which served as an official source for such journalists, authorities, and the public alike.[10] Once the final capture of Dzhokhar Tsarnaev was made, the announcement was not made via press conference but rather on Twitter.[11] The success of the Boston Police Department's Twitter feed has pushed many other police and fire departments to create their own handle. This incident has also started a new conversation centered on the effect of social media during crisis.

HISTORY OF THE BOSTON MARATHON

The Boston Athletic Association has organized the Boston Marathon since it began in 1897. The Boston Marathon is the world's oldest annual marathon and ranks as one of the world's most prestigious road racing events.[12] Typically, the event attracts over 500,000 people per year, making it New England's most widely viewed sport-ing event.[13] The race started with 18 participants in 1897. The event now attracts approximately 20,000 registered participants every year with about 26,839 people registered in 2013.[14] The marathon is considered an American classic and a staple for American athletics. The BAA promotes a healthy lifestyle through the support of various charities, youth, and year-round running programs.[15] The BAA has expanded its presence in the local community through various charity involvements and races. The organization is very much a part of the community's pulse.

MISSION

"Established in 1887, the Boston Athletic Association is a non-profit organization with a mission of managing athletic events and promoting a healthy lifestyle through sports, especially running."[16]

THE PATRIOTS' DAY RACE

During 1897–1968, the Boston Marathon was held on Patriots' Day, April 19. This holiday commemorates the start of the Revolutionary War and is recognized only in Massachusetts and Maine. The only exception allowed was when the nineteenth fell on Sunday. For those years, the race was held the following day (Monday the twentieth). But in 1969, the holiday was officially moved to the third Monday in April. Since 1969 the race has been held on a Monday.[17]

Patriots' Day commemorates the anniversary of the Battles of Lexington and Concord. These victories were the first battles of the Revolutionary War.[18] The day is meant to be a time when Americans celebrate a supreme dedication to freedom while remembering the many battles America had to endure before becoming free.

PAST CRISIS AND MEDIA COVERAGE

Due to the scale of this event, about 1,000 media members from more than 100 outlets receive media credentials. The Boston Marathon has not encountered many crises throughout history. Generally, the press surrounding the race has been very positive and upbeat. Many times any news is related to new partnerships or coverage on runners and their achievements. The most recent issue before the bombing was a scandal involving Rosie Ruiz in the 1980 marathon. Ruiz had been crowned the victor of the 1980 race, but it was later discovered she did not actually finish the entire course. At the time, social media did not exist. However, the reaction of the media was as strong as it is today. Newspaper columnists, television and radio talk show hosts, along with others took part in publicizing the situation with Ruiz.[19] This scandal did shake the BAA but eventually blew over, and the news coverage returned to normal. The only other recorded deaths at the Boston Marathon previous to the bombing were in 1996, when a 62-year-old man died of a heart attack during the one hundredth anniversary event,[20] then again in 2002 when a 28-year-old woman died of hyponatremia.[21] None of these events were as dramatic as what happened at the finish line on Monday, April 15. The tragic event killed three individuals and injured over 200 people, making it the biggest crisis in the marathon's history.

SEQUENCE OF EVENTS

The following is a chronological account of developments in the Boston Marathon bombing case and subsequent investigation, as spelled out in court documents and other official statements, including a federal complaint. The names below reflect authorities' official explanation as to what they believe occurred. The tweets were taken from the Boston Police Department's Twitter account.

Monday, April 15

Morning: The Boston Marathon begins at Hopkinton, Massachusetts, with runners and wheelchair competitors. Almost 23,000 people participate in the race with an abundance of cheering spectators along the 26.2-mile course.[22]

2:38 p.m.: Cameras show two men, later identified by authorities as Tamerlan and Dzhokhar Tsarnaev, turning onto Boylston Street heading east near the location of the finish line and carrying a knapsack.[23]

2:45 p.m.: Dzhokhar Tsarnaev begins walking toward the finish line also carrying a knapsack with a phone in his left hand. He drops the knapsack to the ground at his feet. He remains there for about four minutes, seeming to take a picture with his phone.[24]

2:49 p.m.: Dzhokhar Tsarnaev lifts the phone to his head and speaks for about 18 seconds. He finishes the call, and the first explosion goes off within seconds. He looks to the east, then starts moving west—away from the finish line without the knapsack he had been carrying. Ten seconds later, the second explosion occurs right where Dzhokhar Tsarnaev has left the knapsack.[25]

Wednesday, April 17

Afternoon: Dias Kadyrbayev (a friend of Dzhokhar Tsarnaev since the two enrolled together at the University of Massachusetts-Dartmouth in fall 2011) drives to Tsarnaev's dormitory room and texts his friend to come down and meet him. Kadyrbayev notices that Dzhokhar Tsarnaev has cut his hair short. The two talk, then Tsarnaev goes back to his room.[26]

Evening: Azamat Tazhayakov (Kadyrbayev's roommate at a New Bedford apartment) stays with Dzhokhar Tsarnaev at the apartment until about midnight.[27]

Thursday, April 18

Afternoon: Azamat Tazhayakov attends a class at the University of Massachusetts-Dartmouth, after which Dzhokhar Tsarnaev drives him home to his New Bedford apartment.[28]

5 p.m. ET: The FBI releases pictures of two male suspects being sought in connection with the Boston Marathon bombings.[29]

11 p.m.: Massachusetts Institute of Technology police officer Sean Collier, 26, is shot dead on the school's Cambridge, Massachusetts, campus (the killing is later linked to the Tsarnaevs).[30]

Friday, April 19

Early hours: Police say the two suspects hijack a car at gunpoint in Cambridge, Massachusetts, taking the driver as a hostage. One suspects tells the driver they are the Boston Marathon bombers. Then the suspects talk openly about heading to New York. Eventually, the driver is able to escape his captors by running into a gas station convenience store. From the information gathered from the hostage, authorities track down the suspects. Then, a chase ensues, during which the suspects toss explosives and exchange gunfire with the police. Tamerlan Tsarnaev dies after the gunfight, while Dzhokhar eludes the authorities.[31]

Daytime: Boston and surrounding communities are put on lockdown. Schools are closed, public transit is shut down, and people are ordered off the street.[32] Governor Deval Patrick asks that all residents "shelter in place" and that they not open the door for anyone with the exception of a properly identified law enforcement officer.[33]

6 p.m. to 9 p.m.: After the lockdown is lifted, a resident goes outside to check his boat parked in the backyard. He notices blood inside. This tip leads to a large-scale law enforcement effort that ends with the capture of Dzhokhar Tsarnaev.[34]

BOSTON POLICE DEPARTMENT'S RESPONSE

The Boston Police Department's use of social media was a fairly new concept. Unlike other large-scale city police departments, Boston has invested in its police department's social media presence for a number of years. The department's Twitter account was created in 2009 and was the first to publish public safety information during the St. Patrick's Day parade.[35] Shortly after they opened their Twitter account, the department expanded to Facebook, YouTube, Pinterest, and a video-streaming site, UStream. These sites are all handled by the Bureau of Public Information and provide information to local and national media outlets while handling the majority of media relations functions as part of the Office of the Police Commissioner. The department's Twitter account originally had 54,000 followers. This number grew to over 330,000 people following the account after the events. In total, the account reached approximately 49 million people within five days.[36]

USE OF SOCIAL MEDIA DURING THE BOMBING

The Boston Police team in place during the Boston bombing and the manhunt that occurred in the following days consisted of Bureau Chief Cheryl Fiandaca and three officers responsible for the content on BPD's multiple social media outlets. Fiandaca was a former television news reporter with 16 years of experience working in New York City and Boston.[37] Her ultimate goal was to transform the department into a news organization in addition to carrying out their usual activities. Additionally, Fiandaca stated the department cross-trains staff to perform public relations activities such as writing news releases or posting Facebook and Twitter messages.

"We staffed 24 hours," Fiandaca told the *Huffington Post*. "Someone was always here. We tried to put out as much information as we possibly could without jeopardizing the investigation."

Cheryl Fiandaca, Bureau Chief[38]

During the crisis the Boston Police had blocked cell phone reception due to speculation that phones might have detonated the bombs. The department's blog was a popular source of information (30,000 views monthly), but it crashed due to heavy user traffic.[39] The department's official Twitter account published updates about the incident quickly after the first blast. Fiandaca tweeted from the Boston Police handle @BostonPolice 10 times during approximately a 90-minute time span.[40]

"It was difficult to communicate. When I finally got a call and spoke to the commissioner, he said, 'We need to push this out and let people know what's happening,'" Fiandaca recalled. "That's what I did, I started tweeting from my phone at that mall."

Cheryl Fiandaca, Bureau Chief[41]

The department understood Twitter was the quickest and most reliable way to communicate with Boston residents, marathon runners, friends and family members, the news media, BPD employees, and other law enforcement agencies. The team was briefed by commanders three to five times per day.[42] The department posted 148 tweets during the five-day manhunt that concluded with the capture of Dzhokhar Tsarnaev.

However, early on Friday, April 19, the Boston Police changed their approach.[43] Instead of posting updates alone, they tried to counteract false information that was spreading rapidly throughout various social networks. A vast amount of misinformation was being published in newspapers and broadcasted on networks. This prompted rumors to become perceived reality and led to false accusations. A missing student from Brown University had been incorrectly identified as a suspect, and confusion spread over a number of people who were held as suspects.[44] These misunderstandings had far-reaching effects for law enforcement and the individuals who were eventually proven innocent. Additionally, multiple news sources including AP and CNN had erroneously reported a suspect was in custody.

Fiandaca said she had to address the issue of misinformation and the multitude of information that was being spread rapidly throughout various social media outlets. It all came to a boiling point when she received a phone call from an official stating a local radio station was reporting locations of officers involved in the manhunt. While the department has the ability to release information in real time, they have a responsibility to ensure safety first.[45]

"These guys know not to do that. They don't give away where officers are," said Fiandaca, in reference to local media. "But there were hundreds of reporters from all over the country here. We wanted to let other media folks who aren't as familiar know what's commonplace in Boston."

Cheryl Fiandaca, Bureau Chief[46]

After releasing several tweets asking people to stop compromising officer safety and broadcasting live video of officers, the department observed the tone and speed of coverage change instantly.

INFLUENCE OF SOCIAL MEDIA

While the Boston Police and the FBI were working hard to locate the two suspects who were responsible for the bombing, it became a trend for mainstream media, including established and professional forces, to follow the lead of the plethora of information being released on various social media outlets.[47] According to a recent report from the Pew Research Center, a quarter of Americans received information about the explosions and the manhunt for the bombers on a social networking site like Facebook or Twitter.[48] This trend promoted a new wave of crowdsourcing, therefore bypassing more traditional methods.

Reddit

Soon after the bombing at the Boston Marathon, a "hive community"—Reddit— set into motion a collaborative effort to identify who was potentially responsible for the devastation.[49] Essentially, Reddit serves as a community board that posts any and all new pieces of information. While the intention may have been noble, innocent bystanders were labeled as suspicious or worse simply because they were near the scene during the time of the explosion.

> "Activity on Reddit fueled online witch hunts and dangerous speculation which spiraled into very negative consequences for innocent parties. The Reddit staff and the millions of people on Reddit around the world deeply regret that this happened."
>
> Erik Martin, Reddit's General Manager[50]

In many cases, it was from this massive cloud of information that news outlets chose to report. One instance in particular involved CNN reporting on arrests that were never made and suspects who were deemed innocent.[51] The *New York Post* also published a front-page photo of two dark-skinned males, implying they were the suspects.[52] Reddit's work was being cited by major publications. Each time the group targeted a now-wronged bystander, they had the potential to ruin a life. Hence, ground rules were set forth requiring that photos that had been thoroughly examined and vindicated were to be clearly marked in old threads.[53] However, the site had proven its worth. One user uploaded a photo taken during the destruction; it contained a shot of Dzhokhar Tsarnaev. Various other photos were questioned by the *New York Times*, but some have since been verified as authentic.[54]

Twitter

On Friday morning among the multitudes of broadcasts from Watertown, Massachusetts, a Twitter account claiming to belong to the suspect's brother started posting threats to the police. After earning a great number of retweets, it was picked up by a police scanner, which added authenticity to the user. Once the scanner decided to broadcast the threats, journalists started to tweet about them as well, which essentially created a credibility-building feedback loop.[55] Terrorism experts said social media helped those in Boston and played a role in determining next steps after the explosions.

> "Authorities have recognized that one of the first places people go in events like this is to social media, to see what the crowd is saying about what to do next. And today authorities went to Twitter and directed them to traditional media environments where authorities can present a clear calm picture of what to do next."
>
> Bill Braniff, executive director of the National Consortium for the Study of Terrorism and Response to Terrorism[56]

Initially, law enforcement asked for the public's aid via Twitter and other social media outlets. However, it became clear the frenzy of information was harming the integrity of the investigation and jeopardizing officer safety as well as leading to numerous false accusations.[57] Yet Cheryl Fiandaca's use of Twitter remained separate from the rest due to the credibility of the content being posted. Twitter said the department's tweets acted as "a lifeline of communication for the entire city, and served as a defense against miscommunication" during the uncertain days after the April 15 bombings.[58] However, this was not the only time the department's use of social media was applauded. After the capture of Dzhokhar Tsarnaev, the social media news site *Mashable* ran the headline, "Boston Police Schooled Us All on Social Media."[59] The *Huffington Post* also ran with, "How Cop Team Led City From Terror To Joy."[60] The department's Twitter account was able to memorialize the horror of the bombs and the elation of the final capture in real time.[61]

> "If I'm here in Washington, D.C., and I'm on Twitter and can demonstrate my empathy, it helps create this idea of resolve or community solidarity with people who are there on the ground in a way that uni-dimensional media doesn't do," said Braniff. "Online, I can express outrage or sympathy. I get a greater sense of unity—the we is a much bigger we."
>
> Bill Braniff, executive director of the National Consortium for the Study of Terrorism and Response to Terrorism[62]

Facebook

Many people who were concerned about family and friends in the Boston area turned to Facebook as a source of news.[63] As the word spread about the blasts on Monday afternoon, social media was contoured by runners, authorities, and the general public. "I have been following my friend's Facebook [account] who is near the scene and she is updating everyone before it even gets to the news," said Sara Bozorg, doctor at Massachusetts Eye and Ear Infirmary.[64] "Sites like Facebook offer a convenient way to retrieve news especially since many users are constantly on them," says Michael Dimock, director of Pew's public opinion and polling project. They "are on Facebook, and the information is just flowing at them."[65] Some found different platforms were suitable for different purposes. Facebook can improve the overall image of a crisis if used correctly. In the end, Facebook was best for care and support.[66]

IMPLICATIONS FOR THE FUTURE

The biggest source of information in this crisis came from the public via social media outlets. Social media can be effective in a crisis when used to gain awareness of the situation. Listening to the conversation and noticing what is being said, then appropriately responding, was crucial for the police department during the event. By providing real-time updates, the Boston Police Department was able to control the tone of the conversation. Additionally, this case was perhaps the best illustration of a crowdsourcing investigation in recent history.[67] The public quickly and adamantly responded to the FBI's request for information. Ultimately, it all ended with a tweet.[68] A citizen's tip led to the capture of the surviving suspect. Meanwhile, major networks turned to Twitter and other social media platforms for breaking news coverage. Many Boston residents offered aid and shelter to those impacted by the bombings via social media. As news broke about the devastating bombings, many were desperate to connect with family and friends who were running the race or in the area. Yet with cell-phone service cut off, people turned to social media to connect and check in.[69] Lastly, the Boston Police Department's and Cheryl Fiandaca's smart use of Twitter set a new precedent for other authorities to follow during emergencies. As the city of Boston and all of America continues to recover from the devastation, developments in technology such as social media continue to shape and define our responses to crisis.[70]

REFERENCES

1. Anderson, N. (2013, April 29). [Web log message]. Retrieved from http://www.aml.ca/boston-marathon-bombing-as-case-study/.

2. PR Daily. (2013, April 16). *PR firms in Boston and nationwide react to marathon bombing.* Retrieved from http://www.prdaily.com/Main/Articles/ PR_firms_in_Boston_and_nationwide_react_to_maratho_14286.aspx#.

3. Henn, S. (Performer) (2013). Social media's rush to judgement in the Boston bombings [Radio series episode]. In *All Tech Considered*. NPR. Retrieved from http://www.npr.org/blogs/alltechconsidered/2013/04/23/178556269/Social-Medias-Rush-To-Judgment-In-The-Boston-Bombings.

4. Harshaw, T. (2013, April 19). *Social media's manhunt for the Boston bombers.* Retrieved from http://www.bloomberg.com/news/2013-04-19/social-media-s-manhunt-for-the-boston-bombers.html.

5, 6. Gross, D. (2013, April 17). *5 viral stories about Boston attacks that aren't true.* Retrieved from http://www.cnn.com/2013/04/16/tech/social-media/social-media-boston-fakes/.

7. Stein, L. (2013, April 16). Former comms director praises Boston PD's use of social media after bombing. *PRWeek*, Retrieved from http://www.prweekus.com/former-comms -director-praises-boston-pds-use-of-social-media-after-bombing/article/289118/.

8. Chang, D. (2013, October 22). *Boston police chief shares lessons learned from marathon explosion.* Retrieved from http://www.nbcphiladelphia.com/news/local/Boston-Police-Chief -Shares-Lessons-Learned-From-Marathon-Explosion-228844981.html.

9. Barker, G. (2013, November 11). Social media lessons from the Boston bombings and Australian bush fires. *The Guardian.* Retrieved from http://www.theguardian.com/public -leaders-network/2013/nov/11/social-media-boston-bombings-bush-fires.

10. Seitz, J. (2013, May 1). [Web log message]. Retrieved from http://nieman.harvard .edu/ reportsitem.aspx?id=102877.

11. PRSA. (2013, April 30). *Boston police mastered social media after marathon bombings.* Retrieved from http://www.prsa.org/SearchResults/view/10172/105/Boston_Police_mas tered_social_media_after_marathon.

12, 13, 18. *Boston marathon history: Boston marathon facts.* Retrieved from http://216 .235.243.43/races/boston-marathon/boston-marathon-history/boston-marathon-facts.aspx.

14. *2013 Boston marathon statistics.* Boston Athletic Association. Retrieved from http:// www.baa.org/error-404.aspx?reqUrl=/statistics.html.

15, 16. *About the Boston Athletic Association.* Retrieved from http://www.baa.org/about.aspx.

17. Flynn, D. *The meaning of Patriots' Day.* Retrieved from http://spectator.org/ar ticles/55737/meaning-patriots-day.

19. RT Archive. (1980, July 1). *Rosie Ruiz tries to steal the Boston marathon.* Retrieved from http://www.runnersworld.com/rt-miscellaneous/rosie-ruiz-tries-steal-boston-marathon.

20. Burfoot, A. (2011, April 5). *April 5: Boston marathon appears to have a lower heart- attack death rate than other marathons.* Retrieved from http://www.runnersworld.com/running -tips/april-5-boston-marathon-appears-have-lower-heart-attack-death-rate-other-marathons.

21. *Fluid cited in marathoner's death.* (2002, August 13). Retrieved from http:// www.apnewsarchive.com/2002/Fluid-Cited-in-Marathoner-s-Death/id-424edce6ed89d8ad cb14d4d97c0448a3.

22, 23, 24, 25, 26, 27, 28, 29, 30, 31, 32, 34. Botelho, G. (2013, May 2). *Timeline: The Boston marathon bombing, manhunt and investigation.* Retrieved from http://www.cnn .com/2013/05/01/justice/boston-marathon-timeline/.

33. Greenblatt, A. (2013, April 19). *Boston on lockdown: 'Today is so much scarier.'* Retrieved from http://www.npr.org/blogs/thetwo-way/2013/04/19/177934915/The-Scene-In-Boston -Today-Is-So-Much-Scarier.

35, 36, 37, 38, 44, 46. Keller, J. (2013, April 26). *How Boston police won the Twitter wars during the marathon bomber hunt.* Retrieved from http://www.businessweek.com/ar ticles/2013-04-26/how-boston-police-won-the-twitter-wars-during-bomber-hunt.

39, 40, 43, 45. Swann, P. (2013, May 24). *How the Boston police used Twitter during a time of terror.* Retrieved from http://www.prsa.org/Intelligence/Tactics/Articles/view/10197/1078/ How_the_Boston_Police_used_Twitter_during_a_time_o.

41, 42, 61. Bindley, K. (2013, April 26). Boston police Twitter: How cop team tweets led city from terror to joy. *The Huffington Post.* Retrieved from http://www.huffingtonpost .com/2013/04/26/boston-police-twitter-marathon_n_3157472.html.

47, 49, 51, 52, 53, 54, 55. Zarkarin, J. (2013, April 19). Boston bombing: How Reddit, Twitter and the internet helped and hurt the manhunt. *The Hollywood Reporter*. Retrieved from http:// www.hollywoodreporter.com/news/boston-bombing-how-reddit-twitter-442946.

48, 65. Petrecca, L. (2013, April 23). After bombings, social media informs (and misin-forms). *USA Today*. Retrieved from http://www.usatoday.com/story/news/2013/04/23/ social -media-boston-marathon-bombings/2106701/.

50. Kaufman, L. (2013, April 28). Bombings trip up Reddit in its turn in spotlight. *The New York Times*. Retrieved from http://www.nytimes.com/2013/04/29/business/media/ bombings-trip-up-reddit-in-its-turn-in-spotlight.html?_r=0.

56, 62, 64. Gilgoff, D., & Lee, J. (2013, April 15). *Social media shapes Boston bombings response*. Retrieved from http://news.nationalgeographic.com/news/2013/13/130415-boston -marathon-bombings-terrorism-social-media-twitter-facebook/.

57. Mack, E. (2013, April 19). *Authorities in Boston bombing helped, hindered by social media*. Retrieved from http://news.cnet.com/8301-17938_105-57580456-1/authorities-in -boston-bombing-helped-hindered-by-social-media/.

58, 59, 60. Randall, E. (2013, November 7). Boston police's spokeswoman helped ring the bell for the Twitter IPO. *Boston Magazine*. Retrieved from http://www.bostonmagazine.com/ news/blog/ 2013/11/07/boston-polices-spokeswoman-helped-ring-bell-twitter-ipo/.

63, 66. Kane, G. C. (2013, April 25). [Web log message]. Retrieved from http:// sloanreview.mit.edu/ article/what-can-managers-learn-about-social-media-from-the-boston -marathon-bombing/.

67, 69. Konkel, F. (2013, April 26). *Boston probe's big data use hints at the future*. Retrieved from http://fcw.com/articles/2013/04/26/big-data-boston-bomb-probe.aspx.

68, 70. CBS News. (2013, April 21). *Lessons to be learned from the Boston bombing*. Retrieved from http://www.cbsnews.com/news/lessons-to-be-learned-from-the-boston-bombing/.

69. Butter, M. (2013, April 16). *Boston bombing: How Google, social media and cloud bring hope amid tragedy*. Retrieved from http://www.forbes.com/sites/netapp/2013/04/16/boston -bomb-cloud-hope/.

Notes

CHAPTER 1—WHY ETHICS MATTER

1. Brown University, "A framework for making ethical decisions," Science and Technology Studies, accessed June 19, 2017, https://www.brown.edu/academics/science-and-technology-studies/framework-making-ethical-decisions.

2. Brown University, "A framework for making ethical decisions," Science and Technology Studies, accessed June 19, 2017, https://www.brown.edu/academics/science-and-technology-studies/framework-making-ethical-decisions.

3. WPSU—Penn State Public Media, Public Relations Ethics Module, "Understanding Ethics As a Decision-Making Process," accessed June 18, 2017, http://pagecentertraining.psu.edu/public-relations-ethics/introduction-to-public-relations-ethics/lesson-1/understanding-ethics-as-a-decision-making-process.

4. P. Seib and K. Fitzpatrick, *Public Relations Ethics* (Orlando: Harcourt Brace and Company, 1995).

5. Timothy Coombs and Robert Heath, *Today's Public Relations: An Introduction* (Thousand Oaks, CA: SAGE Publications, 2006).

6. R. A. Nelson, "Issues communication and advocacy: Contemporary ethical challenges," *Public Relations Review* 20 (1994) 225–32.

7. "Public Relations Society of America (PRSA) Member Code of Ethics," Public Relations Society of America (PRSA), accessed January 6, 2017, https://apps.prsa.org/About PRSA/Ethics/CodeEnglish/index.html.

8. J. Booth & Son, 147 Fulton St., NY—Somers Historical Society, P.O. Box 336, Somers, NY 10589 Printed Handbill—12 × 6½" Title: The Greatest Natural & National Curiosity in the World Joice Heth.

9. Eric Lott, *Love and Theft: Blackface Minstrelsy and the American Working Class* (New York: Oxford University Press, 1993).

10. Jessie Szalay, "The Feejee Mermaid: Early Barnum Hoax," LiveScience, accessed December 14, 2016, http://www.livescience.com/56037-feejee-mermaid.html.

11. Jessie Szalay, "The Feejee Mermaid: Early Barnum Hoax," LiveScience, accessed December 14, 2016, http://www.livescience.com/56037-feejee-mermaid.html.

12. Tim Morris, "Ivy Lee and the origins of the press release," *Behind the Spin*, August 25, 2014, accessed May 30, 2017, http://www.behindthespin.com/features/ivy-lee-and-the -origins-of-the-press-release.

13. Edward L. Bernays, "The engineering of consent," *Annals of the American Academy of Political and Social Science* 250 (March 1947): doi:10.1177/000271624725000116.

14. "Propaganda by Edward Bernays (1928)," accessed December 15, 2016, http://www .historyisaweapon.org/defcon1/bernprop.html.

15. "The trolley dilemma and how it relates to ethical communication," The Trolley Dilemma, accessed October 7, 2017, http://www.trolleydilemma.com/.

16. Jeremy Bentham, 1789 [PML] *An Introduction to the Principles of Morals and Legislation* (Oxford: Clarendon Press, 1907).

17. Stephen Nathanson, "Act and rule utilitarianism," Internet Encyclopedia of Philosophy, accessed October 7, 2017, http://www.iep.utm.edu/util-a-r/.

18. Craig E. Johnson, *Organizational Ethics: A Practical Approach* (Thousand Oaks, CA: SAGE Publications, 2012), 20.

19. John Stuart Mill, "Utilitarianism by John Stuart Mill," Utilitarianism by John Stuart Mill, 6, accessed January 4, 2017, https://www.utilitarianism.com/mill2.htm.

20. Michael Sandel, "Episode 06," *Justice with Michael Sandel*, accessed January 4, 2017, http://www.justiceharvard.org/2011/02/episode-06/.

21. Immanuel Kant and Mary J. Gregor, *Groundwork of the Metaphysics of Morals* (Cambridge, UK: Cambridge University Press, 1998).

22. Immanuel Kant and Mary J. Gregor, *Groundwork of the Metaphysics of Morals* (Cambridge, UK: Cambridge University Press, 1998).

23. Katie Reilly, "Disney worker fired—then rehired—after tweet about alligators at the park," *Time*, accessed January 3, 2017, http://time.com/4409314/disney-world-alligators -worker-fired/.

24. Travis M. Andrews, "Disney fires, rehires intern who tweeted sign telling employees to deny on-site alligators" Chicagotribune.com, July 18, 2016, accessed October 7, 2017, http:// www.chicagotribune.com/news/nationworld/ct-disney-intern-alligator-sign-20160718-story .html.

25. Nancy J. Hirschmann, *Gender, Class, and Freedom in Modern Political Theory* (Princeton, NJ: Princeton University Press, 2009, p. 79).

26. Michael Zuckert, *The Natural Rights Republic* (Notre Dame, IN: Notre Dame University Press, 1996, pp. 73–85).

27. John Locke, "John Locke: Two treatises of government (1680-1690)," LONANG Institute, accessed January 4, 2017, http://lonang.com/library/reference/locke-two-treatises -government/.

28. George Rede, "Same-sex couple in Sweet Cakes controversy should receive $135,000, hearings officer says," OregonLive.com, April 24, 2015, accessed January 5, 2017, http:// www.oregonlive.com/business/index.ssf/2015/04/same-sex_couple_in_sweet_cakes.html.

29. George Rede, "Same-sex couple in Sweet Cakes controversy should receive $135,000, hearings officer says," OregonLive.com, April 24, 2015, accessed January 5, 2017, http:// www.oregonlive.com/business/index.ssf/2015/04/same-sex_couple_in_sweet_cakes.html.

30. Lawrence Kohlberg, "Moral stages and moralization: The cognitive-developmental approach," in *Moral Development and Behavior: Theory, Research and Social Issues* (New York: Holt, Rinehart and Winston, 1976).

31. Lawrence Kohlberg, "Moral stages and moralization: The cognitive-developmental approach," in *Moral Development and Behavior: Theory, Research and Social Issues* (New York: Holt, Rinehart and Winston, 1976).

32. "Internet Marketing—Chapter 6-Kohlberg," accessed January 5, 2017, http://education.smartpros.com/internetmarketing/ch06/kohlberg.html.

33. Joseph Fletcher and James F. Childress, *Situation ethics: The new morality* (Louisville: Westminster John Knox Press, 2006).

34. Kim Harrison, "Ensure you bring ethics into your PR activities," 2013, accessed May 12, 2017, http://www.cuttingedgepr.com/articles/bring-ethics-into-pr-activities.asp.

35. "Ethical Orientations: Situational Ethics," accessed May 12, 2017, http://pagecentertraining.psu.edu/public-relations-ethics/core-ethical-principles/lesson-1-title/ethical-orientations-situational-ethics/.

36. Kim Harrison, "Ensure you bring ethics into your PR activities," Cutting Edge PR, 2013, accessed October 7, 2017, http://www.cuttingedgepr.com/articles/bring-ethics-into-pr-activities.asp.

37. Shannon Bowen, "Ethics and public relations," Institute for Public Relations, June 9, 2015, accessed October 7, 2017, http://www.instituteforpr.org/ethics-and-public-relations/.

38. 2015 Cone Communications Ebiquity Global CSR Study, PDF, Cone Communications, 2015.

39. 2015 Cone Communications Ebiquity Global CSR Study, PDF, Cone Communications, 2015.

40. Doug Ireland, *Village Voice*, March 26, 1991.

41. The use of the Big Lie to manipulate public opinion and neutralize opposition to a particular war was not invented by Bush. See, for instance, James Laxer, "Iraq: US has match, seeks kindle: American leaders have often falsified reasons to attack other countries" (Action-Greens, March 31, 2001). Laxer is a political science professor at York University, Toronto.

42. *ABC World News Tonight*, March 15, 1991.

43. Sharon Beder and Richard Gosden, *PR Watch* 8, no. 2, 2nd Quarter 2001. The PR firm has since been working at the behest of the pharmaceutical industry to ban over-the-counter vitamin and nutritional supplement sales in Europe.

CHAPTER 2—ETHICS IN PUBLIC RELATIONS

1. "Public Relations Society of America (PRSA) Member Code of Ethics," accessed February 17, 2017, https://apps.prsa.org/AboutPRSA/Ethics/CodeEnglish/index.html#.WKcb528rLIU.

2. "Fact Sheet," PRSA Newsroom, accessed February 21, 2017, http://media.prsa.org/about prsa/fact sheet/.

3. "Fact Sheet," PRSA Newsroom, accessed February 21, 2017, http://media.prsa.org/about prsa/fact sheet/.

4. "Public Relations Society of America (PRSA) Member Code of Ethics," accessed February 17, 2017, https://apps.prsa.org/AboutPRSA/Ethics/CodeEnglish/index.html#.WKcb528rLIU.

5. "Public Relations Society of America (PRSA) Member Code of Ethics," accessed February 17, 2017, https://apps.prsa.org/AboutPRSA/Ethics/CodeEnglish/index.html#.WK cb528rLIU.

6. "Statement of Ethics," American Marketing Association, accessed February 21, 2017, https://www.ama.org/AboutAMA/Pages/Statement-of-Ethics.aspx.

7. "CIPR," Charter, Regulations and Code of Conduct, Chartered Institute of Public Relations, accessed February 21, 2017, https://www.cipr.co.uk/content/our-organisation/charter-regulations-and-code-conduct.

8. "SPJ Code of Ethics," Society of Professional Journalists, accessed February 17, 2017, https://www.spj.org/ethicscode.asp.

9. "Code of ethics and standards," PRISA, accessed February 21, 2017, http://www.prisa .co.za/index.php/membership/code-of-ethics-and-standards.

10. "Ethics and social media," PDF, New York City, The Public Relations Society of America, 2015.

11. Donald K. Wright, "Enforcement dilemma: Voluntary nature of public relations codes," *Public Relations Review* 19, no. 1 (1993): doi:10.1016/0363-8111(93)90026-9.

12. Shannon Bowen, "Ethics and public relations," Institute for Public Relations, June 9, 2015, accessed February 21, 2017, http://www.instituteforpr.org/ethics-and-public-relations/.

13. Stephen Daly, "Black Ops 3's story revealed through Twitter campaign," Gameranx, February 3, 2016, accessed February 21, 2017, http://gameranx.com/updates/id/30694/article/black-ops-3-s-story-revealed-through-twitter-campaign/.

14. "Treyarch shocked by reaction to Call of Duty: Black Ops 3 Twitter marketing stunt," AR12 Gaming, accessed February 21, 2017, https://ar12gaming.com/articles/treyarch -shocked-by-reaction-to-call-of-duty-black-ops-3-twitter-marketing-stunt.

CHAPTER 3—ADVOCACY

1. "Children and Teens: Statistics," RAINN, accessed January 9, 2017, https://www.rainn .org/statistics/children-and-teens.

2. Holly Bentley, Orla O'Hagan, Annie Raff, and Iram Bhatti, "How safe are our children? The most comprehensive overview of child protection in the UK 2016," London: NSPCC, accessed November 8, 2016, https://www.nspcc.org.uk/services-and-resources/research-and -resources/2016/how-safe-are-our-children-2016/.

3. "Sexual victimization of children in South Africa: Final report of the Optimus Foundation Study: South Africa," UBS Optimus Foundation, June 2016, accessed November 8, 2016, http://www.cjcp.org.za/uploads/2/7/8/4/27845461/08_cjcp_report_2016_d.pdf.

4. Wpadmin, "37 scarey repeat sex offenders statistics," HRFnd, November 13, 2014, accessed November 3, 2016, http://healthresearchfunding.org/37-scarey-repeat-sex-offenders -statistics/.

5. C. R. Hollin, "Does punishment motivate offenders to change?" In M. McMurran (ed.), *Motivating Offenders to Change. A Guide to Enhancing Engagement in Therapy*, Wiley Series in Forensic Clinical Psychology, 2002, 235–46.

6. Klaus M. Beier et al., "Encouraging self-identified pedophiles and hebephiles to seek professional help: First results of the Prevention Project Dunkelfeld (PPD)," *Child Abuse and Neglect* 33, no. 8 (2009): doi:10.1016/j.chiabu.2009.04.002.

7. Klaus M. Beier et al., "Encouraging self-identified pedophiles and hebephiles to seek professional help: First results of the Prevention Project Dunkelfeld (PPD)," *Child Abuse and Neglect* 33, no. 8 (2009): doi:10.1016/j.chiabu.2009.04.002.

8. Wpadmin, "37 scarey repeat sex offenders statistics," HRFnd, November 13, 2014, accessed November 3, 2016, http://healthresearchfunding.org/37-scarey-repeat-sex-offenders-statistics/.

9. James E. Grunig, "Ethics problems and theories in public relations," *Communiquer*, online since April 21, 2015, connection on January 14, 2017, http://communiquer.revues.org/559; doi:10.4000/communiquer.559; Kathy Fitzpatrick and Carolyn Bronstein, *Ethics in Public Relations: Responsible Advocacy* (Thousand Oaks, CA: SAGE Publications, 2006); Ruth Edgett, "Toward an ethical framework for advocacy in public relations," *Journal of Public Relations Research* 14, no. 1 (2002):1–26, doi:10.1207/s1532754xjprr1401_1; Jay Black, "Semantics and ethics of propaganda," *Journal of Mass Media Ethics* 16, no. 2–3 (2001):121–37, doi:10.1080/08900523.2001.9679608; Sherry Baker and David L. Martinson "The TARES test: Five principles for ethical persuasion," *Journal of Mass Media Ethics* 16, no. 2–3 (2002): 148–75, doi:10.1080/08900523.2001.9679610; Stanley B. Cunningham, "Responding to Propaganda: An Ethical Enterprise," *Journal of Mass Media Ethics* 16, no. 2–3 (2001), 138–47.

10. Robert Jackall, *Moral Mazes: The World of Corporate Managers* (New York: Oxford University Press, 1988); Robert Jackall and Janice M. Hirota, *Image Makers: Advertising, Public Relations, and the Ethos of Advocacy* (Chicago: University of Chicago Press, 2000).

11. Robert Jackall, *Moral Mazes: The World of Corporate Managers* (New York: Oxford University Press, 1988), 185.

12. Patricia Parsons, *Ethics in Public Relations: A Guide to Best Practice* (London: Kogan Page, 2004), 105.

13. Dean Kruckeberg and Kenneth Starck, *Public Relations and Community: A Reconstructed Theory* (New York: Praeger, 1988), 4.

14. "Public Relations Society of America (PRSA) Member Code of Ethics," accessed December 13, 2016, https://www.prsa.org/aboutprsa/ethics/codeenglish#.WHmBXLYrJPN.

15. "Public Relations Society of America (PRSA) Member Code of Ethics," accessed December 13, 2016, https://www.prsa.org/aboutprsa/ethics/codeenglish#.WHmBXLYrJPN.

16. Ruth Edgett, "Toward an ethical framework for advocacy in public relations," *Journal of Public Relations Research* 14, no. 1 (2002):1, doi:10.1207/s1532754xjprr1401_1.

17. G. R. Miller, "Persuasion and public relations: Two 'Ps' in a pod," in *Public Relations Theory*, ed. C. H. Botan and V. Hazelton (Hillsdale, NJ: Lawrence Erlbaum Associates, Inc., 1989), 45.

18. Sherry Baker, "Five baselines for justification in persuasion," *Journal of Mass Media Ethics* 14, no. 2 (1999): doi:10.1207/s15327728jmme1402_1.

19. Sherry Baker, "Five baselines for justification in persuasion," *Journal of Mass Media Ethics* 14, no. 2 (1999): doi:10.1207/s15327728jmme1402_1.

20. Sherry Baker, "Five baselines for justification in persuasion," *Journal of Mass Media Ethics* 14, no. 2 (1999): doi:10.1207/s15327728jmme1402_1.

21. Thomas Bivins, "Public relations, professionalism and the public interest," *Journal of Business Ethics* 12, no. 2 (1993) 117–26.

22. Thomas Bivins, "Responsibility and accountability," in K. Fitzpatrick and C. B. Bronstein (eds.), *Ethics in Public Relations: Responsible Advocacy* (Thousands Oaks, CA: SAGE Publications, 2006).

23. Kathy Fitzpatrick and Caroline Bronstein, *Ethics in Public Relations Responsible Advocacy* (London: SAGE Publications, 2006).

24. Ruth Edgett, "Toward an Ethical Framework for Advocacy in Public Relations," *Journal of Public Relations Research* 14, no. 1 (2002), doi:10.1207/s1532754xjprr1401_1.

25. Ruth Edgett, "Toward an Ethical Framework for Advocacy in Public Relations," *Journal of Public Relations Research* 14, no. 1 (2002), doi: 10.1207/s1532754xjprr1401_1.

26. Sherry Baker and David L. Martinson, "The TARES test: Five principles for ethical persuasion," *Journal of Mass Media Ethics* 16, no. 2–3 (2001): doi:10.1080/08900523.2001.9679610.

27. Ralph B. Potter, *The Structure of Certain American Christian Responses to the Nuclear Dilemma, 1958–1963*. Doctoral thesis, Harvard University, 1965.

28. WPSU—Penn State Public Media, Public Relations Ethics Module, "Understanding Ethics As a Decision-Making Process," accessed June 18, 2017, http://pagecentertraining.psu.edu/public-relations-ethics/introduction-to-public-relations-ethics/lesson-1/understanding-ethics-as-a-decision-making-process.

29. Shannon A. Bowen, "A practical model for ethical decision making in issues management and public relations," *Journal of Public Relations Research* 17, no. 3 (2005): doi:10.1207/s1532754xjprr1703_1.

30. WPSU—Penn State Public Media, Public Relations Ethics Module, "Understanding Ethics As a Decision-Making Process," accessed June 18, 2017, http://pagecentertraining.psu.edu/public-relations-ethics/introduction-to-public-relations-ethics/lesson-1/understanding-ethics-as-a-decision-making-process.

31. Immanuel Kant and Mary J. Gregor, Groundwork of the Metaphysics of Morals (Cambridge, UK: Cambridge University Press, 1998).

32. Sarah Kliff, "Martin Shkreli raised his drug's prices 5,500 percent because, in America, he can," *Vox*, December 17, 2015, retrieved January 4, 2017, https://www.vox.com/2015/9/22/9366721/daraprim-price-shkreli-turing.

33. Stephen B. Calderwood and Adaora Adimora, "Letter from Stephen B. Calderwood, MD, FIDSA (President, IDSA) and Adaora Adimora, MD, MPH, FIDSA (Chair, HIVMA) to Mssrs. Tom Evegan (Head of Managed Markets) and Kevin Bernier (National Director Alliance Development & Public Affairs), both of Turing Pharmacauticals" (PDF). Arlington, VA: Infectious Diseases Society of America (IDSA), HIV Medicine Association (HIVMA). Retrieved December 10, 2015, http://www.hivma.org/uploadedFiles/HIVMA/HomePage Content/PyrimethamineLetterFINAL.pdf.

34. Jason Tannahill, "PR man Allan Ripp representing the most hated man in America," *EverythingPR*, October 9, 2015.

35. John Stuart Mill, "Utilitarianism by John Stuart Mill," Utilitarianism by John Stuart Mill, 6, accessed January 4, 2017, https://www.utilitarianism.com/mill2.htm.

36. John Locke, "John Locke: Two Treatises of Government (1680-1690)," LONANG Institute, accessed January 4, 2017, http://lonang.com/library/reference/locke-two-treatises-government/.

37. Maggie Fox, "Competitor to offer $1 pill after Turing price hike outrage," NBC News, October 22, 1015, retrieved December 5, 2016, https://www.nbcnews.com/health/health-news/competitor-offer-1-pill-after-turing-price-hike-outrage-n449661.

38. Jeremy, Bentham, 1789 [PML], *An Introduction to the Principles of Morals and Legislation* (Oxford: Clarendon Press, 1907).

39. "Echo chamber (media)," Wikipedia, accessed February 11, 2017, https://en.wikipedia.org/wiki/Echo_chamber_(media).

40. "Public Relations Society of America (PRSA) Member Code of Ethics," accessed December 13, 2016, https://www.prsa.org/aboutprsa/ethics/codeenglish#.WHmBXLYrJPN.

41. "Social media is lost without a social compass," Brian Solis, accessed February 20, 2017, http://www.briansolis.com/2014/07/social-media-lost-without-social-compass/.

42. Clay Shirky, *Here Comes Everybody: The Power of Organizing without Organizations* (New York: Penguin, 2008).

43. Henry Jenkins, "The cultural logic of media convergence," *International Journal of Cultural Studies* 7, no. 1 (2004): doi:10.1177/1367877904040603.

44. Alexandra Sifferlin, "Here's how the ALS Ice Bucket Challenge actually started," *Time*, August 18, 2014, retrieved from http://time.com/3136507/als-ice-bucket-challenge-started/.

45. Beth Kanter, *Ice Bucket Challenge: Can Other Nonprofits Reproduce It?* [Web log post] 2014, retrieved from http://www.bethkanter.org/icebucket-2/.

46. Alexandra Sifferlin, "Here's how the ALS Ice Bucket Challenge actually started," *Time*, August 18, 2014, retrieved from http://time.com/3136507/als-ice-bucket-challenge-started/.

CHAPTER 4—HONESTY

1. Http://kdvr.com/fox31-kdvr-channel-2-kwgn-on-facebook/, "By the numbers: Here are the 20 'most dangerous' cities in America," FOX31 Denver, May 8, 2015, accessed January 16, 2017, http://kdvr.com/2015/05/08/by-the-numbers-here-are-the-most-dangerous-cities-in-america/.

2. Monica Davey, "Flint officials are no longer saying the water is fine," *New York Times*, October 7, 2015, accessed July 2, 2016, https://www.nytimes.com/2015/10/08/us/reassurances-end-in-flint-after-months-of-concern.html?_r=0.

3. Ron Fonger, "Flint River water complicating city's efforts to battle contamination, boil advisories," Mlive, September 18, 2014, accessed July 2, 2016, http://www.mlive.com/news/flint/index.ssf/2014/09/dpw_director_says_flint_river.html.

4. Ron Fonger, "Lead leaches into 'very corrosive' Flint drinking water, researchers say," Mlive, September 2, 2015 accessed July 3, 2016, http://www.mlive.com/news/flint/index.ssf/2015/09/new_testing_shows_flint_water.html

5. "Public health emergency declaration for people using the Flint City water supply with the Flint River as the source," Genesee County, Michigan, accessed July 15, 2016, http://www.gc4me.com/departments/emg_mgt_homeland_sec/docs/Water_Emergency_Declaration_12_4_15.pdf.

6. Jack Lessenberry, "Flint's water crisis another example of how Gov. Snyder seems incapable of admitting mistakes," Michigan Radio, October 2, 2015, accessed July 16, 2016, http://michiganradio.org/post/flints-water-crisis-another-example-how-gov-snyder-seems-incapable-admitting-mistakes#stream/0.

7. "Public Relations Society of America (PRSA) Member Code of Ethics," accessed December 13, 2016, https://www.prsa.org/aboutprsa/ethics/codeenglish#.WHmBXLYrJPN.

8. James E. Grunig and Todd Hunt, *Managing Public Relations* (New York: Holt, Rinehart and Winston, 1984).

9. James E. Grunig and Todd Hunt, *Managing Public Relations* (New York: Holt, Rinehart and Winston, 1984).

10. "Magic bullet or hypodermic needle theory of communication," *Communication Theory*, accessed January 16, 2017, http://communicationtheory.org/magic-bullet-or-hypo dermic-needle-theory-of-communication/.

11. Bill Sledzik, "The '4 Models' of public relations practice: How far have you evolved?" *ToughSledding: Challenging the status quo in public relations* (web log), August 10, 2008, accessed June 6, 2016, https://toughsledding.wordpress.com/2008/08/10/the-4-models-of -public-relations-practice-how-far-have-you-evolved/.

12. Allen H. Center and Scott Cutlip, *Effective Public Relations* (New York: Pearson, 1952).

13. Rex F. Harlow, "Building a public relations definition," *Public Relations Review* 2, no. 4 (1976): doi:10.1016/s0363-8111(76)80022-7.

14. Ruth Edgett, "Toward an ethical framework for advocacy in public relations," *Journal of Public Relations Research* 14, no. 1 (2002):17, doi: 10.1207/s1532754xjprr1401_1.

15. J. Vernon Jensen, *Ethical Issues in the Communication Process* (Mahwah, NJ: Erlbaum, 1997), 88.

16. Sissela Bok, *Lying: Moral Choice in Public and Private Life* (New York: Pantheon Books, 1978).

17. Sissela Bok, *Lying: Moral Choice in Public and Private Life* (New York: Pantheon Books, 1978).

18. Doug Newsom, Judy VanSlyke Turk, and Dean Kruckeberg, *This Is PR: The Realities of Public Relations* (Belmont, CA: Wadsworth Publishing, 1996).

19. Young Entrepreneur Council, "The 3 T's of a great PR experience: Truth, trust and transparency," *Forbes*, June 22, 2013, accessed January 16, 2017, http://www.forbes .com/sites/theyec/2013/06/20/the-3-ts-of-a-great-pr-experience-truth-trust-and-transpar ency/#2ad0585b2fde.

20. Lisa Goldsberry, "Is there honesty in PR?" *Axia Public Relations* (web log), June 20, 2016, accessed August 11, 2016, http://www.axiapr.com/blog/is-there-honesty-in-pr.

21. Lisa Goldsberry, "Is there honesty in PR?" *Axia Public Relations* (web log), June 20, 2016, accessed August 11, 2016, http://www.axiapr.com/blog/is-there-honesty-in-pr.

22. Lisa Goldsberry, "Is there honesty in PR?" *Axia Public Relations* (web log), June 20, 2016, accessed August 11, 2016, http://www.axiapr.com/blog/is-there-honesty-in-pr.

23. Sapna Maheshwari, "Samsung's response to Galaxy Note 7 crisis draws criticism," *New York Times*, October 11, 2016, accessed January 16, 2016, https://www.nytimes .com/2016/10/12/business/media/samsungs-passive-response-to-note-7s-overheating-prob lem-draws-criticism.html

24. Sapna Maheshwari, "Samsung's response to Galaxy Note 7 crisis draws criticism," *New York Times*, October 11, 2016, accessed January 16, 2016, https://www.nytimes .com/2016/10/12/business/media/samsungs-passive-response-to-note-7s-overheating-prob lem-draws-criticism.html

25. Cal-jeffrey, "Galaxy Note 7: Samsung facing PR disaster and sobering losses after pull ing the plug on its flagship smartphone," The Inquisitr News, January 16, 2017, accessed January 16, 2017, http://www.inquisitr.com/3593141/galaxy-note-7-samsung-facing-pr -disaster-and-sobering-losses-after-pulling-the-plug-on-its-flagship-smartphone/.

26. Christian Red, Michael O'Keeffe, and Nathaniel Vinton, "Alex Rodriguez's career over shadowed by steroid scandals," *NY Daily News*, August 7, 2016, accessed January 16, 2017, http://www.nydailynews.com/sports/baseball/yankees/alex-rodriguez-career-overshadowed -steroid-scandals-article-1.2741694.

27. Mike Bauman, "Mike Bauman: Drug policy, appeal process prevail in Alex Rodriguez A-Rod case," Major League Baseball, January 11, 2014, accessed January 16, 2017, http://m.mlb.com/news/article/66498146/mike-bauman-drug-policy-appeal-process-prevail-in-alex-rodriguez-a-rod-case/.

28. Darren Rovell, "Maria Sharapova suspended 2 years over positive doping test," ESPN, June 9, 2016, accessed January 16, 2017, http://www.espn.com/tennis/story/_/id/16044538/maria-sharapova-suspended-two-years-international-tennis-federation-positive-drug-test-meldonium.

29. Darren Rovell, "Maria Sharapova suspended 2 years over positive doping test," ESPN, June 09, 2016, accessed January 16, 2017, http://www.espn.com/tennis/story/_/id/16044538/maria-sharapova-suspended-two-years-international-tennis-federation-positive-drug-test-meldonium.

30. Marcia W. DiStaso, and Denise Sevick Bortree, *Ethical Practice of Social Media in Public Relations* (New York: Routledge, 2014).

31. Cheryl Conner, "Is ghostwriting ethical?" *Forbes*, March 13, 2014, accessed February 17, 2017, http://www.forbes.com/sites/cherylsnappconner/2014/03/13/is-ghostwriting-ethical/#d4e721733a0d.

32. Cheryl Conner, "Is ghostwriting ethical?" *Forbes*, March 13, 2014, accessed October 7, 2017, https://www.forbes.com/sites/cherylsnappconner/2014/03/13/is-ghostwriting-ethical/#71c0fffc40a3.

33. Steve Farnsworth, "Ghostwriting isn't unethical (most of the time)," June 20, 2012, accessed February 17, 2017, https://www.ragan.com/Main/Articles/Ghostwriting_isnt_unethical_most_of_the_time_45078.aspx#.

CHAPTER 5—EXPERTISE

1. "Statement by Press Secretary Sean Spicer," The White House, January 21, 2017, accessed February 11, 2017, https://www.whitehouse.gov/the-press-office/2017/01/21/statement-press-secretary-sean-spicer.

2. "Sean Spicer stands by false claim over inauguration crowd size," *Time*, accessed February 11, 2017, http://time.com/4643927/sean-spicer-white-house-donald-trump-inauguration-press-briefing/.

3. "Conway: Trump White House offered 'alternative facts' on crowd size," CNN, accessed February 11, 2017, http://www.cnn.com/2017/01/22/politics/kellyanne-conway-alternative-facts/.

4. "Meet The Press 01/22/17," NBCNews.com, January 22, 2017, accessed February 11, 2017, http://www.nbcnews.com/meet-the-press/meet-press-01-22-17-n710491.

5. "Meet The Press 01/22/17," NBCNews.com, January 22, 2017, accessed February 11, 2017, http://www.nbcnews.com/meet-the-press/meet-press-01-22-17-n710491.

6. "Meet The Press 01/22/17," NBCNews.com, January 22, 2017, accessed February 11, 2017, http://www.nbcnews.com/meet-the-press/meet-press-01-22-17-n710491.

7. "Meet The Press 01/22/17," NBCNews.com, January 22, 2017, accessed February 11, 2017, http://www.nbcnews.com/meet-the-press/meet-press-01-22-17-n710491.

8. "Public Relations Society of America (PRSA) Member Code of Ethics," accessed February 11, 2017, https://apps.prsa.org/AboutPRSA/Ethics/CodeEnglish/index.html?seMobiPref=true.

9. Aristotle, *Nicomachean Ethics*, bk. VI (H. Rackbam trans. 1962).

10. Daryl Koehn, "What is practical judgement?" *Professional Ethics, A Multidisciplinary Journal* 8, no. 3 (2000): doi:10.5840/profethics200083/420.

11. Rhonda Breit and Kristin Demetrious, "Professionalisation and public relations: An ethical mismatch," *Ethical Space: The International Journal of Communication Ethics* 7, no. 4 (2010), 20–29.

12. Dennis L. Wilcox, Glen T. Cameron, Bryan H. Reber, and Jae-Hwa Shin, *Think Public Relations* (Boston: Pearson, 2013).

13. Rhonda Breit and Kristin Demetrious, "Professionalisation and public relations: An ethical mismatch," *Ethical Space: The International Journal of Communication Ethics* 7, no. 4 (2010), 20–29.

14. Rhonda Breit and Kristin Demetrious, "Professionalisation and public relations: An ethical mismatch," *Ethical Space: The International Journal of Communication Ethics* 7, no. 4 (2010): 20–29.

15. Michael Schudson and Chris Anderson, "Objectivity, professionalism and truth seeking in journalism," Karen Wahl-Jorgenson and Thomas Hanitzsch (eds.), *The Handbook of Journalism Studies* (New York and London: Routledge, 2009), 88–101.

16. Rhonda Breit and Kristin Demetrious, "Professionalisation and public relations: An ethical mismatch," *Ethical Space: The International Journal of Communication Ethics* 7, no. 4 (2010), 20–29.

17. Rhonda Breit and Kristin Demetrious, "Professionalisation and public relations: An ethical mismatch," *Ethical Space: The International Journal of Communication Ethics* 7, no. 4 (2010), 20–29.

18. Rudi Volti, *An Introduction to the Sociology of Work and Occupations* (Los Angeles: Pine Forge Press, 2008).

19. Rudi Volti, *An Introduction to the Sociology of Work and Occupations* (Los Angeles: Pine Forge Press, 2008).

20. Andrew Laird, "Ringing the changes on Gyges: Philosophy and the formation of fiction in Plato's Republic," *The Journal of Hellenic Studies* 121 (2001): doi:10.2307/631825.

21. "Great Philosophers: Plato—Ethics—The Ring of Gyges," accessed February 11, 2017, http://oregonstate.edu/instruct/phl201/modules/Philosophers/Plato/plato_dialogue _the_ring_of_gyges.html.

22. The Internet Classics Archive. *The Republic by Plato*, accessed February 11, 2017, http://classics.mit.edu/Plato/republic.3.ii.html.

23. The Internet Classics Archive. *The Republic by Plato*, accessed February 11, 2017, http://classics.mit.edu/Plato/republic.3.ii.html.

24. Massimo Pigliucci, "Crimes, misdemeanors, and Gyges' ring," Rationally Speaking, December 22, 2005, accessed June 18, 2017, http://rationallyspeaking.blogspot.com/ 2005/12/crimes-misdemeanors-and-gyges-ring.html.

25. Mark Renfree, "Ryan Lochte and the 3 F's of crisis communications," *PR News*, August 22, 2016, accessed February 11, 2017, http://www.prnewsonline.com/ryan-lochte-crisis?hq _e=el&hq_m=3280668&hq_l=7&hq_v=69836be966.

26. Jane Dvorak, "PRSA statement on 'alternative facts,'" PRSA Newsroom, January 24, 2017, accessed February 17, 2017, http://media.prsa.org/news-releases/prsa-opinions-and -commentary/prsa-makes-statement-on-alternative-facts.htm.

27. Anne Green, "FROM," PR Council, February 1, 2017, accessed February 17, 2017, http://prcouncil.net/blog/truthiness-alternative-facts-must-recommit-core-communications -values/.

CHAPTER 6—INDEPENDENCE

1. "Leslie Roberts resigns from Global News in wake of internal investigation," Global News, January 16, 2015, accessed February 12, 2017, http://globalnews.ca/news/1774336/ leslie-roberts-resigns-from-global-news-in-wake-of-internal-investigation/.

2. Kevin Donovan, "Leslie Roberts quits Global TV after Star investigation," Thestar.com, January 15, 2015, accessed February 12, 2017, https://www.thestar.com/news/ gta/2015/01/15/leslie-roberts-quits-global-tv-after-star-investigation.html.

3. Kevin Donovan, "Leslie Roberts quits Global TV after Star investigation," Thestar.com, January 15, 2015, accessed February 12, 2017, https://www.thestar.com/news/ gta/2015/01/15/leslie-roberts-quits-global-tv-after-star-investigation.html.

4. Kevin Donovan, "Leslie Roberts quits Global TV after Star investigation," Thestar.com, January 15, 2015, accessed February 12, 2017, https://www.thestar.com/news/ gta/2015/01/15/leslie-roberts-quits-global-tv-after-star-investigation.html.

5. Jennifer Deutschmann, "News anchor Leslie Roberts suspended amid 'journalistic integrity' probe," The Inquisitr News, January 9, 2015, accessed February 12, 2017, http:// www.inquisitr.com/1739968/leslie-roberts-suspended/.

6. Jennifer Deutschmann, "News anchor Leslie Roberts suspended amid 'journalistic integrity' probe," The Inquisitr News, January 9, 2015, accessed February 12, 2017, http:// www.inquisitr.com/1739968/leslie-roberts-suspended/.

7. "Leslie Roberts resigns from Global News in wake of internal investigation," Global News, January 16, 2015, accessed February 12, 2017, http://globalnews.ca/news/1774336/ leslie-roberts-resigns-from-global-news-in-wake-of-internal-investigation/.

8. Anne W. O'Connell, "Top 10 reasons for earning the APR," PRSay, September 28, 2015, accessed February 12, 2017, https://prsay.prsa.org/2015/09/28/top-10-reasons-for -earning-the-apr/.

9. "APR: Accredited in Public Relations—Universal Accreditation Board," accessed February 12, 2017, http://www.praccreditation.org/apply/apr/.

10. Gini Dietrich, "A crisis communications plan to prepare for a sexist tweet," Spin Sucks, November 2, 2016, accessed June 2, 2017, http://spinsucks.com/communication/crisis -communications-plan-sexist-tweet/.

11. Jon Ronson, "When online shaming goes too far," TED Talk Subtitles and Transcript, TED.com, accessed February 12, 2017, https://www.ted.com/talks/jon_ronson_what_hap pens_when_online_shaming_spirals_out_of_control/transcript?language=en.

12. Jon Ronson, "When online shaming goes too far," TED Talk Subtitles and Transcript, TED.com, accessed February 12, 2017, https://www.ted.com/talks/jon_ronson_what_hap pens_when_online_shaming_spirals_out_of_control/transcript?language=en.

13. Jon Ronson, "When online shaming goes too far," TED Talk Subtitles and Transcript, TED.com, accessed February 12, 2017, https://www.ted.com/talks/jon_ronson_what_hap pens_when_online_shaming_spirals_out_of_control/transcript?language=en.

14. Jon Ronson, "When online shaming goes too far," TED Talk Subtitles and Transcript, TED.com, accessed February 12, 2017, https://www.ted.com/talks/jon_ronson_what_hap pens_when_online_shaming_spirals_out_of_control/transcript?language=en.

15. Lucy Waterlow, "'I lost my job, my reputation and I'm not able to date anymore': Former PR worker reveals how she destroyed her life one year after sending 'racist' tweet before trip to Africa," Daily Mail Online, February 16, 2015, accessed February 12, 2017, http://www.dailymail.co.uk/femail/article-2955322/Justine-Sacco-reveals-destroyed-life-rac ist-tweet-trip-Africa.html.

16. Jon Ronson, "When online shaming goes too far," TED Talk Subtitles and Transcript, TED.com, accessed February 12, 2017, https://www.ted.com/talks/jon_ronson_what_hap pens_when_online_shaming_spirals_out_of_control/transcript?language=en.

17. Sam Biddle, "Justine Sacco is good at her job, and how I came to peace with her," Gawker, accessed February 12, 2017, http://gawker.com/justine-sacco-is-good-at-her-job -and-how-i-came-to-pea-1653022326.

18. "How can you manipulate the media to promote your self-interest?—with Ryan Holiday," Mixergy, accessed February 12, 2017, https://mixergy.com/interviews/ryan-holiday -interview/.

19. Ryan Holiday, *Trust Me, I'm Lying: Confessions of a Media Manipulator* (New York, NY: Portfolio, 2013).

20. Ryan Holiday, *Trust Me, I'm Lying: Confessions of a Media Manipulator* (New York, NY: Portfolio, 2013).

21. Shannon Bowen, "Ethics and public relations," Institute for Public Relations, June 9, 2015, accessed February 20, 2017, http://www.instituteforpr.org/ethics-and-public-relations/.

22. Admin, "History of public relations," InfoRefuge, May 31, 2011, accessed February 22, 2017, https://www.inforefuge.com/history-of-public-relations.

23. Thierry C. Pauchant and Ian I. Mitroff, *Transforming the Crisis-Prone Organization: Preventing Individual, Organizational, and Environmental Tragedies* (San Francisco: Jossey-Bass, 1992), 193.

24. Matthew W. Seeger and Robert R. Ulmer, "Explaining Enron: Communication and responsible leadership," *Management Communication Quarterly* 17, no. 1 (2003): doi:10.1177/0893318903253436; Robert Jackall, *Moral Mazes: The World of Corporate Managers* (Oxford University Press, 1988); Richard L. Johannesen, Kathleen S. Valde, and Karen E. Whedbee, *Ethics in Human Communication* (Long Grove, IL: Waveland Press, 2008).

25. Craig E. Johnson, *Meeting the Ethical Challenges of Leadership: Casting Light or Shadow* (Thousand Oaks, CA: SAGE Publications, 2001), 50.

26. Richard Burnor and Yvonne Raley, *Ethical Choices: An Introduction to Moral Philosophy with Cases* (New York: Oxford University Press, 2011), 222.

27. Leo V. Ryan, F. Byron Nahser, and Wojciech Gasparski, *Praxiology and Pragmatism* (New Brunswick, NJ: Transaction Publishers, 2002).

28. Patricia Parsons, *Ethics in Public Relations: A Guide to Best Practice* (London, UK: Kogan Page Limited, 2016), 133.

29. Ralph B. Potter, *The Structure of Certain American Christian Responses to the Nuclear Dilemma, 1958-1963*. Doctoral thesis, Harvard University, 1965.

30. Pierre Kiami, "Perspective," Individual Ethics—Tools and Methods for Empowering Ethical Decisions, November 2011.

31. Lucinda Austin, "Student's guide: Examining principles for ethical public relations through social media," http://comm.psu.edu/assets/uploads/AustinStudentGuideEthicsin PRNewMediav.pdf.

32. David Vinjamuri, "Ethics and the five deadly sins of social media," *Forbes*, March 5, 2012, accessed February 20, 2017, http://www.forbes.com/sites/davidvinjamuri/2011/11/03/ethics-and-the-5-deadly-sins-of-social-media/#d69364437ad2.

CHAPTER 7—LOYALTY

1. "Government Whistleblower, Paula Pedene, Named PRSA's 2015 Public Relations Professional of the Year," PRSA Newsroom, November 3, 2015, accessed November 8, 2016, http://media.prsa.org/news-releases/government-whistleblower-paula-pedene-named-prsas -2015-public-relations-professional-of-the-year.htm.

2. "Government Whistleblower, Paula Pedene, Named PRSA's 2015 Public Relations Professional of the Year," PRSA Newsroom, November 3, 2015, accessed November 8, 2016, http://media.prsa.org/news-releases/government-whistleblower-paula-pedene-named-prsas -2015-public-relations-professional-of-the-year.htm.

3. United States Department of Veterans Affairs, VA Office of Inspector General, "Review of alleged mismanagement of non-VA fee care funds at the Phoenix VA Health Care System," 1-12, November 8, 2011, accessed January 5, 2017, https://www.va.gov/oig/pubs/VAOIG-11-02280-23.pdf.

4. "Government Whistleblower, Paula Pedene, Named PRSA's 2015 Public Relations Professional of the Year," PRSA Newsroom, November 3, 2015, accessed November 8, 2016, http://media.prsa.org/news-releases/government-whistleblower-paula-pedene-named-prsas -2015-public-relations-professional-of-the-year.htm.

5. United States Department of Veterans Affairs, VA Office of Inspector General, "Review of alleged patient deaths, patient wait times, and scheduling practices at the Phoenix VA Health Care System," August 26, 2014, accessed January 5, 2017, https://www.va.gov/oig/pubs/VAOIG-14-02603-267.pdf.

6. "Government Whistleblower, Paula Pedene, Named PRSA's 2015 Public Relations Professional of the Year," PRSA Newsroom, November 3, 2015, accessed November 8, 2016, http://media.prsa.org/news-releases/government-whistleblower-paula-pedene-named-prsas -2015-public-relations-professional-of-the-year.htm.

7. "Loyal," *Merriam-Webster*, accessed February 17, 2017, https://www.merriam-webster .com/dictionary/loyal.

8. Patricia Houlihan Parsons, "Framework for analysis of conflicting loyalties," *Public Relations Review* 19, no. 1 (1993): doi:10.1016/0363-8111(93)90029-c.

9. "Public Relations Society of America (PRSA) Member Code of Ethics," accessed February 17, 2017, https://apps.prsa.org/AboutPRSA/Ethics/CodeEnglish/index.html.

10. Doug Newsom, Alan Scott, and Judy VanSlyke Turk, *This Is PR: The Realities of Public Relations* (Belmont, CA: Wadsworth, 1989.)

11. Philip M. Seib and Kathy Fitzpatrick, *Public Relations Ethics* (Mason, OH: Thomson Wadsworth, 2006).

12. Patricia Parsons, *Ethics in Public Relations: A Guide to Best Practice* (London, UK: Kogan Page Limited, 2016), 27.

13. Fraser P. Seitel, *The Practice of Public Relations*, 4th ed. (Columbus, OH: Merrill Publishing Co., 1989), 104.

14. "Public Relations Society of America (PRSA) Member Code of Ethics," accessed February 17, 2017, https://apps.prsa.org/AboutPRSA/Ethics/CodeEnglish/index.html.

15. "SPJ Code of Ethics," Society of Professional Journalists, accessed February 18, 2017, http://www.spj.org/ethicscode.asp.

16. "CIPR," Charter, Regulations and Code of Conduct, Chartered Institute of Public Relations, accessed February 18, 2017, https://www.cipr.co.uk/content/our-organisation/charter-regulations-and-code-conduct.

17. "Code of ethics and standards," PRISA, accessed February 18, 2017, http://www.prisa.co.za/index.php/membership/code-of-ethics-and-standards.

18. Michael D. Bayles, *Professional Ethics* (Pacific Grove: International Thomson Publishing, 1996).

19. Patricia Houlihan Parsons, "Framework for analysis of conflicting loyalties," *Public Relations Review* 19, no. 1 (1993): 49–57. doi:10.1016/0363-8111(93)90029-c.

20. Kevin Stoker (2005), "Loyalty in public relations: When does it cross the line between virtue and vice?" *Journal of Mass Media Ethics* 20, no. 4, 269–87, doi: 10.1207/s15327728jmme2004_4.

21. Kevin Stoker (2005), "Loyalty in public relations: When does it cross the line between virtue and vice?" *Journal of Mass Media Ethics* 20, no. 4, 269–87, doi: 10.1207/s15327728jmme2004_4.

22. Kevin Stoker (2005), "Loyalty in public relations: When does it cross the line between virtue and vice?" *Journal of Mass Media Ethics* 20, no. 4, 269–87, doi: 10.1207/s15327728jmme2004_4.

23. Kevin Stoker (2005), "Loyalty in public relations: When does it cross the line between virtue and vice?" *Journal of Mass Media Ethics* 20, no. 4, 269–87, doi: 10.1207/s15327728jmme2004_4.

24. "Ethics and social media," http://www.prsa.org/wp-content/uploads/2016/10/Ethics-and-Social-Media.pdf, September 1, 2015.

25. "Ethics and social media," http://www.prsa.org/wp-content/uploads/2016/10/Ethics-and-Social-Media.pdf, September 1, 2015.

26. Marc Graser, "Consumer-made commercials blast Chevy," *Ad Age*, April 5, 2006.

27. Frank R. Kardes, Maria L. Cronley, and Thomas W. Cline, *Consumer Behavior* (Stamford, CT: Cengage Learning, 2015).

28. "Chevy history: Defining our spirit, style & dependability," www.chevrolet.com, accessed February 18, 2017, http://www.chevrolet.com/culture/category/history.html.

CHAPTER 8—FAIRNESS

1. "About," *Blackfish*, accessed February 19, 2017, http://www.blackfishmovie.com/about.

2. "Saving SeaWorld," Bloomberg.com, November 20, 2014, accessed February 19, 2017, https://www.bloomberg.com/news/articles/2014-11-20/facing-blackfish-backlash-seaworld-tries-to-save-itself.

3. Austen Hufford, "SeaWorld revenue and attendance fall," *The Wall Street Journal*, November 8, 2016, accessed February 19, 2017, https://www.wsj.com/articles/seaworld-revenue-and-attendance-falls-1478616894.

4. John Paul Titlow, "SeaWorld is spending $10 million to make you forget about 'Blackfish,'" *Fast Company*, August 4, 2015, accessed February 19, 2017, https://www.fastcompany .com/3046342/seaworld-is-spending-10-million-to-make-you-forget-about-blackfish.

5. John Paul Titlow, "SeaWorld is spending $10 million to make you forget about 'Blackfish,'" *Fast Company*, August 4, 2015, accessed February 19, 2017, https://www.fastcompany .com/3046342/seaworld-is-spending-10-million-to-make-you-forget-about-blackfish.

6. John Paul Titlow, "SeaWorld is spending $10 million to make you forget about 'Blackfish,'" *Fast Company*, August 4, 2015, accessed February 19, 2017, https://www.fastcompany .com/3046342/seaworld-is-spending-10-million-to-make-you-forget-about-blackfish.

7. "Public Relations Society of America (PRSA) Member Code of Ethics," accessed February 18, 2017, https://www.prsa.org/aboutprsa/ethics/codeenglish/#.Vwfab2PSfVo.

8. "Fairness," Merriam-Webster, accessed February 18, 2017, https://www.merriam-web ster.com/dictionary/fairness.

9. Santa Clara University, "Justice and Fairness," accessed February 18, 2017, https:// www.scu.edu/ethics/ethics-resources/ethical-decision-making/justice-and-fairness/.

10. John Rawls, *A Theory of Justice* (Boston, MA: Belknap Press, 1999).

11. Samuel Freeman, "Original position," *Stanford Encyclopedia of Philosophy*, February 27, 1996, accessed February 18, 2017, https://plato.stanford.edu/entries/original-position/.

12. John Rawls, *A Theory of Justice* (Boston, MA: Belknap Press, 1999).

13. John Rawls, *A Theory of Justice* (Boston, MA: Belknap Press, 1999).

14. "Original position," *Stanford Encyclopedia of Philosophy*, December 20, 2008, accessed February 20, 2017, https://plato.stanford.edu/archives/spr2009/entries/original-position/.

15. Christopher Panza and Adam Potthast, *Ethics for Dummies* (Hoboken, NJ: Wiley, 2010).

16. Christopher Panza and Adam Potthast, *Ethics for Dummies* (Hoboken, NJ: Wiley, 2010).

17. John Rawls, *A Theory of Justice* (Boston, MA: Belknap Press, 1999).

18. Elizabeth Lance Toth, "Whose freedom and equity in public relations? The gender balance argument," ERIC, August 1989, accessed February 20, 2017, https://eric.ed.gov/?id= ED311479.

19. Aarti Shah, "Why aren't there more female CEOs in PR?" The Holmes Report, November 24, 2015, accessed February 20, 2017, http://www.holmesreport.com/long-reads/ article/why-aren't-there-more-female-ceos-in-pr.

20. Keith Trivitt, "General public relations ethics case studies," accessed February 19, 2017, http://apps.prsa.org/AboutPRSA/Ethics/Resources/PublicRelationsEthicsCaseStudies/.

21. Dan Lyons, "Facebook busted in clumsy smear on Google," The Daily Beast, May 11, 2011, accessed February 19, 2017, http://www.thedailybeast.com/articles/2011/05/12/ facebook-busted-in-clumsy-smear-attempt-on-google.html.

22. "From Mercurio, John to Christopher Soghoian," Pastebin, May 3, 2011, accessed January 3, 2016, http://pastebin.com/zaeTeJeJ.

23. Michael Arrington, "Facebook loses much face in secret smear on Google," TechCrunch, accessed February 19, 2017, https://techcrunch.com/2011/05/12/facebook-loses -much-face-in-secret-smear-on-google/.

24. Keith Trivitt, "General public relations ethics case studies," accessed February 19, 2017, http://apps.prsa.org/AboutPRSA/Ethics/Resources/PublicRelationsEthicsCaseStudies/.

25. Keith Trivitt, "General public relations ethics case studies," accessed February 19, 2017, http://apps.prsa.org/AboutPRSA/Ethics/Resources/PublicRelationsEthicsCaseStudies/.

26. Keith Trivitt, "General public relations ethics case studies," accessed February 19, 2017, http://apps.prsa.org/AboutPRSA/Ethics/Resources/PublicRelationsEthicsCaseStudies/.

27. "Ethics and social media," http://www.prsa.org/wp-content/uploads/2016/10/Ethics-and-Social-Media.pdf, September 1, 2015.

28. Rachel Rosenthal, "Look at how a society treats its animals," *Los Angeles Times*, August 12, 2002, accessed February 20, 2017, http://articles.latimes.com/2002/aug/12/opinion/le-hamlin12.2.

29. M. Alan Kazlev, "Sentientism," July 16, 2010, accessed February 20, 2017, http://kheper.net/topics/sentientism/index.html.

Bibliography

"About." *Blackfish*. Accessed February 19, 2017. http://www.blackfishmovie.com/about.

Admin. "History of public relations." InfoRefuge. May 31, 2011. Accessed February 22, 2017. https://www.inforefuge.com/history-of-public-relations.

"APR: Accredited in Public Relations." APR: Accredited in Public Relations—Universal Accreditation Board. Accessed February 12, 2017. http://www.praccreditation.org/apply/apr/.

Aristotle. *Nicomachean Ethics*. bk. VI. H. Rackbam trans. 1962.

Arrington, Michael. "Facebook loses much face in secret smear on Google." TechCrunch. Accessed February 19, 2017. https://techcrunch.com/2011/05/12/facebook-loses-much-face-in-secret-smear-on-google/.

Austin, Lucinda. "Student's guide: Examining principles for ethical public relations through social media." http://comm.psu.edu/assets/uploads/AustinStudentGuideEthicsinPRNewMediav.pdf.

Baker, Sherry. "Five baselines for justification in persuasion." *Journal of Mass Media Ethics* 14, no. 2 (1999): 69–81. doi:10.1207/s15327728jmme1402_1.

Baker, Sherry, and David L. Martinson. "The TARES test: Five principles for ethical persuasion." *Journal of Mass Media Ethics* 16, no. 2–3 (2001): 148–75. doi:10.1080/08900523.2001.9679610.

Bauman, Mike. "Mike Bauman: Drug policy, appeal process prevail in Alex Rodriguez A-Rod case." Major League Baseball. January 11, 2014. Accessed January 16, 2017. http://m.mlb.com/news/article/66498146/mike-bauman-drug-policy-appeal-process-prevail-in-alex-rodriguez-a-rod-case/.

Bayles, Michael D. *Professional Ethics*. Pacific Grove: International Thomson Publishing, 1996.

Beier, Klaus M., Janina Neutze, Ingrid A. Mundt, Christoph J. Ahlers, David Goecker, Anna Konrad, and Gerard A. Schaefer. "Encouraging self-identified pedophiles and hebephiles to seek professional help: First results of the Prevention Project Dunkelfeld (PPD)." *Child Abuse and Neglect* 33, no. 8 (2009): 545–49. doi:10.1016/j.chiabu.2009.04.002.

Bentham, Jeremy. *An Introduction to the Principles of Morals and Legislation*. Oxford: Clarendon Press, 1907.

Bentley, Holly, Orla O'Hagan, Annie Raff, and Iram Bhatti. "How safe are our children? 2016." NSPCC. Accessed November 8, 2016. https://www.nspcc.org.uk/services-and -resources/research-and-resources/2016/how-safe-are-our-children-2016/.

Biddle, Sam. "Justine Sacco is good at her job, and how I came to peace with her." *Gawker*. Accessed February 12, 2017. http://gawker.com/justine-sacco-is-good-at-her-job-and-how -i-came-to-pea-1653022326.

Bivins, Thomas. "Responsibility and accountability." In *Ethics in Public Relations: Responsible Advocacy*. Thousand Oaks, CA: SAGE Publications, 2006.

Bivins, Thomas. "Public relations, professionalism and the public interest." *Journal of Business Ethics* 12, no. 2 (1993).

Black, Jay. "Semantics and ethics of propaganda." *Journal of Mass Media Ethics* 16, no. 2–3 (2001): 121–37. doi:10.1080/08900523.2001.9679608.

Bok, Sissela. *Lying: Moral Choice in Public and Private Life*. New York: Pantheon Books, 1978.

Booth, J. & Son. *The Greatest Natural & National Curiosity in the World Joice Heth*. Printed Handbill—12 × 6½", 147 Fulton St., NY—Somers Historical Society P.O. Box 336, Somers, NY 10589.

Bowen, Shannon. "Ethics and public relations." Institute for Public Relations. June 9, 2015. Accessed February 24, 2017. http://www.instituteforpr.org/ethics-and-public-relations.

Breit, Rhonda, and Kristin Demetrious. "Professionalisation and public relations: An ethical mismatch." *Ethical Space: The International Journal of Communication Ethics* 7, no. 4, 2010.

Burnor, Richard, and Yvonne Raley. *Ethical Choices: An Introduction to Moral Philosophy with Cases*. New York, NY: Oxford University Press, 2011.

"By the numbers: Here are the 20 'most dangerous' cities in America." FOX31 Denver. May 8, 2015. Accessed January 16, 2017. http://kdvr.com/2015/05/08/by-the-numbers-here-are -the-most-dangerous-cities-in-america/.

Calderwood, Stephen B., and Adaora Adimora. "Letter from Stephen B. Calderwood, MD, FIDSA (President, IDSA) and Adaora Adimora, MD, MPH, FIDSA (Chair, HIVMA) to Mssrs. Tom Evegan (Head of Managed Markets) and Kevin Bernier (National Director Al- lience Development & Public Affairs), both of Turing Pharmacauticals" (PDF). Arlington, VA: Infectious Diseases Society of America (IDSA), HIV Medicine Association (HIVMA). Retrieved December 10, 2015. http://www.hivma.org/uploadedFiles/HIVMA/HomePage Content/PyrimethamineLetterFINAL.pdf.

Center, Allen H., and Scott Cutlip. *Effective Public Relations*. New York: Pearson, 1952.

"Chevy history: Defining our spirit, style & dependability." www.chevrolet.com. Accessed February 18, 2017. http://www.chevrolet.com/culture/category/history.html.

"Children and Teens: Statistics." RAINN. Accessed January 9, 2017. https://www.rainn.org/ statistics/children-and-teens.

CIPR. "Charter, regulations, and code of conduct." Accessed February 21, 2017. https://www .cipr.co.uk/content/our-organisation/charter-regulations-and-code-of-conduct.

"Code of ethics and standards." PRISA. Accessed February 21, 2017. http://www.prisa.co.za/ index.php/membership/code-of-ethics-and-standards.

Conner, Cheryl. "Is ghostwriting ethical?" *Forbes*. March 13, 2014. Accessed February 17, 2017. http://www.forbes.com/sites/cherylsnappconner/2014/03/13/is-ghostwriting-eth ical/#d4e721733a0d.

"Conway: Trump White House offered 'alternative facts' on crowd size." CNN. Accessed Febru- ary 11, 2017. http://www.cnn.com/2017/01/22/politics/kellyanne-conway-alternative-facts/.

Cunningham, Stanley B. "Responding to propaganda: An ethical enterprise." *Journal of Mass Media Ethics* 16, no. 2–3 (2001): 138–47. doi:10.1080/08900523.2001.9679609.

Daly, Stephen. "Black Ops 3's story revealed through Twitter campaign." Gameranx. February 3, 2016. Accessed February 21, 2017. http://gameranx.com/updates/id/30694/article/black-ops-3-s-story-revealed-through-twitter-campaign/.

Davey, Monica. "Flint officials are no longer saying the water is fine." *New York Times.* October 7, 2015. Accessed July 2, 2016. https://www.nytimes.com/2015/10/08/us/reassurances-end-in-flint-after-months-of-concern.html?_r=0.

Deutschmann, Jennifer. "News anchor Leslie Roberts suspended amid 'journalistic integrity' probe." *The Inquisitr News.* January 9, 2015. Accessed February 12, 2017. http://www.inquisitr.com/1739968/leslie-roberts-suspended/.

DiStaso, Marcia W., and Denise Sevick Bortree. *Ethical Practice of Social Media in Public Relations.* New York: Routledge, 2014.

Donovan, Kevin. "Leslie Roberts quits Global TV after Star investigation." Thestar.com. January 15, 2015. Accessed February 12, 2017. https://www.thestar.com/news/gta/2015/01/15/leslie-roberts-quits-global-tv-after-star-investigation.html.

Dvorak, Jane. "PRSA statement on 'Alternative Facts'." PRSA Newsroom. January 24, 2017. Accessed February 17, 2017. http://media.prsa.org/news-releases/prsa-opinions-and-commentary/prsa-makes-statement-on-alternative-facts.htm.

"Echo chamber (media)." Wikipedia. Accessed February 11, 2017. https://en.wikipedia.org/wiki/Echo_chamber_(media).

Edgett, Ruth. "Toward an ethical framework for advocacy in public relations." *Journal of Public Relations Research* 14, no. 1 (2002): 1–26. doi:10.1207/s1532754xjprr1401_1.

"Ethics and social media." http://www.prsa.org/wp-content/uploads/2016/10/Ethics-and-Social-Media.pdf. September 1, 2015.

"Fact sheet." PRSA Newsroom. Accessed February 21, 2017. http://media.prsa.org/about prsa/fact sheet/.

"Fairness." Merriam-Webster. Accessed February 18, 2017. https://www.merriam-webster.com/dictionary/fairness.

Farnsworth, Steve. "Ghostwriting isn't unethical (most of the time)." Ragan.com. June 20, 2012. Accessed February 17, 2017. https://www.ragan.com/Main/Articles/Ghostwriting_isnt_unethical_most_of_the_time_45078.aspx#.

Fitzpatrick, Kathy. "Ethical decision-making guide helps resolve ethical dilemmas." PRSA.org. Accessed November 2, 2016. http://www.prsa.org/AboutPRSA/Ethics/documents/decisionguide.pdf.

Fitzpatrick, Kathy, and Carolyn Bronstein. *Ethics in Public Relations: Responsible Advocacy.* London: SAGE Publications, 2006.

Fonger, Ron. "Flint River water complicating city's efforts to battle contamination, boil advisories." Mlive. September 18, 2014. Accessed July 2, 2016. http://www.mlive.com/news/flint/index.ssf/2014/09/dpw_director_says_flint_river.html.

Fonger, Ron. "Lead leaches into 'very corrosive' Flint drinking water, researchers say." Mlive. September 2, 2015. Accessed July 3, 2016. http://www.mlive.com/news/flint/index.ssf/2015/09/new_testing_shows_flint_water.html.

Foot, Philippa. "The problem of abortion and the doctrine of the double effect." In *Virtues and Vices and Other Essays in Moral Philosophy*, 19–32. Berkeley and Los Angeles: University of California Press, 1978.

Fox, Maggie. "Health competitor to offer $1 pill after Turing price hike outrage." NBC News. October 22, 1015. Retrieved December 5, 2016.

Freeman, Samuel. "Original position." *Stanford Encyclopedia of Philosophy*. February 27, 1996. Accessed February 18, 2017. https://plato.stanford.edu/entries/original-position/.

"From Mercurio, John to Christopher Soghoian." *Pastebin*. May 3, 2011. Accessed January 3, 2016. http://pastebin.com/zaeTeJeJ.

Goldsberry, Lisa. "Is there honesty in PR?" *Axia Public Relations* (web log). June 20, 2016. Accessed August 11. 2016, http://www.axiapr.com/blog/is-there-honesty-in-pr.

"Government whistleblower, Paula Pedene, Named PRSA's 2015 Public Relations Professional of the Year." PRSA Newsroom. November 3, 2015. Accessed November 8, 2016. http://media.prsa.org/news-releases/government-whistleblower-paula-pedene-named -prsas-2015-public-relations-professional-of-the-year.htm.

Graser, Marc. "Consumer-made commercials blast Chevy." *Ad Age*. April 5, 2006.

"Great Philosophers: Plato—Ethics—The ring of Gyges." *Great Philosophers: Plato—Ethics— The Ring of Gyges*. Accessed February 11, 2017. http://oregonstate.edu/instruct/phl201/ modules/Philosophers/Plato/plato_dialogue_the_ring_of_gyges.html.

Green, Anne. "FROM." PR Council. February 1, 2017. Accessed February 17, 2017. http:// prcouncil.net/blog/truthiness-alternative-facts-must-recommit-core-communications-values/.

Grunig, James E. "Ethics problems and theories in public relations." Communiquer. *Revue De Communication Sociale Et Publique*, no. 11 (2014): 1–14. doi:10.4000/communiquer.559.

Grunig, James E., and Todd Hunt. *Managing Public Relations*. New York: Holt, Rinehart and Winston, 1984.

Harlow, Rex F. "Building a public relations definition." *Public Relations Review* 2, no. 4 (1976). doi:10.1016/s0363-8111(76)80022-7.

Hirschmann, Nancy J. *Gender, Class, and Freedom in Modern Political Theory*. Princeton, NJ: Princeton University Press, 2009.

Holiday, Ryan. *Trust Me, I'm Lying: Confessions of a Media Manipulator*. New York: Portfolio, 2013.

Hollin, C. R. "Does punishment motivate offenders to change?" In M. Mc Murran (ed.), *Motivating Offenders to Change. A Guide to Enhancing Engagement in Therapy*. Wiley Series in Forensic Clinical Psychology, 2002.

"How can you manipulate the media to promote your self-interest?—with Ryan Holiday." *Mixergy*. Accessed February 12, 2017. https://mixergy.com/interviews/ryan-holiday-interview/.

Hufford, Austen. "SeaWorld Revenue and attendance fall." *The Wall Street Journal*. November 8, 2016. Accessed February 19, 2017. https://www.wsj.com/articles/seaworld-revenue-and -attendance-falls-1478616894.

"The Internet Classics Archive. The Republic by Plato." Accessed February 11, 2017. http:// classics.mit.edu/Plato/republic.3.ii.html.

"Internet Marketing–Chapter 6-Kohlberg." Accessed January 5, 2017. http://education .smartpros.com/internetmarketing/ch06/kohlberg.html.

Jackall, Robert. *Moral Mazes: The World of Corporate Managers*. Oxford University Press, 1988.

Jackall, Robert, and Janice M. Hirota. *Image Makers: Advertising, Public Relations, and the Ethos of Advocacy*. Chicago: University of Chicago Press, 2000.

Jeffrey, Cal. "Galaxy Note 7: Samsung facing PR Disaster and sobering losses after pulling the plug on its flagship smartphone." *The Inquisitr News*. January 16, 2017. Accessed January 16, 2017. http://www.inquisitr.com/3593141/galaxy-note-7-samsung-facing-pr-disaster -and-sobering-losses-after-pulling-the-plug-on-its-flagship-smartphone/.

Jenkins, Henry. "The cultural logic of media convergence." *International Journal of Cultural Studies* 7, no. 1 (2004). doi:10.1177/1367877904040603.

Jensen, Vernon J. *Ethical Issues in the Communication Process.* Mahwah, NJ: Erlbaum, 1997.

Johannesen, Richard L, Kathleen S. Valde, and Karen E. Whedbee. *Ethics in Human Communication.* Long Grove, IL: Waveland Press, 2008.

Johnson, Craig E. *Organizational Ethics: A Practical Approach.* Thousand Oaks, CA: SAGE Publications, 2012.

Kant, Immanuel, and Mary J. Gregor. *Groundwork of the Metaphysics of Morals.* Cambridge, UK: Cambridge University Press, 1998.

Kanter, Beth. *Ice Bucket Challenge: Can Other Nonprofits Reproduce It?* [Web log post] 2014. Retrieved from http://www.bethkanter.org/icebucket-2/.

Kardes, Frank R., Maria L. Cronley, and Thomas W. Cline. *Consumer Behavior.* Stamford, CT: Cengage Learning, 2015.

Kazlev, M. Alan. "Sentientism." July 16, 2010. Accessed February 20, 2017. http://kheper.net/topics/sentientism/index.html.

Kiami, Pierre. "Perspective." *Individual Ethics—Tools and Methods for Empowering Ethical Decisions.* November 2011.

Kliff, Sarah. "Vox explainers: A drug company raised a pill's price 5,500 percent because, in America, it can." Vox. September 22, 2015.

Koehn, Daryl. "What is practical judgement?" *Professional Ethics, A Multidisciplinary Journal* 8, no. 3 (2000). doi:10.5840/profethics200083/420.

Kohlberg, Lawrence. "Moral stages and moralization: The cognitive-developmental approach." In *Moral Development and Behavior: Theory, Research and Social Issues.* Holt, NY: Rinehart and Winston, 1976.

Kruckeberg, Dean, and Kenneth Starck. *Public Relations and Community: A Reconstructed Theory.* New York: Praeger, 1988.

Laird, Andrew. "Ringing the changes on Gyges: Philosophy and the formation of fiction in Plato's Republic." *The Journal of Hellenic Studies* 121 (2001). doi:10.2307/631825.

"Leslie Roberts resigns from Global News in wake of internal investigation." *Global News.* January 16, 2015. Accessed February 12, 2017. http://globalnews.ca/news/1774336/leslie-roberts-resigns-from-global-news-in-wake-of-internal-investigation/.

Lessenberry, Jack. "Flint's water crisis another example of how Gov. Snyder seems incapable of admitting mistakes." Michigan Radio. October 2, 2015. Accessed July 16, 2016. http://michiganradio.org/post/flints-water-crisis-another-example-how-gov-snyder-seems-incapable-admitting-mistakes#stream/0.

Levick. "It's not just about honesty." *Public Relations and Strategic Communication.* March 23, 2016. Accessed January 2, 2017. http://levick.com/blog/brand/not-just-honesty/.

Locke, John. "John Locke: Two Treatises of Government (1680–1690)." LONANG Institute. Accessed January 4, 2017. http://lonang.com/library/reference/locke-two-treatises-government.

Lott, Eric, and Greil Marcus. *Love and Theft: Blackface Minstrelsy and the American Working Class.* New York: Oxford University Press, 2013.

"Loyal." *Merriam-Webster.* Accessed February 17, 2017. https://www.merriam-webster.com/dictionary/loyal.

Lyons, Dan. "Facebook busted in clumsy smear on Google." *The Daily Beast.* May 11, 2011. Accessed February 19, 2017. http://www.thedailybeast.com/articles/2011/05/12/facebook-busted-in-clumsy-smear-attempt-on-google.html.

"Magic bullet or hypodermic needle theory of communication." *Communication Theory.* Accessed January 16, 2017. http://communicationtheory.org/magic-bullet-or-hypodermic-needle-theory-of-communication/.

Maheshwari, Sapna. "Samsung's response to Galaxy Note 7 crisis draws criticism." *New York Times.* October 11, 2016. Accessed January 16, 2016. https://www.nytimes.com/2016/10/12/business/media/samsungs-passive-response-to-note-7s-overheating-problem-draws-criticism.htm

"Meet The Press 01/22/17." NBCNews.com. January 22, 2017. Accessed February 11, 2017. http://www.nbcnews.com/meet-the-press/meet-press-01-22-17-n710491.

Mill, John Stuart. "Utilitarianism by John Stuart Mill." Utilitarianism by John Stuart Mill. Accessed January 4, 2017. https://www.utilitarianism.com/mill2.htm.

Miller, G. R. "Persuasion and public relations: Two 'Ps' in a pod." In *Public Relations Theory.* Hillsdale, NJ: Lawrence Erlbaum Associates, 1989.

Newsom, Doug, Judy VanSlyke Turk, and Dean Kruckeberg. *Instructor's Guide for Newsom, Turk, Kruckeberg's: This Is PR: The Realities of Public Relations.* Belmont, CA: Wadsworth, 1996.

O'Connell, Anne W. "Top 10 reasons for earning the APR." *PRSay.* September 28, 2015. Accessed February 12, 2017. https://prsay.prsa.org/2015/09/28/top-10-reasons-for-earning-the-apr/.

"Original Position." *Stanford Encyclopedia of Philosophy.* December 20, 2008. Accessed February 20, 2017. https://plato.stanford.edu/archives/spr2009/entries/original-position/.

Panza, Christopher, and Adam Potthast. *Ethics for Dummies.* Hoboken, NJ: Wiley, 2010.

Parsons, Patricia. *Ethics in Public Relations: A Guide to Best Practice.* London, UK: Kogan Page Limited, 2004.

Parsons, Patricia Houlihan. "Framework for analysis of conflicting loyalties." *Public Relations Review* 19, no. 1 (1993). doi:10.1016/0363-8111(93)90029-c.

Pauchant, Thierry C., and Ian I. Mitroff. *Transforming the Crisis-Prone Organization: Preventing Individual, Organizational, and Environmental Tragedies.* San Francisco, CA: Jossey-Bass, 1992.

Potter, Ralph B. *The Structure of Certain American Christian Responses to the Nuclear Dilemma, 1958-1963.* Doctoral thesis, Harvard University, 1965.

"Propaganda by Edward Bernays (1928)." Historyisaweapon.org. Accessed February 24, 2017. http://www.historyisaweapon.org/defcon1/bernprop.html.

"Public health emergency declaration for people using the Flint city water supply with the Flint River as the source." Genesee County, Michigan. Accessed July 15, 2016. http://www.gc4me.com/departments/emg_mgt_homeland_sec/docs/Water_Emergency_Declaration_12_4_15.pdf.

"Public Relations Institute of Australia (PRIA) Code of Ethics." PRIA.com. July 15, 2009. Accessed January 4, 2017. https://www.pria.com.au/documents/item/6317.

"Public Relations Society of America (PRSA) Member Code of Ethics." Public Relations Society of America. Accessed February 24, 2017. https://apps.prsa.org/AboutPRSA/Ethics/CodeEnglish/index.html.

Rawls, John. *A Theory of Justice.* Boston, MA: Belknap Press, 1999.

Red, Christian, Michael O'Keeffe, and Nathaniel Vinton. "Alex Rodriguez's career overshadowed by steroid scandals." *NY Daily News.* August 7, 2016. Accessed January 16, 2017. http://www.nydailynews.com/sports/baseball/yankees/alex-rodriguez-career-overshadowed-steroid-scandals-article-1.2741694.

Rede, George. "Same-sex couple in Sweet Cakes controversy should receive $135,000, hearings officer says." OregonLive.com. April 24, 2015. Accessed January 5, 2017. http://www.oregonlive.com/business/index.ssf/2015/04/same-sex_couple_in_sweet_cakes.html.

Reilly, Katy. "Disney worker fired—then rehired—after tweet about alligators at the park." *Time.* Accessed January 3, 2017. http://time.com/4409314/disney-world-alligators-worker-fired/.

Renfree, Mark. "Ryan Lochte and the 3 F's of crisis communications." *PR News.* August 22, 2016. Accessed February 11, 2017. http://www.prnewsonline.com/ryan-lochte-crisis?hq_e=el&hq_m=3280668&hq_l=7&hq_v=69836be966.

Ronson, Jon. "Transcript of 'When online shaming goes too far.'" TED Talk Subtitles and Transcript, TED.com. Accessed February 12, 2017. https://www.ted.com/talks/jon_ronson_what_happens_when_online_shaming_spirals_out_of_control/transcript?language=en.

Rosenthal, Rashel. "Look at how a society treats its animals." *Los Angeles Times.* August 12, 2002. Accessed February 20, 2017. http://articles.latimes.com/2002/aug/12/opinion/le-hamlin12.2.

Rovell, Darren. "Maria Sharapova suspended 2 years over positive doping test." ESPN. June 9, 2016. Accessed January 16, 2017. http://www.espn.com/tennis/story/_/id/16044538/maria-sharapova-suspended-two-years-international-tennis-federation-positive-drug-test-meldonium.

Ryan, Leo V., F. Byron Nahser, and Wojciech Gasparski. *Praxiology and Pragmatism.* New Brunswick, NJ: Transaction Publishers, 2002.

Sandel, Michael. "Episode 06." Justice with Michael Sandel. Accessed January 4, 2017. http://www.justiceharvard.org/2011/02/episode-06/.

Santa Clara University. "Justice and Fairness." *Ethical Decision Making—Ethics Resources—Markkula Center for Applied Ethics—Santa Clara University.* Accessed February 18, 2017. https://www.scu.edu/ethics/ethics-resources/ethical-decision-making/justice-and-fairness/.

"Saving SeaWorld." Bloomberg.com. November 20, 2014. Accessed February 19, 2017. https://www.bloomberg.com/news/articles/2014-11-20/facing-blackfish-backlash-seaworld-tries-to-save-itself.

Schudson, Michael, and Chris Anderson. "Objectivity, professionalism and truth seeking in journalism." Karen Wahl-Jorgenson and Thomas Hanitzsch (eds.), *The Handbook of Journalism Studies.* NewYork and London: Routledge, 2009.

"Sean Spicer stands by false claim over inauguration crowd size." *Time.* Accessed February 11, 2017. http://time.com/4643927/sean-spicer-white-house-donald-trump-inauguration-press-briefing/.

Seeger, Matthew W., and Robert, R. Ulmer. "Explaining Enron: Communication and responsible leadership." *Management Communication Quarterly* 17, no. 1 (2003). doi:10.1177/0893318903253436.

Seib, Philip M., and Kathy Fitzpatrick. *Public Relations Ethics.* Mason, OH: Thomson Wadsworth, 2006.

Seitel, Fraser P. *The Practice of Public Relations*, 4th ed. Columbus, OH: Merrill Publishing Co., 1989.

Sexual victimization of children in South Africa: Final report of the Optimus Foundation Study. UBS Optimus Foundation, June 2016. Accessed November 8, 2016. http://www.cjcp.org.za/uploads/2/7/8/4/27845461/08_cjcp_report_2016_d.pdf.

Shah, Aarti. "Why aren't there more female CEOs in PR?" *The Holmes Report.* November 24, 2015. Accessed February 20, 2017. http://www.holmesreport.com/long-reads/article/why-aren't-there-more-female-ceos-in-pr.

Shirky, Clay. *Here Comes Everybody: The Power of Organizing without Organizations.* New York: Penguin, 2008.

Sifferlin, Alexandra. "Here's how the ALS Ice Bucket Challenge actually started." *Time.* August 18, 2014. Retrieved from http://time.com/3136507/als-ice-bucket-challenge-started/.

Sims, Ronald R. "Linking groupthink to unethical behavior in organizations." *Journal of Business Ethics* 11, no. 9 (1992): 651–62. doi:10.1007/bf01686345.

Sledzik, Bill. "The '4 models' of public relations practice: How far have you evolved?" *ToughSledding: Challenging the status quo in public relations* (web log). August 10, 2008. Accessed June 6, 2016. https://toughsledding.wordpress.com/2008/08/10/the-4-models -of-public-relations-practice-how-far-have-you-evolved/.

Solis, Brian. "Social media is lost without a social compass." Accessed February 20, 2017. http://www.briansolis.com/2014/07/social-media-lost-without-social-compass/.

"SPJ Code of Ethics." Society of Professional Journalists. September 6, 2014. Accessed February 17, 2014. https://www.spj.org/ethicscode.asp.

"Statement by Press Secretary Sean Spicer." The White House. January 21, 2017. Accessed February 11, 2017. https://www.whitehouse.gov/the-press-office/2017/01/21/statement -press-secretary-sean-spicer.

"Statement of Ethics." American Marketing Association. Accessed February 21, 2017. https:// www.ama.org/AboutAMA/Pages/Statement-of-Ethics.aspx.

Stoker, K. "Loyalty in public relations: When does it cross the line between virtue and vice?" *Journal of Mass Media Ethics* 20, no. 4 (2005). doi: 10.1207/s15327728jmme2004_4.

"Study: 81% of consumers say they will make personal sacrifices to address social, environmental issues." Sustainablebrands.com. Accessed January 3, 2017. http://www.sustainablebrands .com/news_and_views/stakeholder_trends_insights/sustainable_brands/study_81_consum ers_say_they_will_make_.

Szalay, Jessie. "The Feejee Mermaid: Early Barnum hoax." *LiveScience.* Accessed December 14, 2016. http://www.livescience.com/56037-feejee-mermaid.html.

Tannahill, Jason. "PR man Allan Ripp representing the most hated man in America." *EverythingPR.* October 9, 2015.

Titlow, John Paul. "SeaWorld is spending $10 million to make you forget about 'Blackfish'." *Fast Company.* August 4, 2015. Accessed February 19, 2017. https://www.fastcompany .com/3046342/seaworld-is-spending-10-million-to-make-you-forget-about-blackfish.

"Top 10 reasons for earning the APR." *PRSay.* September 28, 2015. Accessed February 13, 2017. http://prsay.prsa.org/2015/09/28/top-10-reasons-for-earning-the-apr/.

Toth, Elizabeth Lance. "Whose freedom and equity in public relations? The gender balance argument." ERIC. August 1989. Accessed February 20, 2017. https://eric.ed.gov/?id=ED311479.

"Treyarch shocked by reaction to *Call of Duty: Black Ops 3* Twitter marketing stunt." AR12 Gaming. Accessed February 12, 2017. https://ar12gaming.com/articles/treyarch-shocked -by-reaction-to-call-of-duty-black-ops-3-twitter-marketing-stunt.

Trivitt, Keith. "General public relations ethics case studies." Public Relations Society of America. Accessed February 19, 2017. http://apps.prsa.org/AboutPRSA/Ethics/Resources/ PublicRelationsEthicsCaseStudies/.

United States. Department of Veteran Affairs. VA Office of Inspector General. Review of Alleged Mismanagement of Non-VA Fee Care Funds at the Phoenix VA Health Care System. 1-12. November 8, 2011. Accessed January 5, 2017. https://www.va.gov/oig/pubs/ VAOIG-11-02280-23.pdf.

Vinjamuri, David. "Ethics and the five deadly sins of social media." *Forbes*. March 5, 2012. Accessed February 20, 2017. http://www.forbes.com/sites/davidvinjamuri/2011/11/03/ethics-and-the-5-deadly-sins-of-social-media/#d69364437ad2.

Volti, Rudi. *An Introduction to the Sociology of Work and Occupations*. Los Angeles: Pine Forge Press, 2008.

Waterlow, Lucy. "'I lost my job, my reputation and I'm not able to date anymore': Former PR worker reveals how she destroyed her life one year after sending 'racist' tweet before trip to Africa." *Daily Mail Online*. February 16, 2015. Accessed February 12, 2017. http://www.dailymail.co.uk/femail/article-2955322/Justine-Sacco-reveals-destroyed-life-racist-tweet-trip-Africa.html.

Wilcox, Dennis L., Glen T. Cameron, Bryan H. Reber, and Jae-Hwa Shin. *Think Public Relations*. Boston: Pearson, 2013.

Wpadmin. "37 scarey repeat sex offenders statistics." HRFnd. November 13, 2014. Accessed November 3, 2016. http://healthresearchfunding.org/37-scarey-repeat-sex-offenders-statistics/.

Wright, Donald K. "Enforcement dilemma: Voluntary nature of public relations codes." *Public Relations Review* 19, no. 1 (1993): 13–20. doi:10.1016/0363-8111(93)90026-9.

Yakowicz, Will. "How loyalty affects your team's ethics." Inc.com. January 7, 2016. Accessed February 28, 2017. http://www.inc.com/will-yakowicz/loyalty-can-improve-moral-judgment.html.

Young Entrepreneur Council. "The 3 T's of a great PR experience: Truth, trust and transparency." *Forbes*. June 22, 2013. Accessed January 16, 2017. http://www.forbes.com/sites/theyec/2013/06/20/the-3-ts-of-a-great-pr-experience-truth-trust-and-transparency/#2ad0585b2fde.

Zuckert, Michael. *The Natural Rights Republic*. Notre Dame, IN: Notre Dame University Press, 1996.

Index

CSR and, 18–19; Hill & Knowlton controversy, 10, 19–21; origins of, 8–10; practitioners guiding code, 26; PRISA, 39–43, 110; with professional values, 8; PRSA, viii–x, 9, 27–32, 55, 68; SPJ, 37–39; Verrengia on, 3–7
Ethics in Public Relations (Parsons), 55
Ethics in Public Relations: Responsible Advocacy (Seib and Fitzpatrick), 57, 108
evaluation, advocacy and, 57
expertise: enhancing, 83; overview, 80–81; Pflanz on, 77–78; PRSA member statement of professional values, 27; public relations and role of, 82–83, 84; PURE model and, 84–85; skills with public relations, 4, 24, 52, 65–66, 78, 89–90, 105, 117–18; social media and, 85–86; White House, 79–80, 86–87

Facebook, 83, 138, 140, 152, 162; Boston Marathon bombing and, 195, 197, 198–99; against Google, 123–24
Facebook Live, 44
fairness: AMA and, 33; defined, 121; Neace on, 117–18; overview, 121–22; PRSA member statement of professional values, 25, 28; in public relations, 122–24; SeaWorld and, 119–20, 125–26; with social media implications, 125
Farnsworth, Steve, 73
Farook, Syed Rizwan, 135–36, 137, 139–40
Federal Bureau of Investigation (FBI): Amtrak and, 150, 154; Apple with privacy and security battle with, 135–45; Boston Marathon bombing and, 194, 197, 199; iPhone and, 135–36, 140, 141, 142; VA and, 177, 179, 180
Federal Railroad Administration, 151
Federal Trade Commission, 101
FeeJee Mermaid, 9
Fiandaca, Cheryl, 192, 195–96, 198, 199
finances: ALS Ice Bucket Challenge, 63; Amtrak, 149, 155; Apple and impact on, 143–44; drug prices, 60; earnings and, 20, 81, 102, 166–67; GM bail out, 12; Starbucks, 166–67; VA, 107, 174

Finn Partners, 75
Fitzpatrick, Kathy, 57, 108
Fletcher, Joseph, 17
Flint water crisis, 67–68, 75
Fombrun, C. J., 154–55, 156
Foote, Sam, 107–8, 176, 177
Formula of Universal Law, 13–14, 59–60, 85
Fortune (magazine), 138, 162
Frates, Peter, 63
freedom, of ideas, 5–6, 25, 52–53, 66, 78, 90, 106, 118
free flow of information, PRSA and, 28, 110
free will, honesty and, 72

Galaxy Note 7 phone, 71
Gallicano, Tiffany Derville, 73
Gallucci, Ryan M., 179
Gandhi, Mahatma, 125
Garner, Eric, 164
Gawker, 98
General Motors (GM), 12, 67
ghostwriting, 73, 108–9
Gibbs, Nancy, 142
GI Bill, 172
Gibson, Sloan, 182
Gino, Francesca, 115
GitHub Inc., 143
Glaucon (brother of Plato), 82
GM. *See* General Motors
Gold, Hadas, 180
Goldsberry, Lisa, 71
Google, 97, 123–24, 138, 140, 143
Gosden, Richard, 21, 205n43
Gotbaum, Josh, 154, 155
Great Depression, 172
Greece, ancient, 55
Griffin, Drew, 180
Griffin, Richard, 177–78
Grossman, Lev, 142
Grunig, James E., 68, 69
guidelines, PRSA, 28–31
guiding code, practitioners, 26
Gulf War, 173

Haid, Phillip, 166
Hajdak, Stacey, 149

240

Index

About the Authors

Regina Luttrell, Ph.D., spent the first half of her career managing high-level public relations and marketing activities for Fortune 500 companies, governmental entities, and nonprofit organizations. She has the keen ability to develop diverse messages through traditional and nontraditional media relations techniques; Internet and Intranet channels; and marketing strategies including lead generation, events promotions, innovative advertising solutions, and social media tactics. Luttrell is currently an assistant professor of social media and public relations at the S.I. Newhouse School of Public Communication at Syracuse University. A contributor to *PR Tactics* and *PR News*, as well as peer-reviewed journals, Luttrell is a noted speaker, frequently presenting at national and international conferences and business events on topics related to the current social media revolution, the ongoing public relations evolution, and millennials within the classroom and workplace. She has (co)authored the following books: *Social Media: How to Engage, Share, and Connect*; *The Millennial Mindset: Unraveling Fact from Fiction*; *Brew Your Business: The Ultimate Craft Beer Playbook*; *Public Relations Campaigns: An Integrated Approach*; and *The PR Agency Handbook*.

Jamie Ward, Ph.D., is an assistant professor of public relations at Eastern Michigan University. As an avid researcher and writer, she publishes and discusses content on public relations, storytelling, crisis communication, and ethics. She is a social scientist who uses methodologies and theories from communications, media studies, cultural studies, sociology, and education. Her work focuses on storytelling for advocacy and engagement. Prior to entering academia, she spent more than a decade in the nonprofit field working to help nonprofit organizations advance their cause through strategic public relations. Ward is author of the following book: *Veteran Friendships Across Lifetimes: Brothers and Sisters in Arms.*

ACKNOWLEDGMENTS

Gina Luttrell would like to acknowledge those she holds dearest, Todd, Emma, and Avery. None of this would have been possible without your support. Thank you for permitting me to soar.

Jamie Ward would like to thank her husband, Joe, and her daughters, Kaia and Izzy, for their continued support throughout this process. Thank you for giving me a reason to push myself beyond my limits. I love you to the moon and back.

The authors would like to to acknowledge Rowman & Littlefield Publishers, specifically Leanne Silverman for understanding the importance of publishing a book on ethics in public relations, Elizabeth Swayze for her shrewd editorial eye, and Carli Hanson for always keeping us organized.

We would like to express our deepest appreciation to the reviewers that provided feedback on how to improve the book. Your insights were indispensable in making the text what it became.

Finally, we would also like to thank the many people and professional associations who have participated in this project, including Rosemary Benzo-Bonacci, Hope Brown, Lexie Broyton, Megan Cauley, Daniel Cherrin, Mitchel Cohen, Gini Dietrich, Teresa Dougherty, Stacey Hajdak, J. Suzanne Horsley, Alison Kangas, Alexander Laskin, Brooke Lichtman, Chelsea Michael, Brenda Middleton, Jason Mollica, Laurence Mussio, Brianna Neace, Anne O'Connell, Jen O'Conner, Lizmarie Orengo, Jack Pflanz, Jaymie Polet, Matthew Ragas, Bria Smith, Rubai Soni, Peter Verrengia, Levick, Mixergy, The Arthur W. Page Society, Public Relations Society of America, American Marketing Association, Chartered Institute of Public Relations, Society of Professional Journalists, Public Relations Institute of Australia, and the Public Relations Institute of Southern Africa.